Catastrophes and Disasters

Roger Smith

Chambers

EDINBURGH NEW YORK

Published 1992 by W & R Chambers Ltd,
43–45 Annandale Street, Edinburgh EH7 4AZ
95 Madison Avenue, New York N.Y. 10016

British Library Cataloguing in Publication Data
A catalogue record for this book is available from the British Library.

Library of Congress Cataloging-in-Publication Data applied for

ISBN 0 550 17015 4

Chambers Compact Reference Series Editor   Min Lee
Typeset by AMA Graphics Ltd, Preston
Printed in England by Clays Ltd, St Ives, plc

Acknowledgements

I would like to extend my extend my sincere thanks to the following, without whom this book could never have been completed: Kitty Boland, Claire and Patricia O'Neill, Becky and Lindsay Smith. And to the staffs of the Mitchell Library, Glasgow; the Sandeman Library, Perth; the British Geological Survey Library, Edinburgh; Hamilton Library; and the New York City Library for their willing help in unearthing relevant books, newspapers and other material. The book has inevitably drawn on previous published work, and a debt is similarly owed to the authors of books covering various parts of the 'disaster' canvas and to a few who, like myself, have attempted a broad sweep of the subject.

Finally, my heartfelt thanks to Min Lee, Reference Manager at Chambers, for her patience with my many changes of plan, her sympathetic handling of the project from beginning to end, her particular assistance with the section on tsunamis, and most importantly, for giving me the assignment in the first place. It has been a fascinating experience from which I have learned a great deal.

R S
April 1992

Contents

Chronological list of events   viii

Introduction   1

Air disasters   7
The R101 crash   8
The Manchester United tragedy   10
The Staines Trident crash   12
Soviet air disasters   13
The Turkish Airlines crash   14
The Tenerife collision   15
The Chicago DC-10 disaster   17
The Mount Erebus crash   18
The Riyadh fire   20
The Korean Air Lines shoot-down   21
Air India flight 182   23
Japan Air Lines flight 123   24
The Lockerbie bombing   25
The Lauda Air explosion   28

Avalanches, rockfalls and mudslides   29
The sufferings of Leukerbad   30
The Plattenbergkopf rockfall   31
The Tyrolean avalanches of
    World War I   32
The white killer   33
Nevada de Huascarán, 1962   34
Nevada de Huascarán, 1970   35

Earthquakes   37
Earthquake severity measurement   38
Major earthquakes   39
Dvin   40
Eastern Mediterranean   41
Shenshi   42
Anatolia   42
Some historic earthquakes   43
The destruction of Lisbon   45
Kuchan   47
Messina   47
San Francisco   48
Tokyo/Yokohama   50
Agadir   52
Alaska   53
Friuli   55

Tang-shan   56
Mexico City   58
Armenia   60
North-west Iran   62
Erzincan   64

Environmental disasters   65
Minamata   66
Kyshtym   67
Torrey Canyon   68
Seveso   70
Amoco Cadiz   72
The Sverdlovsk anthrax release   73
The Aegean Captain/Atlantic Empress
    collision   74
Bhopal   75
Spanish cooking oil tragedy   77
Chernobyl   78
Exxon Valdez   81
Kuwait burns   83

Famine   85
India   86
The Irish potato famine   87
Biafra   89
The Sahel   90
Ethiopia   91

Fire   93
The Great Fire of London   94
La Compania   95
The destruction of Chicago   96
Iroquois Theatre   97
Cocoanut Grove   98
Joelma building   100
Two Australian States burn   101

Floods   103
Noah's flood   104
Yellow River   105
North Sea floods through history   107
Johnstown   109
Mississippi River   110
Lynmouth   111

The North Sea overflows	112	**Space**	177
Vaiont Dam	115	The Tunguska meteorite	178
Florence	116	The Nedelin disaster	180
Big Thompson River	119	The Challenger explosion	181
Sudan	120		
		Sporting disasters	183
Industrial disasters	121	The Le Mans crash	184
The Oaks	122	The Lima riot	185
The Blantyre mine explosion	123	Disaster at Ibrox	186
American mining disasters	126	The Bradford fire	187
The Senghenydd pit fire	127	Riot at Heysel	188
The Halifax Harbour explosion	129	The Hillsborough disaster	189
The Texas City disaster	131		
The Aberfan colliery tip	132	**Tsunamis**	191
Piper Alpha	134	Major tsunamis	192
Incirharmani mine	136	Tsunamis	193
Explosions in Guadalajara	137	Hilo and the Hamakua coast (1946)	194
		Valdivia	195
Pandemics	139	Hilo (1960)	196
The Black Death	140		
Spanish Influenza epidemic	142	**Volcanoes**	197
AIDS	144	Major volcanoes	198
		Vesuvius	199
Rail and road disasters	145	Santorini	200
The Tay Bridge disaster	146	Taupo	201
The Quintinshill rail crash	148	Mount Etna	203
The Tangiwai Bridge collapse	151	Mount Laki	204
The Moorgate underground crash	152	Tambora	205
The Bihar rail disaster	153	Krakatoa	206
The Salang Tunnel	154	Mont Pelée	208
The Trans-Siberian disaster	155	Kelut	210
		Parícutin	210
		Mount St Helens	211
Disasters at sea	157	Nevado del Ruiz	213
Camorta	158		
General Slocum	158	**Windstorms**	215
Titanic	159	The Beaufort scale	216
Empress of Ireland	162	Hurricanes through history	217
The Lusitania torpedoed	163	A British hurricane	219
Principe de Asturias	164	British tornadoes	220
Valbanera	164	Galveston's great storm	221
Afrique	165	The Long Island Express	222
Principessa Mafalda	165	Typhoon Vera	223
Morro Castle	166	Hurricane Camille	225
Toya Maru	168	Midwest tornadoes	226
The Andrea Doria collision	169	Hurricane Fifi	228
Dara	170	A Christmas Day hurricane	229
Heraklion	171	Hurricane David	230
Admiral Nakhimov	172	The one the weathermen missed	232
Herald of Free Enterprise	173	Bangladesh inundated	235
Dona Paz	175		
Salem Express	176	Index	237

Chronological list of events

Date	Event, location	Page
Prehistory	Noah's flood	104
c.1450BC	Eruption, Santorini, Mediterranean	200
79AD, 24 Aug	Eruption, Vesuvius (Pompeii buried)	199
150AD	Eruption, Taupo, New Zealand	201
893, 27 Mar	Earthquake, Dvin, Armenia	40
1099–1947	Floods, North Sea	107–8
1202, 20 May	Earthquake, E Mediterranean	41
1274 and 1281	Typhoons sink Kubla Khan's fleets off Japan	217
1338–51	The Black Death	140
1556, 23 Jan	Earthquake, Shenshi, China	42
1580, 6 Apr	Earthquake, England	43
1666, 2 Sep	Great Fire of London	94
1668, 17 Aug	Earthquake, Anatolia	42
1669, 11 Mar	Eruption, Mt Etna, Sicily	203
1693, Jan	Earthquake, Sicily	43
1703, 26–7 Nov	Severe gales, England and Wales	219
1720	Avalanches, Leukerbad, Switzerland	30
1737, 11 Oct	Earthquake, Bay of Bengal, India	43
1755, 1 Nov	Earthquake, Lisbon	45
1769–70	Famine, India	86
1783, Feb–Mar	Earthquake, Calabria, Italy	43
1783, 8 Jun	Eruption, Mt Laki, Iceland	204
1811–12	Earthquakes, USA	43
1815, Apr	Eruptions, Tambora, Indonesia	205
1819, 16 Jun	Earthquake, Rann of Kutch, India	44
1835, 20 Feb	Earthquake, Chile	44
1845–8	Potato Famine, Ireland	87
1857, 16 Dec	Earthquake, Naples, Italy	44
1863, 8 Dec	Fire, La Compania, Santiago, Chile	95
1866, 12 Dec	Pit disaster, Barnsley, England	122
1871, 8 Oct	Fire destroys much of Chicago	96
1877, 22 Oct	Pit disaster, Blantyre, Scotland	123
1879, 28 Dec	Tay Bridge rail disaster, Scotland	146
1881, 11 Sep	Rockfall, Plattenbergkopf, Switzerland	31
1883, 27 Aug	Eruption, Krakatoa, Java	206
1887, Sep–Oct	Floods, Yellow River, China	105
1889, 31 May	Flood, Johnstown, USA	109
1891, 28 Oct	Earthquake, Japan	44
1893, 12 Jun	Earthquake, Assam	44
1893, 17 Nov	Earthquake, Kuchan, China	47
1900, Sep	Hurricane, Galveston, Texas	221
1902, Apr	*Camorta* sinks, Gulf of Martaban	158
1902, 8 May	Eruption, Mont Pelée, Martinique	208
1903, 30 Dec	Fire, Iroquois Theatre, Chicago	97
1904, 15 Jun	*General Slocum* sinks, New York Harbour	158
1906, 17 Apr	Earthquake, San Francisco	48
1907	Pit disaster, Monongah, W Virginia, USA	126
1908, Jun	Meteorite (Encke's Comet) strikes Siberia	178
1908, 28 Dec	Earthquake, Sicily	47
1909	Pit disaster, Cherry, Illinois, USA	126

1910, 1 Mar	Avalanche, Wellington, USA	33
1912, 14 Apr	*Titanic* sinks, N Atlantic	159
1913, 14 Oct	Pit disaster, Senghenydd, S Wales	127
1914, 29 May	*Empress of Ireland* sinks, off Canada	162
1915, 1 May	*Lusitania* torpedoed off Ireland	163
1915, 22 May	Rail disaster, Quintinshill, Scotland	148
1916–18	Avalanches (World War I), Alps	32
1916, 3 Mar	*Principe de Asturias* sinks, off Brazil	164
1917, 7 Dec	Explosion, Halifax Harbour, Nova Scotia	129
1918–20	Spanish 'Flu epidemic, worldwide	142
1919	Eruption, Kelut, Indonesia	210
1919, 12 Sep	*Valbanera* sinks, Caribbean	164
1920, 12 Jan	*Afrique* sinks, Bay of Biscay	165
1923, 1 Sep	Earthquake, Japan	50
1927, Apr	Floods, Mississippi River, USA	110
1927, 25 Oct	*Principessa Mafalda* sinks, off Brazil	165
1930, 5 Oct	R101 airship crashes, France	8
1934, 8 Sep	Fire on *Morro Castle*, off New Jersey, USA	166
1938, Apr	Floods, Yellow River, China	106
1938, 21 Sep	'Long Island Express' hurricane, USA	222
1942, 28 Nov	Fire, Cocoanut Grove, Boston, USA	98
1943	Famine, India	86
1943, 20 Feb	New volcano born, Parícutin, Mexico	210
1946, 1 Apr	Tsunami, Hawaii	194
1947, 16 Apr	Explosion, Texas City, USA	131
1950s–60s	Mercury poisoning, Minamata, Japan	66
1951, Jan	Avalanches, Switzerland and Italy	33
1953, 31 Jan–1 Feb	Floods, North Sea	112
1954, 26 Sep	*Toya Maru* sinks, Japan	168
1955, 11 Jun	Car crashes into crowd, Le Mans race, France	184
1956, 25 July	*Andrea Doria* sinks, off USA	169
1957, Sep	Radiation escape, Kyshtym, USSR	67
1958, 6 Feb	Air crash, Munich (Manchester United football team)	10
1959, 27 Sep	Typhoon Vera, Japan	223
1960, 29 Feb	Earthquake, Agadir, Morocco	52
1960, 22 May	Tsunami, Valdivia, Chile	195
1960, 23 May	Tsunami, Hawaii	196
1960, Oct	Space rocket explodes on launchpad, USSR	180
1961, 7 Apr	*Dara* sinks, Dubai	170
1962, 10 Jan	Avalanche, Peru	34
1963, 9 Oct	Floods, Vaiont Valley, Italy	115
1963, 24 Dec	Rail disaster, Tangiwei, New Zealand	151
1964, 27 Mar	Earthquake, Alaska	53
1964, 24 May	Football riot, Lima, Peru	185
1966, 21 Oct	Slurry buries school, Aberfan, S Wales	132
1966, 3–4 Nov	Floods, Florence, Italy	116
1966, 12 Dec	*Heraklion* sinks, Aegean Sea	171
1967–70	Famine, Biafra	89
1967, 18 Mar	Oil spill, *Torrey Canyon*, English Channel	68
1968, 20 Nov	Pit disaster, Mannington, W Virginia, USA	126
1969, 16 Aug	Hurricane Camille, USA	225
1970s onward	Spread of AIDS, worldwide	144
1970, 31 May	Avalanche, Peru	35
1971, 2 Jan	Football disaster, Ibrox, Glasgow	186
1972, 2 May	Pit disaster, Kellogg, Idaho, USA	126

1972, 18 Jun	Air crash, Trident, near London Airport	12
1972, 14 Oct	Air crash, IL-162, Moscow	13
1973–4	Famine, Sahel	90
1974, 1 Feb	Fire, Joelma Building, Sao Paulo, Brazil	100
1974, 3 Mar	Air Crash, Turkish Airlines DC10, Paris	14
1974, 2–3 Apr	150 tornadoes, USA	226
1974, 18 Nov	Hurricane Fifi, Honduras	228
1974, 25 Dec	Hurricane Tracy, Darwin, Australia	229
1975, 28 Feb	Underground rail disaster, Moorgate, London	152
1976, 6 May	Earthquake, N Italy	55
1976, 10 Jul	Toxic cloud, Seveso, Italy	70
1976, 28 Jul	Earthquake, Tang-shan, China	56
1977, 27 Mar	Airliner collision on runway, Tenerife	15
1978, 16 Mar	Oil spill, *Amoco Cadiz*, Brittany	72
1979, Apr	Anthrax escape, Sverdlovsk, USSR	73
1979, 25 May	Air crash, American Airlines DC10, Chicago	17
1979, 19 Jul	Oil spill, *Aegean Captain/Atlantic Empress* collision, Caribbean	74
1979, 30 Aug–1 Sep	Hurricane David, Caribbean	230
1979, 28 Nov	Air crash, Air New Zealand DC10, Antarctica	18
1980, 18 May	Eruption, Mount St Helens, USA	211
1980, 19 Aug	Fire, Saudi Air TriStar, Riyadh	20
1981–9	Contaminated olive oil, Spain	77
1981, 6 Jun	Rail disaster, Bihar, India	153
1982, 3 Nov	Road disaster, Salang Tunnel, Afghanistan	154
1983, Feb	Bush fires, Australia	101
1983, 31 Aug	Korean Air Lines Boeing 747 shot down	21
1984–5	Famine, Ethiopia	91
1984, 3 Dec	Chemical gas escape, Bhopal, India	75
1985, 11 May	Fire, Bradford City football club	187
1985, 29 May	Riot at European Cup Final, Heysel, Brussels	188
1985, 23 Jun	Air crash, Air India Boeing 747, Atlantic Ocean	23
1985, 12 Aug	Air crash, Japan Airlines Boeing 747, Japan	24
1985, 19 Sep	Earthquake, Mexico City	58
1985, Nov	Eruption, Nevada del Ruiz, Colombia	213
1986, 28 Jan	*Challenger* space rocket explodes, USA	181
1986, 26 Apr	Radiation escape, Chernobyl, USSR	78
1986, 31 Aug	*Admiral Nakhimov* sinks, Black Sea	172
1987, 6 Mar	*Herald of Free Enterprise* sinks, Zeebrugge	173
1987, 16 Oct	'Great storm', SE England	232
1987, 20 Dec	*Dona Paz* sinks, Philippines	175
1988, 6 Jul	Piper Alpha oil rig disaster, North Sea	134
1988, Aug	Floods, Sudan	120
1988, Dec	Earthquake, Armenia	60
1988, 21 Dec	Air crash, Pan Am Boeing 747, Lockerbie, Scotland	25
1989, 24 Mar	Oil spill, *Exxon Valdez*, Alaska	81
1989, 15 Apr	Football disaster, Hillsborough, Sheffield	189
1989, 4 Jun	Rail disaster, USSR	155
1990, Jun	Earthquake, Iran	62
1991, Feb	Oil wells set alight, Kuwait	83
1991, 30 Apr	Typhoon and flooding, Bangladesh	235
1991, 26 May	Air crash, Lauda Air, Boeing 767, Burma	28
1991, 15 Dec	*Salem Princess* sinks, Red Sea	176
1992, Feb	Avalanches, Turkey	33
1992, 4 Mar	Pit disaster, Turkey	136
1992, 22 Apr	Gas explosions, Guadalajara, Mexico	137

Introduction

What is a catastrophe? The question is not so facile as it might at first appear, and in terms of selecting items for inclusion in this book, it has had to be considered carefully. There is space here only for those events or incidents which have made a large impact by virtue of their scale, significance or their unique character. If a violent but highly localized windstorm (they occur in several parts of the world, including Britain) severely damages your house but leaves neighbouring properties untouched, that is a catastrophe for you but makes little impact on the wider scene. The same wind could, however, drive a 'supertanker' aground and cause a large-scale oil spill with disastrous consequences for the environment, creating a significant catastrophe.

The catastrophes dealt with in this book fall into two main categories — natural and man-made — and, almost in parallel, ancient and modern. There are records of great natural disasters stretching back into antiquity. All of the world's principal civilizations and religions have stories of great floods, famines and windstorms. Earthquakes, volcanic eruptions and tidal waves were just as frequent in ancient times as they are today. There are two principal differences between those times and now.

The first is in the speed and scope of communication. We are still discovering very significant natural events from ancient civilizations. There are, for example, thousands of earth tremors every year and there is no reason to believe that this is a modern phenomenon. The earth has always been a restless, evolving planet. Yet we have records of only a very small number of earthquakes taking place more than a thousand years ago. It is quite likely that whole civilizations were shattered by such events, either lost to us altogether or remembered in legends such as the persistent story of Atlantis.

Visitors from space

Another area where our knowledge is very imperfect is that of impact on the earth's surface by objects from space. Hundreds if not thousands of small pieces of natural space debris rain down on our atmosphere every day. Very few reach the surface, and very few of those are of significant size. The Siberian meteorite of 1908 is included in the book as an event of catastrophic impact on its area, and as the largest known to us, though few if any people died as a result of its arrival. In prehistoric times it could have been different. There is evidence of other large-scale impacts, but what effect they had must remain a mystery. The possibility of such an object striking a large centre of civilization in the future, or hitting the ocean and causing destructive tidal waves, certainly cannot be ruled out.

There must also have been many more destructive fires, floods and windstorms in past eras than are yet known to us. We are fortunate in that the eruption of Pompeii in AD79 happened in an area of highly developed civilization and was thus very well recorded (though the people of Pompeii and the other towns around the Bay of Naples would not feel themselves so fortunate). This event is one of those rare and very special links between the past and the present which makes an impact on us as vivid today as when it happened. The site has been meticulously conserved, and no-one visiting it today can fail to be aware of the significance of the eruption.

The sites of other massive volcanic eruptions in the distant past make less impact simply because they affected only the land- and seascape, and nature heals such scars over a long period of time. The eruption of Mount St Helens in 1980, however, provided vulcanologists and other earth scientists with a unique, large-scale natural laboratory, an opportunity which was eagerly accepted and which will provide material for decades to come.

That eruption is one of a number of events included in this book which are 'catastrophic' in the natural sense of being mighty in scale and impact on the environment without causing large numbers of human deaths (though many animals undoubtedly perished), and because they made a global impact. If Mount St Helens had erupted (as it possibly did) a thousand years ago, we would know virtually nothing about it. Today, any such event will be covered extensively in newspapers and on radio and television. Later on, films will be made about it and articles will appear in both popular and scientific periodicals. As an example, the full scientific report on the Alaskan earthquake of 1964, disastrous in its economic impact though again with relatively few human casualties, runs to eight large volumes and several thousand pages. It will be studied for a long time to come.

Warning but not prevention

The second difference between ancient times and today is in terms of prediction and precaution, which is now a highly developed science. Again looking back to ancient times, any such disaster was inevitably seen as the work of the gods, venting their wrath on an erring or sinful people. Those very words, 'the wrath of God', appear in the contemporary report of the first earthquake described in the book, that which shattered the city of Dvin, Armenia, in 893. In one sense nothing changes. Though scientists may use other terms, the people of Spitak and Leninakan in that same area undoubtedly felt that the wrath of God had descended on them when earthquake struck again in December 1988.

Natural disasters of several kinds can now be predicted with reasonable accuracy. Hurricane and typhoon warning services are well developed, and have saved many lives by triggering evacuation or shelter procedures. Earthquake prediction is less accurate, but some warning can often be given. The Chinese are at the forefront of this science, though even there, nothing could be done to prevent the awful tragedy of July 1976 when Tangshan, a city of a million people, was reduced to rubble in a few minutes. Interestingly, instinctive means used in ancient times are now arousing considerable scientific interest. The Chinese, again, have found that certain patterns recur in animal behaviour in the days before major earth tremors. If your goldfish jumps out of its bowl, watch out — the earth could open up beneath you at any time.

However good our predictive sciences become, we cannot prevent natural disasters happening. A tremendous amount of effort has gone into predicting the next major earthquake along the San Andreas Fault in California. What happened to San Francisco in 1906 could happen again at almost any time: a major quake is predicted for early in the 21st century. Buildings have been designed to withstand shock, as far as possible, and there are well-developed warning procedures for the people of the area, but a really significant quake, that is one registering 8 or more on the Richter scale, would still cause immense damage.

The same is true of other natural disasters. In less developed parts of the world, even warning will be of little use. Where can the people of the teeming cities of Bangladesh go when a typhoon approaches? How could the citizens of Yungay, in Peru, have escaped the awful avalanche, triggered by an earthquake, that engulfed them so suddenly and completely in 1970? Dominica, Cuba and Haiti can batten down the hatches when a hurricane approaches but they cannot stop it destroying their houses, or flattening their vital crops of sugar cane and banana.

International aid

At least we are better organized now in providing relief on an international scale when such disasters do strike. Here modern communications do help. It was first still and then television pictures that shocked the world into responding to the plight of the African peoples stricken by drought and famine in recent years (and still suffering, in many areas). International teams with highly developed skills flew to Mexico, Armenia and Iran to help with rescue and relief work after recent earthquakes, and in many cases of disaster, money and materials has been generously provided. After Tang-shan, the Chinese government did not seek outside help but poured its own resources in on an extraordinary scale. Tens of thousands of relief workers arrived to restore services, repair damage and provide medical aid, and Tang-shan was recreated with amazing speed.

International efforts have long been directed towards the eradication of disease. A small section on epidemics includes the medieval Black Death and the exceptional 'Spanish 'flu' epidemic of 1918–20, which killed more people than the Great War with which it overlapped. AIDS — a modern equivalent of the Black Death? — is also included. The forward forecasting for this viral disease throws up horrifying numbers, and so far no cure is in sight. Its full impact may well be just as bad as any previous world pandemic.

Man-made catastrophes

The book also covers many man-made catastrophes and disasters. There is no shortage of these. Whatever technology man develops, it seems inevitably to bring disaster in some form as well as benefits. Sea, rail and most recently air travel have opened up the world as never before. With this development, accidents (to use the common, though very euphemistic, term) inevitably happen, and a number of them are described here. The story is all too frequently one of human frailty.

Aircraft navigation systems are wrongly programmed and the craft fly into mountains or, in one case, into hostile airspace to be shot down. Despite the sophistication of modern radar and computers, ships still collide and run aground. The best signalling devices fail to prevent trains arriving together on tracks where they should be apart.

In the case of air travel, still statistically extremely safe, terrorist action has been the cause of a number of recent disasters such as that over Lockerbie in Scotland when a PanAm airliner was blown out of the sky, needlessly killing all on board and a number of people on the ground as well. With continuing unrest in many parts of the world, such incidents are likely to continue, and so far we do not seem to be able to prevent the explosive devices — simple and small — from finding their way on board.

Sea disasters of many kinds are covered. Some have quite bizarre origins such as the sudden death of a ship's master (the *Morro Castle*) or a main ferry loading door left open (the *Herald of Free Enterprise*). The worst tragedies in recent times have nearly all been ferries, the worst of all being the sinking of a Philippine ferry after collision in December 1987. That is one of a number of incidents where the exact loss of life can probably never be established.

Industry too has been responsible for its share of disasters. Mining was always a hazardous occupation, taking place in a volatile and often literally explosive environment. The human cost was extremely high and a number of tragic incidents where great loss of life occurred are related here, as is the gruesome incident at Aberfan in South Wales when a colliery waste tip, poorly managed and overloaded, slid down, engulfing a school and entombing over a hundred children.

Offshore oil exploration in such places as the North Sea, between Britain and Norway, is in some ways the more modern equivalent of coal mining. It too takes place in an extremely hazardous environment with constant risks which can be reduced by careful management but never eliminated, as was tragically shown in the Piper Alpha explosion in July 1988. A volatile mix of gases and oils is being extracted from under the sea and it is hardly surprising, perhaps, that occasionally something goes wrong and the spark — all that is necessary to set off an explosion — occurs, spreading fire with a speed too great to counter.

A number of intriguing disasters from the former Soviet Union are described. Several of these have only come to light very recently through diligent research or through Soviet scientists defecting and bringing information with them. The situation in that vast region now seems more open, though economically less secure. Famine has become a possibility in several areas.

There is even a section on sporting disasters. Sport should be a relaxation and a recreation, but international competitive sport arouses strong emotions and passions in people, and those feelings have, unfortunately, overspilled into riot at times, as at Heysel and Lima. Poor crowd control and fire led to other disasters described here, and the tragedy at the Le Mans motor race in 1955 is also covered.

Environmental hazards

There is a substantial section devoted to environmental catastrophes and disasters. The earliest of these dates only from the 1950s, and most have occurred since 1970. Our capacity for meddling with the environment seems never-ending. The incidents related here are bad enough, including as they do oil spills on a vast scale, chemical escapes causing thousands of deaths, the awful 'olive oil' case from Spain when huge numbers of people were affected by contaminated cooking oil, and the explosion at Chernobyl, the worst nuclear incident so far and a classic example of the way pollution knows no boundaries.

In compiling this section, a strong feeling remains that, were it to be revised in 10 or 20 years time, it would become the largest and most significant in the book. And this despite the fact that, simply because they cannot be dealt with adequately in the limited space available for each entry, the really big catastrophes (or at the least, potential catastrophes) such as global warming, depletion of the ozone layer and acid rain have been left out.

Man persists in thinking that he can control nature, and that his science and technology is equal to anything nature can throw at us. This is a foolish and misguided belief. Ask the people of Tang-shan, Armenia or Dominica if we can control nature. They will say no; we can warn, we can repair afterwards, but we cannot control.

Ask the people of the Chernobyl region if our technology is foolproof. We have been given ample warning, but the warnings have not, so far, been adequately heeded, and one can only guess at what catastrophes lie in wait in the future.

Overlapping categories

The 16 categories of disaster included here frequently overlap. Very often a catastrophe is a combination of events rather than a single incident. Earthquakes are associated with tsunamis and landslides; volcanoes can also create massive waves, as at Krakatoa, and landslides; windstorms are very often associated with floods. Fire, though worthy of the separate category it is given, has many causes and is a part of the majority of catastrophes.

You will only find war here as an overlapping factor. The suffering, death and destruction caused by war has truly been catastrophic, almost since history began, but a decision was made not to include it as a separate section. The same applies to insurrection, which continues to take many thousands of lives in dozens of countries and is a festering sore on the face of humanity. The exceptions are incidents such as the deliberate torpedoing of the liner *Lusitania* in 1915 and a number of transport accidents with a military connection.

Within each section, incidents are arranged chronologically, and an overall chronological list is also provided. The boxes included with most entries provide an opportunity, which the author has been glad to take, for some intriguingly quirky and humorous happenings, a slight leavening of what must inevitably be a rather serious subject. Thus, as well as the jumping goldfish, we have the origin of the *Frankenstein* story, the original Mad Hatters and the sad end of the rhubarb-gatherers of Baalbek.

From Noah to Chernobyl

It is a long way, in time and human development, from Noah and his Ark to reactor no 4 at Chernobyl, but that is the span encompassed by this book. It describes about 150 events or incidents, all of which are selected as warranting the description 'catastrophic'. This can still only be seen as a representative selection. Many important events have had to be omitted or covered only briefly. What seems a catastrophe in one part of the world, or in one scientific discipline, may seem insignificant in another, and the author is only too well aware that the selection of events, while wide-ranging, is inevitably imperfect.

Nonetheless, there is much of interest here. Catastrophes have a fascination for us. Perhaps a morbid fascination, but it is undoubtedly there. We can learn much from the great natural events such as earthquakes and volcanic eruptions about the way our earth works; we should also learn much from our own mistakes, those that lead to man-made disasters. It is tempting to hope that a revised version of this book in 20 years' time would contain no new environmental, transport or industrial disasters, but that is an unrealistic hope. Catastrophe is an inevitable part of our lives.

Air disasters

Air travel is still less than a century old: passenger travel by air has only been developed on a large scale within the last 50 years. As with any other mode of mechanical transport, there have been mishaps since the beginning, but as the numbers of airliners have grown in recent years, and the aircraft themselves have got larger, so the scale of incidents has also increased. The 14 disasters described here are a representative cross-section ranging from the crash of the R101 in 1930 which effectively ended the era of the large airship to a number of 'jumbo jet' crashes from the past few years. If there is a thread running through them it is, sadly, that of human frailty and error. Maintenance checks are not carried out properly; air traffic control instructions are ignored; navigational errors cause aircraft to fly into mountains.

Two, possibly three, of the tragedies detailed here have another more sinister cause, that of international terrorism. A large aircraft loaded with passengers and luggage is an obvious target and despite the best efforts of security services, explosive devices can be hidden in very small packages or inside innocuous items such as tape recorders.

There is also one crash — that of a Korean Air Lines Boeing 747 in 1983 — caused by military action. The aircraft — unwittingly, it would appear, and as the result of either human or computer navigational error, despite accusations of spying at the time — strayed into Soviet airspace and in the tense atmosphere of the cold war, a fighter was scrambled to shoot it down.

The cockpit voice recorders or 'black boxes' of modern aircraft are so constructed as to withstand any emergency or crash, and from their recovery the last fateful moments leading up to calamity can be relived. These recorders often give investigators vital clues as to the causes of air crashes. Sometimes, as with the December 1988 Lockerbie tragedy, what happened was so sudden that the tape is blank. In that case, police investigation recovered vital evidence from a wide area and the exact point where the bomb went off inside the aircraft could be pinpointed.

Unlike a ship or train, there is little hope of escape from an aircraft in flight if things do go badly wrong. However, it should not be thought that air travel is inherently unsafe: on statistics per passenger-mile it is still among the safest forms of travel. The disasters, when they come, tend to be spectacular and to hit the headlines. The many hundreds of flights that arrive without incident go unrecorded.

The R101 crash

5 October 1930

Britain's Air Minister dies

Explosion and fire ends government interest in airships.

In the latter part of the 1920s there was great debate about the future of international air travel. Some services had already started on routes such as London to Paris, and within the USA, using fixed-wing aircraft, but there was considerable doubt as to whether such aircraft would ever be suitable for the longer-haul intercontinental routes.

Instead, attention was focused on the development of airships, large dirigibles filled with gas and powered by conventional engines. Germany started regular services in 1928 with the *Graf Zeppelin*. In Britain, two teams were working simultaneously on such craft; one was the commercial firm of Vickers (the R100), and the other was an Air Ministry team (the R101). With hindsight, it can be seen that the failure of the two teams to discuss common problems led not only to a great waste of time, effort and money, but also to the difficulties encountered by the Air Ministry team working on R101 remaining unsolved at the time of the craft's demise.

Development proceeded for five years. The R101 was better streamlined than its rival, but its propulsion system and steerage were less efficient — a crucial factor, as things turned out. The R101 was powered by diesel, whereas R100 used lighter petrol engines. More seriously, the valves controlling the gas on R101 were too sensitive. They opened automatically if the ship tilted more than three degrees, and she was always likely to do this as the tail fin design was imperfect.

First flight

Both ships were completed in 1929. R101 made a successful first flight from its base at Cardington, near Bedford, on 14 October, circling London before returning. R100 flew from Howden in Yorkshire, where it had been built, to Cardington on 16 December. There were problems with the gas bags and outer covers of both machines, with numerous tears and holes appearing on each test flight. Despite this, long journeys were planned for both: R100 to Canada and R101, with the Air Minister, Lord Thomson on board, to India.

R100 completed its flight to Canada and back in July and August 1930, but the problems with the cover had not been resolved. The R101 team were also encountering considerable difficulties. On a test flight from the airfield at Hendon, North London, the craft was almost impossible to control, the nose swaying alarmingly up and down. An observer from the R100 team was aboard, and commented afterwards that he had never felt so concerned aboard an airship.

Despite this, Lord Thomson insisted that R101 be made ready to take him to India and back. The airship was cut in two and an extra section was inserted with more gas bags, to increase buoyancy. The flight was set for 5 October. The airship had never been flown at full speed, or in bad weather, and the inspector in charge, Frank McWade, had refused to renew its airworthiness certificate; he was over-ruled. The weather outlook was poor, with rains and high winds forecast.

Palm trees

Before take-off, four tons of water ballast had to be jettisoned to get the weight down. R101 was luxuriously fitted out with heavy furniture and carpets, and potted palm trees in the public rooms, which all added to the weight. Lord Thomson brought luggage and effects with him weighing over 250 lbs, including a carpet over 100 lbs in weight which had to be stored in the nose.

The 770-foot (235m) craft took off at 6:30pm, slowly gaining height. It crossed the coast near Hastings at 9:35pm, watched by crowds on the cliffs, and continued across the Channel, but over northern France the winds grew stronger and the crew struggled to keep height. At 2am, it seems that the forward gas bags ruptured. The airship's nose dipped sharply. It just cleared the houses of the small village of St Valery-sur-Somme, near Beauvais, then hit a wood at Allonne. Within seconds a fire started and five million cubic feet of hydrogen exploded.

Of the 56 people on board, 48 were killed instantly and two died later of their injuries. The six who survived were all at the rear of the craft, and some were saved through being drenched by a burst water ballast tank. Lord Thomson had gone down with the craft he had supported, and the British government's interest in airships was ended. Within a few years, fixed-wing aircraft were on service on intercontinental routes.

The Hindenburg crash

The German government continued to back airships, even after the R101 crash. The *Graf Zeppelin* flew over a million miles between 1928 and 1937 in perfect safety, carrying over 16 000 passengers. The *Hindenburg*, a larger craft which could carry 70 passengers and 13 tons of freight, went into service in May 1936. On 6 May 1937 the big airship reached Lakehurst, New Jersey at the end of a transatlantic flight. As it was being moored it exploded in a sheet of flame, killing 35 people. Sabotage was suspected as a cause of the crash, which ended German airship services.

*Wreckage of the **R101** airship.*

The Manchester United tragedy
6 February 1958

The loss of the 'Busby Babes'

A winter crash at Munich takes the lives of many fine young footballers.

Manchester United were the first British football team invited to play in the prestigious European Cup. In 1957 the young side reached the semi-finals of the competition before losing to the winners, Real Madrid. The following season they set out again on the European trail.

The side — none of them over 30 and most home-grown talent nurtured by their famous manager Matt Busby — were nicknamed the 'Busby Babes' and there was nationwide interest in their progress. They survived the first round, beating Dukla Prague 3–1 on aggregate (European matches are played over two legs). In the next round, the quarter-finals, United were drawn against Red Star Belgrade.

United won the home leg 2–1 on 14 January. The away leg was set for Wednesday 5 February. Because they had to be back promptly for an important league match, and following difficulties with scheduled flights on their trip to Prague, the club took the then novel step of chartering an aircraft — an Airspeed Ambassador of British European Airlines, known by the airline as the *Elizabethan*.

Exciting match

The players, manager, trainers and press corps left on Monday 3 February, travelling via Munich. The weather on arrival in Belgrade was poor, with low cloud and snow, but the aircraft landed safely. The match was an exciting one. At the final whistle the score was 3–3 and United were through to the semi-finals on a 5–4 aggregate. The jubilant team and staff were treated to a reception at the British Embassy.

The return flight was next day, Thursday 6 February. There were 38 people on board. The Ambassador landed in Munich at 2:15pm in very poor conditions, with the runway covered in slush and wet snow. The aircraft was refuelled for the long flight back to Manchester, and taxied out to the runway at 3:20pm. Captain James Thain and his co-pilot Captain Kenneth Rayment went through the pre-take off drills and set the aircraft rolling. Partway down the runway the take-off was abandoned due to fluctuating oil pressure. On a second try the same thing happened, and the aircraft returned to the terminal.

The problem was one known to Ambassador crews as 'boost surging', due to an over-rich fuel mixture upsetting the distribution. It was decided to try again, opening the throttles some way before releasing the brakes and then easing the power on more gently.

The crash

The passengers re-embarked and the Ambassador set off again at 4pm. At the end of the runway the throttles were eased open and the aircraft began rolling through the slush, which had been added to by fresh falls of snow. Acceleration came slowly, but the nose was pulled up and it seemed all was well. However, at the critical speed of around 115 knots, there was no further acceleration; instead, the speed began to drop.

The aircraft was too far down the runway to stop and the crew made desperate efforts to get it into the air, to no avail. As it left the runway and tore on across snow-covered grass, Captain Rayment shouted 'Christ, we're not going to make it!'

As the Ambassador ripped through the perimeter fence, the two pilots saw a house and a tree directly ahead. Thain pulled the undercarriage up in a last attempt to get airborne, and the aircraft began to turn slowly to the right. It was now invisible from the airport control tower in the thickly falling snow.

The aircraft struck the house, setting it on fire, and spun into the tree, which hit the left side of the cockpit, breaking the windows. The nightmare continued as the Ambassador slid on through the snow, striking a garage with a truck inside. The tail section was ripped off and the truck exploded in flames. Seventy yards (60m) further on the aircraft finally stopped.

Sold for scrap

Inside the aircraft, those who had survived started trying to escape. They included the two stewardesses and a number of players and pressmen. James Thain was badly shocked but unhurt, but Kenneth Rayment was trapped in his seat, unable to move. It seemed at first that the casualty list was relatively light but in fact, of the 44 people on board — 38 passengers and six crew — 20 were already dead, including seven players and an equal number of journalists.

Among those seriously injured were the team's manager, Matt Busby, and perhaps its greatest player, Duncan Edwards. Busby survived, and was later knighted, but Ed-wards, after fighting for his life for nearly two weeks, finally succumbed. Kenneth Rayment lapsed into a coma from which he never recovered, and he too died, on 15 March, bringing the total number lost in the crash to 23.

Investigations into the cause of the accident started a few days after it took place, but after a BEA engineering team had made a thorough inspection, the German authorities sold the wreckage for scrap, less than a week after the incident took place! Such an action seems unbelievable to us today.

The tragedy caused national grief in Britain. When the flag-draped coffins returned to Manchester, a crowd estimated at over 100 000 lined the route to United's Old Trafford ground. The team was rebuilt, with a mixture of experienced players hastily signed from other clubs and raw juniors, and before a crowd of 60 000, amazingly won their next match 3–0.

Ice or slush?

The inquiry into the crash, in Germany, concluded that ice on the aircraft's wings was the primary cause. Captain Thain, whose licence was suspended, never accepted this and with his wife, a qualified chemist, began a long fight to prove that the deep slush and wet snow on the runway had critically slowed the aircraft. He was not vindicated until June 1969, when the re-opened inquiry (now in Britain) concluded that 'the cause of the accident was slush on the runway . . . blame is not to be imputed to Captain Thain'.

The Staines Trident crash

18 June 1972

A mysterious stall

An airliner crashes shortly after take-off from London Heathrow.

British European Airways Flight 548 from London Heathrow to Brussels on the afternoon of Sunday 18 June 1972 was fully booked, with 109 passengers, plus its crew of six. Just before the aircraft was due to take off — the engines had already been started — three extra passengers scrambled aboard. They were a BEA Vanguard freighter crew who were needed urgently in Brussels. The aircraft was thus over its payload carrying limit, but this was compensated for by the fact that, due to the short flying time to Brussels, it had a light fuel load; it was well below the maximum take-off weight.

Flight 548 had a standby crew, the original crew having been delayed in return to London. At the time there was considerable unrest among BEA pilots and strike action had been discussed. Captain Stanley Key, in charge of the Trident, was a very experienced senior officer of 51, and totally opposed to strike action. In the crew room prior to the flight, he had a violent argument with a younger colleague over the matter. Unknown to Captain Key or anyone else, including the airline medical staff, he had a deteriorating heart condition. The argument may well have caused an arterial rupture and he was almost certainly in severe pain during the last moments of the stricken aircraft.

Strong wind

The weather conditions as Bealine 548 taxied out were poor, with heavy rain and a strong, gusting wind. The aircraft set off at 4:08pm. A normal take-off was achieved but the crew had some difficulty keeping the Trident on line, so bad was the buffeting it was getting from the wind. Captain Key selected the autopilot, as was his normal practice, to take the aircraft to its next significant height of 6 000 feet. The autopilot mechanism struggled to cope with the conditions and the aircraft's speed must have dropped below the safe climb level of 180 knots.

Two minutes after take-off, Flight 548, heading south towards the town of Staines, went into stall. By now the aircraft's 'stick shaker', which alerts the crew to stall, would have activated, and a loud audible warning would be sounding in their headsets. If Stanley Key was experiencing severe chest pain all this must have been impossibly confusing. The aircraft dropped steadily through the cloud.

It emerged at only 1 000 feet, but in the poor visibility and concentrating on their instruments, the crew may not even have seen how close the ground was. Flight 548 crossed the busy A30 highway and smashed into a field. It had been airborne just three minutes. Within 15 minutes full rescue services were on hand, but the crash impact had been too severe and everyone on board died. It was the worst British air crash up to that time.

A minor miracle

Those who believe in the hand of Providence have their belief supported by the Trident crash. The aircraft fell, miraculously, on a small patch of open ground almost surrounded by housing, and just beyond a main road. If it had hit the ground five seconds earlier or later, the casualties could have been very much higher.

Soviet air disasters

1972–86

A catalogue of accidents

For many years, these crashes went unreported in the West.

As in other areas, many air crashes happening within the boundaries of the Soviet Union went either unreported or with only the briefest details disclosed. Researchers, and more recent openness, have unearthed some of the facts.

We are not even certain as to the largest single Soviet air disaster. It may be the Il-62 airliner of the major airline Aeroflot which crashed near Moscow in heavy rain on 14 October 1962. All 176 people aboard died, and something is known of this crash because there were about 40 non-Soviet citizens on board, including one Briton and one Frenchman. The accident was reported in a mere 42 words in *Pravda*, but unofficial reports say that the aircraft's instrument landing system had failed and that it made three unsuccessful attempts at a landing before hitting the ground short of the runway on the fourth attempt.

Official figures

In the 18 months following that crash, it is believed that over 600 people died in Soviet air disasters. The accidents included a Tu-154 airliner crash on approach to Prague Airport, which killed 66 people, and a mysterious incident involving a Tu-104 which may have been 'skyjacked' before exploding in midair, killing about 100. By the end of 1973 the list of crashes had reached 17 in little over a year. The official figures given to the International Civil Aviation Organization by the Soviet authorities detailed three crashes with 98 fatalities.

Other serious incidents have included a crash on 27 April 1974 when an Il-18 turbo-prop caught fire on take-off from Leningrad, killing 118 people. In January 1976 a Tu-124 also caught fire on take-off, this time from Moscow; the death toll was 87. A collision near Sochi, the Black Sea resort, in September, killed about 90 people.

The toll has continued. On 11 August 1979 two Tu-134 airliners collided at 25 000 feet over the Ukraine, with a death toll of 173. There was no official announcement of this crash, but unofficial reports spread rapidly, apparently because members of a top Soviet soccer team were on board. On 7 July 1980 a Tu-154 crashed just after take-off at Alma Ata. Everyone on board — 163 in all — was killed.

Omsk crash

The worst Soviet disaster may have occurred on 15 October 1985 when another Tu-154 was lost on landing at Omsk, seemingly after hitting a fuel truck that was on the runway. The incident went unreported in the major Soviet media but was described by a French correspondent in Moscow. It is known that the Tu-154 has a passenger capacity of 167 and carries a crew of up to 12. Since domestic flights are frequently fully booked, this could have resulted in a death toll of 179, which would exceed the October 1972 crash by three.

Since 1985, with the introduction of Mr Gorbachev's glasnost policy, air crashes have been more fully reported. There have been, as far as known, no major disasters in recent years, and certainly none on the scale of the other crashes listed in these pages. But we shall probably never know how many people died, or how many real disasters there were, in the pre-Gorbachev era.

The Turkish Airlines crash

3 March 1974

Major disaster near Paris

A faulty cargo door causes a DC-10 to crash in a French wood shortly after take-off.

On 3 March 1974 a DC-10 of Turkish Airlines left Istanbul on a normal scheduled flight to London Heathrow, with an intermediate stop at Paris Orly. The first leg of the flight was trouble-free, and the aircraft took off from Orly at 11:30am for the short hop across the English Channel with 334 passengers and a crew of 10 on board. The aircraft's passenger load was increased by over 150 in Paris because of a strike by BEA ground engineers in London which led to the cancellation of many BEA flights.

Radar contact with the aircraft was maintained for only a few minutes before it disappeared off the screens. The DC-10 had crashed in the Forest of Ermenonville, in a rugged valley called Bosquet de Dammartin, about 22 miles (37km) northeast of Paris. The aircraft cut a broad swathe extending for half a mile (800m) through the forest, and broke into a large number of pieces. Rescue services were quickly on the scene, but there were no survivors.

Emergency landing

When the crash was investigated, it was found that a rear cargo door had blown out. The same thing had happened to another DC-10, on a flight from Detroit to Buffalo in 1972. It made a successful emergency landing back at Detroit, but following that incident the plane's makers, McDonnell Douglas, recalled all DC10s in order that a special support plate with ex-

tended locking pins should be fitted to these doors. At the time, the Turkish Airlines plane had just been completed but had not gone into service. Its record file showed that this modification had been carried out in July 1972, but it was clear to the crash investigators that the support plate had never been fitted, and the locking pins were incorrectly adjusted.

After conducting their own enquiries, and while admitting that the support plate had not been fitted, McDonnell Douglas disputed that this was the cause of the crash. They found that the 'make-sure' device on the cargo door, which ensures it is properly locked, was not operating correctly, blaming this on faulty maintenance by the plane's operators, Turkish Airlines. The airline denied responsibility.

In May 1975 McDonnell Douglas offered out-of-court settlements to those people — mainly bereaved families — who were seeking compensation, without which the matter would have come to public trial. The full truth behind the Ermenonville crash will most probably never be revealed.

Stamps that never were
The investigation into this crash brought out a most curious and still unexplained mystery. The aircraft's file contained the personalized stamps of three Douglas inspectors verifying that the modification to the cargo door had been carried out. Under questioning, two of the three swore that (a) their stamps had never left their possession, and (b) they had not worked on Ship 29, as the Turkish Airlines DC-10 was known. The third man, Edward Evans, could not remember working on Ship 29 either but accepted that he must have stamped the file without the work having been done. How these three stamps got onto the file remains a mystery.

The Tenerife collision

27 March 1977

The worst air disaster of all

A mistaken instruction leads to a runway collision between two fully loaded jumbo jets.

Up to the end of 1991, the collision which occurred on the runway at Tenerife in March 1977 has taken the greatest toll of any single air disaster — 583 lives lost. The accident showed that airports themselves can be dangerous places, and that loaded aircraft can come to grief before they take to the air, with disastrous results.

Los Rodeos Airport, Tenerife, is busy with holiday traffic all year round, and weekends are a peak time. The day of the disaster was even busier than a Sunday in spring would normally have been, for on that day a terrorist bomb had gone off in the shopping area of Las Palmas, on Grand Canary, and Tenerife had to take much of the traffic that would otherwise have gone to Las Palmas.

To make matters worse, the weather was poor; by the afternoon mist and rain had covered the airport, which at the time had only one main runway. The chapter of accidents is still not completed: two of the airport's three main radio frequencies had been out of action for some time. All flights were therefore having to share one frequency. And, perhaps crucially in view of the fog, the central runway lights were not working. The KLM captain had asked for them to be turned on.

Two 747s

The two aircraft involved were both Boeing 747s. One, belonging to the Dutch airline KLM, had arrived from Amsterdam earlier in the day. The other, a PanAm plane, had come from Los Angeles. Each was delayed in taking off due to the weather and the overcrowded schedule of flights.

Both aircraft were in the hands of very experienced captains — Victor Grubbs of Pan Am and Veldhuizen van Zanten, known as Jaap, of KLM. The KLM aircraft was carrying 230 passengers and a crew of 14; the PanAm plane was more fully loaded, with 364 passengers and a crew of 16. At 5pm both were in the queue of aircraft waiting for take-off clearance from the Los Rodeos tower. The KLM flight was given taxiing instructions first. Jaap van Zanten was told to taxi across a link to the end of the main runway, where he would swing round and prepare for take-off. The PanAm flight was to follow down the runway, but turn off before the end on a short diagonal link which would enable it to swing round behind the KLM aircraft and then follow it into the air.

Waiting for clearance

The KLM flight reported to the tower: 'We are ready for take-off and are waiting for ATC (air traffic control) clearance'.

Tower: 'You are cleared to the Papa Beacon, climb to and maintain flight level nine zero (9 000 feet), right turn after take-off, proceed on heading 040 until intercepting the 325 radial from Las Palmas VOR.'

The PanAm aircraft then called the tower with 'Clipper 1736' (his callsign).

Tower: 'Papa Alpha 1736, report runway cleared.'

PanAm: 'We'll report runway cleared.'

Tower: 'OK. Thank you.'

There is nothing further recorded, but the most likely theory to have emerged is that the KLM crew heard just 'runway cleared' and not the vital preceding words 'we'll report' and therefore assumed that the PanAm aircraft had made its turn off onto the link and that the runway was clear. But they should still have waited for explicit take-off clearance from the tower.

What happened next is described by the PanAm flight's first officer, Robert Bragg, who survived the crash. 'We saw lights ahead of us in the fog. At first we thought it was the KLM aircraft standing at the end of the runway. Then we realized they were coming towards us.' Bragg shouted into the radio 'Get off! Get off!' Captain Grubbs called to the tower: 'We're still on the runway!' and made a desperate attempt to swing his aircraft left onto the grass.

The collision

The KLM aircraft by now had its nose off the ground, so the crew would probably not have seen the other 747. Van Zanten's plane got airborne for a few brief seconds, then collided with the roof of the PanAm aircraft, ripping it open, bounced back onto the runway, slid along for 600 yards, then exploded. Everyone on board was killed. The PanAm aircraft did not catch fire immediately, and 54 people managed to escape before it too went up in flames.

The tower had seen nothing of all this due to the fog, and kept repeating the two callsigns — 'KLM 4805, PA 1736' over and over again. Fire on the runway was then reported by another aircraft, and the emergency services went into action, but too late to save any lives.

Another runway collision

The Tenerife disaster was not the first runway collision between two large jets. At Sydney, Australia, in January 1971, the captain of a Canadian Pacific Airlines DC-8 misunderstood an instruction from the tower and made a U-turn on the runway just as a Trans-Australia Airlines Boeing 727 was starting to take off. The TAA aircraft just managed to get enough height to avoid a major disaster. It clipped the tail of the DC-8. The 727 was still airworthy, and after dumping fuel at sea, returned to Sydney, where it landed safely.

Wreckage of one of the jumbo jets which collided.

The Chicago DC-10 disaster

25 May 1979

America's worst air disaster

A stall after take-off leads to crash and fire.

American Airlines Flight 191 taxied out to runway 32 right at Chicago's O'Hare International Airport at one minute to three in the afternoon of 25 May 1979, on time to begin its scheduled cross-America flight to Los Angeles. There were 258 passengers and 13 crew on board. Little did they imagine that they had only five minutes to live.

The weather was good, with clear visibility and a ground temperature of 17°C. At 3:02pm the aircraft was cleared for take-off and began its roll down the runway, with First Officer James Dillard at the controls. Just as the aircraft reached take-off speed, the instruments registered a complete loss of power from number one engine (suspended below the port wing).

The crew could not see this engine from the flight deck and were thus unaware that the whole engine and its support pylon had fallen off, taking with them a 3ft (1m) section of the leading edge of the wing containing vital hydraulic power lines. For some reason it seems that the crew did not have warning indicators showing the loss of control mechanisms, and they reacted as they had been trained to do in the event of a straightforward engine failure.

Port wing stall

The DC-10 has an engine under each wing and another in the tail, and can fly satisfactorily on two engines. The aircraft had reached its 'lift-off' speed of 145 knots, and

First Officer Dillard brought the nose up. The DC-10 became airborne but the port wing began to drop. The aircraft reached a maximum speed of 172 knots then began decelerating under the influence of the port wing stall.

Twenty seconds after take-off, only 300ft (90m) above the ground, the aircraft began a rapid roll to the left. Ten seconds later, a mile from the end of the runway, it struck the ground and exploded. A fierce fire started immediately and despite the closeness of the airport rescue services, nothing could be done. Everyone on board perished, and this remains the worst single air crash on American soil. Two people on the ground were also killed.

Close examination of the wreckage revealed a fracture in part of the engine pylon. This had led to overloading of the stressed section, and the consequent separation of the engine assembly from the wing. The Federal Aviation Administration ordered an immediate check of all pylons on DC-10s. Further damage was found, and on 6 June the FAA took the unprecedented action of grounding all DC-10s worldwide, a total of 270 aircraft in service with 40 airlines. After stringent checks and the alteration of maintenance and inspection procedures to try to ensure that a similar accident could not happen again, the DC-10 resumed service.

No stall warning
The AA DC-10 suffered an exceptional combination of failures, perhaps the most critical of which was the severing of a number of electrical circuits by the fallen engine and pylon left the pilot with no stall warning system and no 'stick shaker', a system that agitates the controls if the aircraft is in danger of stalling.

The Mount Erebus crash

28 November 1979

An inexplicable navigational error

An Air New Zealand flight to see the spectacular scenery of Antarctica ends in tragedy.

Air New Zealand began operating special 'sightseeing' flights to Antarctica in February 1977. Using DC-10 aircraft, the flights lasted 11 hours and gave passengers spectacular views of the Antarctic ice shelf around McMurdo Sound — where there was an American air base on the ice, Williams Field, and two scientific stations, Scott and McMurdo — and Mount Erebus, an active volcano rising to over 12 000 feet (3 800m).

The flights were popular from the start. Two were flown in February 1977 and more in October and November of that year — the beginning of the Antarctic summer. The flights were strenuous for the crew, as the flying time was at the limit of the fuel load and there was little margin for error.

Initially the flight path took the DC-10s directly over a radio beacon near Williams Field, which enabled a very accurate check to be made. However, this also meant overflying Mt Erebus, so a height of 16 000 feet had to be maintained. To improve the passengers' view, the flight path was changed enabling a descent to 6 000 feet in McMurdo Sound, provided that the cloud base was at least 7 000 feet, visibility was at least 12 miles (20km), and there were no snow showers reported in the area. The aircraft flew in two large circles within McMurdo Sound, giving magnificent views of the ice shelf and the mountains, before starting its long return flight to New Zealand.

Magnetic pole

The navigation on these flights were complicated by the proximity of the South Magnetic Pole, and the crews were given special charts with 'waypoints' inserted to help them keep track. In August 1978 Air New Zealand acquired a new ground computer which was programmed with all the company's routes, including that to Antarctica. Unfortunately, it seems that one of the co-ordinates of Williams Field was entered as 164 degrees east instead of 166, which would move the aircraft's track about 25 miles to the west. The final part of the route was changed to avoid overflying Mt Erebus.

Three flights were planned for November 1979. The first two, on 14 and 21 November, went ahead without problems. The beacon at Williams Field was out of service but another radio aid called TACAN (tactical air navigation aid) was used. On the first flight, on 14 November, Captain Leslie Simpson thought he had located an error in the flight measurements, but his results were inconclusive.

The 28 November flight was commanded by Captain Jim Collins. As he slept the night before, the computer programme for the flight track was checked. By an error, the route was altered to the original bearing which took the flight over Mt Erebus. This change was, by a further error, not communicated to the flight crew. They should have had a 'flash ops' message, but they did not get it.

Inaccurate navigation

The aircraft took off with an enhanced crew of 20 and 237 passengers, including Peter Mulgrew, a distinguished New Zealand mountaineer and polar explorer who was to add a commentary while the aircraft was over Antarctica. The route co-ordinates were entered into the aircraft's AINS (area inertial navigation) system, a spin-off from space flights which provides exceptional navigational accuracy over long distances. The aircraft was now programmed to fly straight towards Mt Erebus; the crew thought it was programmed to fly down McMurdo Sound.

The flight proceeded normally towards Cape Hallett at the tip of the Antarctic continent, with the disappointment that there was extensive cloud reported in the area where these flights normally circled for close-up viewing. The McMurdo weather station reported cloud at 2 000 feet but Captain Collins decided to continue in the hope of getting some breaks in the cloud. At about 40 miles out, the aircraft orbited. VHF contact with McMurdo was frustratingly intermittent — unbeknown to the crew, because Erebus was blocking the line of transmission.

The aircraft continued to descend to 3 000 feet. They could see land on either side and assumed they were flying down McMurdo Sound; they were in fact flying into Lewis Bay, which in appearance was very similar, without being able to see the higher mountains obscured by the cloud. The crew began to feel concern at their position. Flight Engineer Brooks is recorded as saying 'I don't like this' and Captain Collins said 'We'll have to climb out of this'. Peter Mulgrew had indicated that he thought Mt Erebus was about 20 miles to their left: they were in fact flying straight towards it.

Warning system

At 12:50pm the ground proximity warning system sounded with a loud 'whoop' and an electronic voice command *'pull up, pull up'*. There was nothing visible ahead but the crew responded, opening the throttles and pulling the nose up. It was too late. The DC-10 struck the lower slopes of Mt Erebus and broke up, catching fire as it did so. All on board, 257 people in all, were killed instantly.

The aircraft was not located until 1am on 29 November (still in daylight), by which time there was great concern in New Zealand. It was by far the worst air disaster to have befallen that small country. At first pilot error was thought to have caused the crash, but a Royal Commission completely exonerated Captain Collins and his crew in April 1981, concluding that 'the dominant cause of the disaster was the act of the airline in changing the computer track of the aircraft without telling the crew'.

A sad anniversary
The 1979 flights marked the 50th anniversary of Admiral Byrd's first-ever flight over the South Pole. Part of the area overflown by the Air New Zealand flights, the Ross Dependency, is administered by New Zealand. The area commemorates Captain James Clark Ross, who discovered it in 1843. He named Mt Erebus after one of his ships: the name comes from the Greek word for 'darkness'.

The Riyadh fire

19 August 1980

Disastrous errors of judgement

Failure by the flight crew to put emergency procedures into operation leads to 301 deaths.

The problem which affected Saudi Arabian Airlines flight SV 163 on 19 August 1980 need not have killed anybody. But an inexplicable lack of effective action by the crew once the aircraft had safely returned to land led directly to tragedy.

The flight was a scheduled service from Riyadh to Jeddah, carrying 288 passengers and 13 crew in a Lockheed TriStar aircraft. When the aircraft had been airborne only seven minutes, a warning light came up on the instrument panel indicating a possible fire in one of the cargo holds. For several minutes the crew tried to locate the appropriate part of the aircraft manual to see what action they should take.

Checks were carried out to see if there was a fault or if the instruments were faulty. The flight engineer Bradley Curtis asked the captain if he should go back and see if he could see or smell anything. Unable to deal with the problem, Captain Mohammed Ali Khowyter decided to turn back to Riyadh. By now, toxic fumes from the cargo hold were beginning to seep into the main cabin. Nobody told the passengers to pull the oxygen masks down.

No problem

Instead, a message from the cockpit, in three languages, advised passengers to stand by for 'a possible crash landing'. Curtis reported 'everybody's panicking in the back. No problem. No problem at all'.

The aircraft landed safely at Riyadh just under half an hour after taking off, and ground crew could see smoke coming from the hold. The normal procedure would be for the aircraft to stop as soon as possible and for the emergency chutes to be deployed so that everyone could escape. If this had been done many lives would have been saved.

Captain Khowyter taxied the aircraft back towards the terminal building, and kept the engines idling for a further three minutes before shutting them down, at which point a flash fire started in the cabin. It is now known that such fires start as the result of gases emitted by the furnishings overheating. They engulf a closed space in seconds. It took the emergency services 26 minutes to break into the aircraft. By that time all 301 people on board were dead.

The cause of this tragic error was kept secret for months, but eventually it came out, and the inquiry into the disaster concluded that 'the crew responded appallingly slowly to warnings of imminent disaster and made inexplicable errors of judgement'.

Toxic danger

There have been two further incidents where toxic fumes in the cabin have killed large numbers. In 1973 a Varig Airlines flight made a successful crash-landing short of the runway at Orly Airport, Paris. Everyone on board is believed to have survived the landing, but 123 people died when toxic fumes engulfed the cabin. And in August 1985 a British Airtours Boeing 737 caught fire on takeoff at Manchester. Despite fire crews being on the scene in under a minute, 55 people died from fumes. After this incident there were calls for aircraft to be fitted with passenger smokehoods and sprinklers.

The Korean Air Lines shoot-down

31 August 1983

Violation of Soviet airspace

An off-course airliner is gunned down by fighters.

Why did Korean Air Lines Flight 007 violate Soviet military airspace? It is a mystery which seems unlikely ever to be solved. At the time it was said that the aircraft was on a spy mission and even that the violation was pre-arranged to test the Soviet reaction.

From the much-changed political perspective of only a decade later, it seems hard to accept that any airliner could be deliberately shot down, and navigational error seems the most likely cause of the doomed plane flying the wrong course. It was argued that since KAL007 was equipped with the latest inertia navigation system (INS) it was impossible for it to be nearly 200 miles off its intended track. However, no system is infallible, and the plane's co-ordinates could have been incorrectly programmed.

KAL007 was a scheduled Boeing 747 flight from New York to Seoul with a stopover in Anchorage, Alaska. This is a long and tiring trip for both crew and passengers. With a departure time of 20 minutes after midnight (local) from New York and heading west, the aircraft would follow the night round the globe, crossing a number of time zones, with most of the flight being in darkness. The crew was changed at Anchorage while the passengers relaxed for an hour in the lounge.

Departure delayed

Departure from Anchorage was delayed for half an hour after it was found that tailwinds would give the aircraft an arrival time of 5:30am local in Seoul. In common with a number of other major airports, Seoul Kimpo does not accept night flights and opens at 6am.

The crew programmed the INS system ready for departure and the aircraft left Anchorage at 5am local with 246 passengers and 23 crew on board. Its first check was the radar station at Bethel on the Alaskan coast, 300 miles west of Anchorage. From here it was to fly track 'Romeo 20' on a south-westerly curve, passing over pre-plotted but imaginary checkpoints in the North Pacific Ocean which were given codenames such as Nabie, Neeva and Nippi.

In the event it flew some way north of this track. Three hours into the flight, the Korean airliner was 150 miles off course, in Soviet airspace over Kamchatka. The presence of this large, unexpected blip on their radar screens caused great alarm and Soviet fighters were scrambled to intercept. They never made contact with the airliner and returned to base.

The airliner reported to Tokyo that it was over 'Nippi' and heading for the next tracking point, 'Nokka'. In fact it was 185 miles north of Nippi, heading towards Sakhalin Island, where there were Soviet military stations and a missile launching site — an extremely sensitive location. Once again fighter crews were scrambled.

Target destroyed

Western intelligence managed to pick up the voice of the pilot of the SU-15 fighter that closed in on the airliner. If the airliner crew saw the fighter, they did not report it; their only radio contact requested permission to climb to 35 000 feet, which was given. This manoeuvre seems to have caught the fighter pilot by surprise and he overshot the airliner, then circled to place himself behind it again.

The SU-15 pilot must then have received instructions to fire, for the words 'I have executed the launch' were heard followed by 'target is destroyed'. There was one brief startled message from KAL007 saying 'all engines lost . . . rapid decompression' then silence. The airliner crashed into the sea off Sakhalin Island, and all 269 people aboard were killed. The incident provoked international outrage. Unusually, the Soviet military command gave a press conference in Moscow to explain their actions, accusing the 747 of being a reconaissance plane and blaming the incident on the US government.

IFALPA, the airline pilots' body, banned flights to and from Moscow on 12 September. The International Civil Aviation Organization (ICAO) called a special meeting of its Council, at which the USSR representative reiterated the claim that KAL007 was 'a sanctioned and organized provocative flight'. The Council issued a statement deploring the incident and urging the Soviet authorities to do everything it could to recover the bodies of those killed. Following these decisions, IFALPA lifted its ban on 3 October.

ICAO published a full report on 30 December 1983. It said that there was no evidence of any major failure in the aircraft's navigational systems, though confirming that KAL007 had strayed gradually further and further north of its planned route. There was no indication that the flight crew, who were all properly qualified, were at any time aware of the deviation from course, although it lasted for over five hours.

One problem which emerged was that there was no coordination between the US military authorities and the Federal Aviation Authority regarding radar checks on civil aircraft using the North Polar routes. Had there been, KAL007's diversion might have been picked up much earlier.

Spy planes

It also emerged that US authorities had complained of no fewer than 16 off-course diversions by Aeroflot airliners over the USA in 1981–2, one resulting in an overfly of a naval base in Connecticut at the exact time the first Trident nuclear submarine was being launched. The Soviet authorities meanwhile continued to allege that KAL007 was on a spy mission until a year later, when they admitted that a serious mistake had been made.

As a result of the incident, flight procedures on North Polar routes were changed. New communications links were set up and the USSR was informed of all civilian air traffic in the area. In return, the Soviet air authorities offered to assist aircraft in emergencies, and to use the English language in communicating with airliners.

A previous attack

This was not the first KAL airliner to be attacked. On 20 April 1978, a Boeing 707 of the airline also got off course — by no less than 1 000 miles — and was intercepted by Soviet fighters. The airliner came under fire and was badly damaged. Two passengers were killed. Despite losing 15 feet from the left wing, Captain Kim Chang Kyu nursed the plane down to a wheels-up landing on a frozen lake south of Murmansk without further loss of life — an exceptional piece of flying.

Air India flight 182

23 June 1985

An explosion over the Atlantic

All on board die in an accident that can be seen as a tragic forerunner of Lockerbie.

Looking back at the circumstances surrounding the loss of Air India Flight 182 over the Atlantic in June 1985, it is possible to draw disturbing parallels with the Lockerbie disaster three and a half years later. It is always easy to be wise after the event in these matters but aircraft are such an obvious, large target for terrorist activity that it does have to be said that clues were missed which might have saved Pan Am Flight 103.

The Air India Boeing 747 flight, from Toronto to London, left early on a Sunday morning carrying 307 passengers and 22 crew, with Captain Hanse Narendra in charge. Weather conditions were excellent, with a tailwind, and by 8am the aircraft was approaching the coast of Ireland, flying at a height of 31 000 feet.

At 7:05am GMT Captain Narendra called Shannon ground control. The ground controller asked for a 'squawk'. This is a signal which activates the aircraft's transponder, locking it into the ground control computer. From then on signals would be sent and responded to automatically until the aircraft transferred from Shannon's area to that of London Heathrow.

Image fades

The image on Shannon's radar only lasted eight minutes before it faded unexpectedly. It could have been an instrument fault, but there was no response to any signal from the ground, electronic or verbal. Nor would there be: Flight 182 had been blown out of the sky with the loss of 329 lives. Despite the wreckage lying in over 6 000 feet of water, the vital voice and data recorders were recovered within a week in a remarkable salvage operation.

Five weeks before the crash, the Indian High Commission in Ottawa had issued a warning to airports and airlines of possible terrorist attacks against Indian aircraft or flights carrying Indian diplomats. Security in Toronto Airport was considerably tightened, and a private security company guarded all Air India aircraft.

Bomb missed

However, this failed to stop the extremists who got a bomb on board Flight 182. They used the same method as the bombers of PanAm 103. The device was loaded not at Toronto but at Vancouver, on a feeder flight, and transferred to Flight 182. On that day the X-ray machine at Toronto had broken down and a hand-held device was in use. It failed to pick up the bomb which was hidden among clothes in a suitcase, quite possibly disguised as a cassette player, another echo of Lockerbie.

Amazing escape

In 1972 a JAT flight between Copenhagen and Belgrade disappeared at 33 000 feet after an explosion on board. Rescuers searching the wreckage were amazed to find Vesna Vulovic, a stewardess, alive, with only a leg injury. She had landed in deep, soft snow and, possibly due to the angle of impact, had miraculously survived. She was able to give a detailed account of the events on board. Her escape did not put her off flying, and she continued to fly with JAT for another 20 years.

Japan Air Lines flight 123

12 August 1985

The largest single-aircraft disaster

A ruptured bulkhead leads to collision with a mountain.

The Boeing 747 has been the mainstay of Japan Air Lines. By the mid-1980s they had over 60 of these large 'jumbo jets', and expected to increase the fleet to nearly 100 by the end of the century. The aircraft was also in service with many other airlines. It had a reasonable safety record, though an alarming number of minor defects had been reported. On Tuesday 12 August 1985 one of JAL's 747s left Tokyo Haneda at 6:12pm on a routine one-hour trip to Japan's second largest city, Osaka. The plane was fully loaded with 509 people, mainly Japanese flying home or to visit relatives for the three-day Bon holiday, and 15 crew. At 6:24 a loud bang was heard from the tail, and Captain Takahama found he had lost all hydraulic control. The aircraft began a 'Dutch roll', pitching and rolling about the sky and losing height. The captain radioed Haneda requesting permission to return for an emergency landing. Ground control responded, saying that 'Haneda and Yokota (an American Air Force base not far from Tokyo) are ready for your emergency landing. You can begin your approach any time'.

The crash

Captain Takahama and his crew were trying everything they knew to fly the 747. They could only use engine power to control their direction. They turned north, back towards Tokyo, and managed to avoid Mount Fuji. The aircraft flew in a tight circle over Otsuki City and continued north, still losing height. As the crew fought desperately to get it into position to make an approach to one of the airfields, it hit Mount Osutaka, 70 miles (110km) north-west of Tokyo, at a height of about 5 000 feet, in an area of forest where not even a helicopter could land.

Rescuers did not reach the wrecked plane for 14 hours. Amazingly, they found four survivors, all from row 56 of the cabin; the death toll of 520 makes this the worst incident so far involving a single aircraft. An investigation was immediately started to try to uncover the cause of this crash, which caused great public distress in Japan. A year later, it was announced that the aircraft had crashed because the aft pressure bulkhead had ruptured.

The blame was laid at the door of Boeing. In June 1978 this same aircraft had made a heavy landing at Osaka, damaging the tail and the aft part of the fuselage. It had been returned to Boeing for checking and repair, and the crash investigators concluded that the repair had not been carried out to a sufficiently high standard. Eventually, metal fatigue and cracking had occurred and the bulkhead had ruptured. The crew were unable to see the damage to the tail section of the plane, though they were only too well aware that something must be wrong as the plane was not responding to rudder control.

The Boeing witch-hunt

The Boeing company suffered something of a witch-hunt in the 1980s. They were accused by a number of airlines — including JAL and British Airways — of shoddy workmanship, and between 1984 and the end of 1988 were fined 14 times by the Federal Aviation Administration, incurring a total of $245 000 in penalties.

The Lockerbie bombing

21 December 1988

A terrorist attack that shocked the world

A small Semtex bomb destroys a PanAm flight over southern Scotland.

Other aviation incidents are known by the type of aircraft or the flight number: the disaster of 21 December 1988 will always be known simply as Lockerbie, after the small Scottish town on which the major part of PanAm flight PA103 landed after it was destroyed in mid-air by an explosion.

Flight 103 started in Frankfurt as a Boeing 727 feeder to London, taking off at 4:50pm local time and landing normally at 5:20pm London time. The flight continued with the same number but on a different aircraft, a 747, its destination New York, with a departure time of 6pm. There were 211 passengers booked from London to New York, joined by 17 people who had come from Frankfurt, and by a container of luggage which contained the bomb that would kill them all. Unusually for a Christmas flight, there were 159 empty seats.

North then west

The aircraft left London about 20 minutes late and, because of strong winds, headed north before swinging west across the Atlantic. Inside, the passengers settled in their seats, looking forward to Christmas at home. Then, 54 minutes into the flight, the plane was blown out of the sky. Wreckage was scattered over a large area; fortunately for the post-crash investigation, nearly all of it was on land. The main parts of the aircraft, including the engines,

dropped from the sky onto the town of Lockerbie, destroying a number of houses and killing 11 people, bringing the total number of lives lost to over 260.

It was midwinter, the longest night of the year, and investigators were unable to start a detailed search until next morning. There was suspicion from the start that the aircraft might have been blown up, and over the ensuing weeks a remarkable piece of painstaking detective work was carried out. Wreckage was brought into a military warehouse in Longtown, Cumbria from an area more than 40 miles across which included large forests, farmland, towns and villages. Some 10 000 items of personal belongings were assembled, catalogued and X-rayed.

The investigators knew what they were looking for. Twelve days prior to the disaster, warnings had been issued by the US Federal Aviation Administration, on the basis of a call received by the US Embassy in Helsinki, that 'within the next two weeks there would be a bombing attempt against a PanAm aircraft flying from Frankfurt to the US'. And on 19 December, Jim Jack, Principal Aviation Security Adviser to the British Department of Transport, issued a long memorandum to all UK airports and airlines including PanAm that there was a strong likelihood of explosive devices being smuggled aboard aircraft inside small radio-cassette players. Despite these warnings, security was not tightened up and the onward luggage from the Frankfurt flight was loaded onto the New York-bound 747 without being re-checked at London Heathrow.

Police investigation

By the end of January, DCS John Orr, the senior police officer on the investigating team, knew what had been used and exactly where inside the plane the bomb had gone off. An international police investigation lasting nearly three years ended with the naming of two Libyans as suspects for an operation which had begun in Malta before moving to Frankfurt, London and finally the skies over Lockerbie. Airport security arrangements were altered as a result of the crash, and a great deal was learned about terrorist operations and about the way in which small explosive devices can be hidden in seemingly innocuous pieces of luggage.

Although the bomb on PA103 was relatively small, its effect was magnified because the luggage area where it was stored was made of aluminium. Recent research has shown that if plastic lining is used, the effects of such explosions can be largely contained. As a result of this research, some airlines plan to instal such linings for luggage holds. They should be in service by 1994. It has also been alleged that the x-ray machines used at Frankfurt airport were incapable of detecting Semtex explosive, and further research is continuing into how to improve the detecting capability of these machines.

The legal case over compensation still continues as this book goes to press. The situation has been complicated by the PanAm airline, one of the world's largest, going bankrupt in 1992. The compensation case is thus against the airline's insurers, the US Aviation Insurance Group. The defence case maintains that the airline was not aware of the warnings about possible terrorist attacks in December 1988. A total of up to $500 million is sought by lawyers representing bereaved families.

Life in Lockerbie has returned to normal, but the town will never forget that long December night when an aircraft fell out of the sky and it became, unwittingly, the centre of attention for the world's media. Many relatives of the victims have visited the town and through support groups, friendships and associations have been formed, both for the purpose of comforting and counselling the bereaved and to ensure that those responsible for the bombing are brought to justice.

An unlucky placement

The people on board PanAm 103 will never know how unlucky they were: the bomb had by chance been loaded alongside a stressed riveted seam in the fuselage, and when it exploded this seam ripped like paper, causing instant decompression and tearing the aircraft apart before the crew had the chance to send any message. One of the senior investigators said: 'If the bomb had been placed almost anywhere else, it might have killed half a dozen people or just shredded some bags.' The people of Lockerbie were similarly unlucky. The bomb should have gone off over the sea, as in the case of the Air India flight, but because of the aircraft's delayed departure and the strong winds, the plane took a more northerly track than usual for the first part of the flight, and was still over land when the device exploded.

*Part of the passenger cabin from the 747 which crashed at **Lockerbie**.*

The Lauda Air explosion

26 May 1991

Thailand's worst air crash

Another disaster that might have been caused by a terrorist bomb.

The Lauda Air company, based in Austria, was set up by the former world motor racing champion Niki Lauda. It operated regular services to the Far East, and on Sunday 26 May 1991 one of its Boeing 767s took off from Hong Kong bound for Vienna. The aircraft made a routine stop in Bangkok, the Thai capital, and took to the air again carrying 213 passengers and ten crew.

The 767, Flight NG004, headed northwest but when it had gone only about 120 miles, about 15 minutes after take-off, all contact with it was lost. There was no emergency call or other indication of trouble from the aircraft. Shortly afterwards reports were received of a blazing aircraft crashing into an area of bamboo jungle, 1 500 feet up on a hillside.

Drug control agent

All on board were killed. The passengers were of mixed nationality, and included 74 Austrians, 52 Hong Kong Chinese and 39 Thais. Also on board was Don McIntosh, a 43-year-old British drug control agent working for the United Nations. He was based in Bangkok, working on the eradication of heroin trafficking in the area, and it was suggested that he might have been the target for a bomb attack.

Debris from the crash was spread over a large area, and police and rescue services reported that their efforts were hampered by large numbers of people who went to the crash site to loot the wreckage for clothing, valuables, and anything else they could find. The search for bodies was also made difficult by the wide area covered and the awkward terrain. The fact that debris was so widespread is a further indication that an explosion occurred, and that the aircraft was crippled instantly.

This was the worst disaster so far recorded in Thai air space.

A safe design
The Boeing 767, a twin-engine jet, was introduced to service in 1982, and is used by many airlines on medium to long haul services. Before the Lauda Air crash, the aircraft had an unblemished safety record, and there was no indication of any mechanical or other problem with Flight NG004 before the crash happened.

Avalanches, rockfalls and mudslides

Snow is very beautiful, but it can be deadly too. In many of the world's mountain ranges, accumulations of snow under particular weather patterns (generally repeated freeze and thaw) can lead to the snow becoming very unstable, and finally slipping from the mountainsides. As it falls it gathers in more snow, ice, rocks and other debris, and by the time it reaches a valley bottom or run-out slope, can be moving with terrifying force and power. Deaths and injury from avalanches occur in two ways: either from people being buried in the snow itself, which then closes round them, making escape impossible, or from the tremendous 'air blast' that precedes avalanches and can shatter houses with the force of an explosion.

There are two other phenomena like avalanches, equally as deadly as the 'white killer' of the snow. Major rockfalls can be exceptionally destructive. Again there is an accumulative effect, and blast is also a factor here. There is also the mudslide, often associated with an earthquake or with volcanic activity. Some are referred to in those sections of the book, but two dreadful tragedies are included here, both originating from Nevada de Huascarán, the highest mountain in Peru. They occurred within 10 years of each other and the same communities were affected on both occasions; scarcely had they rebuilt their shattered towns and villages after the 1962 avalanche that the mountain struck again with an even worse fall in 1970.

Well-established warning systems for snow avalanches are set up in areas such as the Alps and the Rockies. But even when the avalanche risk is known to be high, there is little that can be done in the way of protecting those below. The best defence is to try to stabilize the slopes with trees, or to construct deflectors which turn avalanches away from centres of population. Even these precautions are no real defence against a major avalanche.

Viewed from a safe distance, a big snow avalanche is an awesome sight, the snow thundering down the mountainside in a reverse 'V' shape, spreading out at its foot and with clouds of spindrift above it. If you are in its path, all you can do is hope you stay near enough to the surface to be dug out afterwards. The white killer continues to take lives every winter.

The sufferings of Leukerbad

1518–1720

A Swiss village buried by the snows

Several times over the centuries tragedy has struck through major avalanches.

Avalanches are regular occurrences in the Alps. They have been recorded for many centuries, and still occur today. Nowadays, a great deal is known about the structure of snow and the various climatic factors that can trigger off avalanches. A large avalanche can move at 200mph (320kph) and an impact pressure of 22 000 lbs per square foot has been recorded. Under such impact it is little wonder that houses crumble and people die.

In the past, avalanches were often thought to be acts of God or or black magic. They were described as 'that which flies without wings, strikes without hand and sees without eyes', and in the Wyler Valley there were stories of an old woman dressed in black who rode down on the snow. In a witch trial at Avers in 1652 it was stated that 'witches are the cause of avalanches'.

Some places seemed to be more prone to avalanches than others. Leukerbad in the Swiss Valais was such a place. Beautifully set at the head of a valley, its waters have long been famed for their curative powers. Pilgrims went there at least as early as the 16th century, but in winter Leukerbad braced itself against the snow's destructive power.

Village flattened

A serious avalanche was recorded here in 1518, when the village was flattened and 61 people died. There were other less serious avalanches in the next 200 years, but in the space of under three years in the early 18th century, Leukerbad suffered grievously. The first disastrous fall occurred on 17 January 1718. During December 1717 there had been a great deal of snow. There was more snow in mid January, then the temperature rose. Under these circumstances an avalanche is always likely, and at 10am on the 17th a fall reached the village, burying three men on its outskirts. Worse was to follow.

At 8pm on the same day a very large powder avalanche crashed down the slopes and swept right through the village. Over 50 houses, the Chapel of St Laurentius, the public baths, every inn — all were destroyed, and only a few houses were left standing. Survivors started a search, but 55 people had died. One man, Stephen Roten, was found alive after eight days, but died later from the after-effects of severe frostbite. The body of the final victim, a young girl, was not found until the snows melted weeks later — still in her bed, yards away from her house in a meadow.

By 1720 the village had been rebuilt, but that was a very bad winter for avalanches, and Leukerbad was struck again. The new houses, inns and baths were severely damaged and there was further loss of life. In 1758, for the third time in 40 years, the village was hit, though less seriously this time.

A British avalanche

There is an inn in Sussex called *The Snowdrop*. Its name recalls the tragic happenings of 27 December 1836 when a huge mass of snow slid off the smooth grass slopes of the South Downs — normally innocuous hills, even in winter — and completely buried a row of cottages.

The Plattenbergkopf rockfall

11 September 1881

The Swiss village of Elm is buried

*Thousands of tons of rock fall
from a mountain.*

Switzerland is known for its snow avalanches, but large rockfalls are also a regular occurrence in the Alps, as they are in other great mountain ranges of the world. One of the worst in recent times happened in September 1881; as with other falls, man's activities had some part to play in precipitating it.

The Plattenbergkopf is one of the outliers of the Glarner Alpen, and there was extensive slate-mining on the mountain in the 18th and 19th centuries. This activity must have steadily reduced the underlying stability of the hill, and a number of small rockfalls had taken place before 1881.

The great avalanche that September may also have been precipitated by heavy rainfall in the preceding days. There were, again, small rockfalls, and these became so regular that people gathered to watch them. On 11 September, a larger fall brought rocks down almost to the valley where the watchers had gathered. Less than half an hour later, another, still greater fall detached a large amount of rock from the side of the mountain.

The mountain moves

The top section of the Plattenbergkopf was by now resting precariously on a narrow base, much of its previous supporting rock having fallen. It was plain that this could not continue, and before long the now alarmed watchers saw the whole top part of the mountain begin to move. Gathering speed and accumulating more mass as it came, the rockfall hurtled down the mountain towards Elm.

By the time it reached the valley, the fall probably contained some 10 million cubic yards (7.5 million square metres) of rock and dust. Much of the mass hit another hill, the Düniberg, and ricocheted off. Accompanied by a thunderous roaring, groaning sound, the rock covered a mile (1.5km) in less than a minute, burying much of the valley around Elm and the village itself.

Where there had been green fields, houses and crops there was now a grey mass of rock, and the air was thick with dust. The village schoolmaster survived, and described what the experience was like. He talked of a great wind which uprooted trees and moved houses bodily. This 'air blast' is a common feature of all avalanches, and is often more destructive than the avalanche material itself. The edge of the fall cut one house in two, slicing through it like a knife through butter. People were annihilated in an instant — 'just as an insect is crushed into a red streak under a man's foot' was the vivid analogy used.

Elm lost 150 men, women and children, and all its productive land.

The Plurs rockfall

Another major rockfall occurred in Switzerland on 4 September 1618. A vast amount of rock became detached from the mountainside above the town of Plurs, completely burying it and all its people. From a population of 1 500, none survived. Four of the townspeople were away on business elsewhere on that day; they returned to find nothing left of their houses or their families. It seems significant that both these major rockfalls occurred in September, at the end of the dry season.

The Tyrolean avalanches of World War I

1916–18

Colossal loss of life through snowfall

Natural risk is deliberately exacerbated by human action.

Generally speaking, this book does not deal with the catastrophes and disasters of war, many and vast in scale though they have been throughout human history. There are a few exceptions, where human intervention has resulted in a natural or semi-natural disaster. The Tyrolean avalanches of World War I are such an example.

In early December 1916 there was a very substantial snowfall in the eastern Alps, continuing on and off for two weeks. Vast amounts of snow were accumulated in the mountains, and the avalanche risk was clearly high. In mid December there was a brief thaw, and many avalanches were set off. A large avalanche from the Marmolada crashed down on a barracks, killing at least 250 soldiers.

Hannibal's losses

Hannibal's crossing of the Alps in 218BC has become a world-famous event. There is a strong possibility that on the descent towards Italy he lost thousands of men and animals through avalanches. The Roman poet Silius Italicus wrote that: 'Hannibal pierced the ice with his lance. Detached snow dragged his men into the abyss and the living squadrons were engulfed'. It is known that on the crossing Hannibal lost 18 000 men and 2 000 horses, as well as several of his famous elephants, so this could be one of the worst avalanche disasters of all time.

Terrifying weapon

Somebody realized that the snow could be used as a terrifying and highly effective weapon. If avalanche slopes were bombed, the falls created would be unstoppable; they could even be directed. The numbers of soldiers annihilated by a few shells would be far greater than through the straightforward use of artillery.

The facts of what happened were suppressed by censorship, and it is difficult to put a figure on the number of fatalities. A conservative estimate puts the number killed in this way as 40 000, on both sides. Matthias Zdarsky, a well-known skier of the time who was involved in training Austrian troops in mountain warfare, is quoted as saying that: 'The mountains themselves were far more dangerous than the Italians'. Zdarsky also claimed to have evidence that 3 000 Austrian soldiers died in only 48 hours through avalanches, and that Italian losses were at least as heavy. A Swiss expert, André Roch, has said that the estimate for avalanche victims throughout the war is 40 000 to 80 000.

The 'avalanche war' became known as the White Death. A German book on the campaign says that: 'Whole barracks, dashing patrols and marching columns were buried in the raging avalanches. Hundreds of men were gripped by the white strangler; even the bravest of the brave had no escape from the winding-sheet of the avalanche. I have seen the corpses. It is no glorious death. It is a pitiful way to die, a comfortless suffocation in an evil element'.

Doubtless there would have been many casualties in the mountains anyway, but the actions of war multiplied the deaths a hundredfold.

The white killer

1910–92

Major avalanches in the Alps, North America and Turkey

Great masses of snow have claimed many victims over the years.

Large snow avalanches occur in many parts of the world. They often occur in clusters, taking many lives with their combined efforts. Such was the case in the winter of 1950–1 in the Alps.

The snowfall in January 1951 was exceptionally high. Between 15 and 22 January, some places had up to seven feet (two metres) of snow. Such a rapid build-up is the perfect preparation for avalanches as the vast weight of the snow accumulates and gradually becomes more unstable on the steep mountainsides.

In the last week of January the 'white killer' began to strike. There were more than 1 000 avalanches in the eastern Alps. The Swiss canton of Graubunden recorded 650, with a total of 54 people killed. The February snowfall was heaviest in the Italian Alps. In Bedretto, in the Ticino, four feet of snow (1.3m) fell on one day, 12 February. There were again many large avalanches; the small village of Airolo was virtually wiped out, with ten people killed. In all, that terrible winter claimed 279 victims in the Alps.

Cascade killer

The worst avalanche tragedy in the USA occurred at Wellington, Washington on 1 March 1910, and became known as the Wellington Snowslide. A vast mass of snow avalanched from the Cascade Mountains

and swept down on the town, striking the railway station area. The whole station building together with three locomotives, carriages, rails and other debris were swept away into a gorge 150 feet (45m) below, and over 100 people lost their lives.

Turkish tragedy

In February 1992 large-scale avalanches caused many deaths in eastern Turkey, an area which often experiences heavy snowfall. The falls of early 1992 were particularly heavy, with more than 30 feet (9m) reported in some areas, and large avalanches began to fall from Mount Gabar onto the villages of Gormec, Sirnak and Seslice. Gormec virtually disappeared under the snow, and more than half its population of 250 were killed.

Snow also engulfed a military post outside the village, killing 70 of the 120 troops stationed there. Those that survived joined in the rescue efforts in the village. Medical teams and emergency supplies were flown in from American bases elsewhere in Turkey, and the Turkish government declared the region a disaster zone as more snow fell and further avalanches were a constant fear.

Snow shower
One strange escape from an avalanche occurred at Bingham, Utah. On 17 February 1926 a man there was taking a shower when a large avalanche roared down Sap Gulch behind the town onto his house. He was lifted from the shower and carried bodily for nearly 100 yards (90m) before being set down unharmed. The incident is recorded in the monthly *Review* of the United States Weather Bureau.

Nevada de Huascarán, 1962

10 January 1962

Ice and rock buries a town

Peru's great peak shows its deadly face.

Nevada de Huascarán is the highest mountain in Peru. A superbly sculptured peak, it thrusts its icy head far into the sky of western Peru. This is an area of great instability in geological terms; earthquakes and other disturbances are common, and the people have become inured to natural disaster. Even so, there is still shock and dismay when disasters occur.

On 10 January 1962 the weight of a vast accumulated mass of ice on the north peak of Huascarán became too much for the mountain to bear and it broke away. As it fell, it gathered up ever larger chunks of rock. The avalanche, travelling at over a mile a minute, was funnelled into the valley of the Ranrahirca River. The town of Ranrahirca was directly in its path.

Irresistible force

Experts from the US Geological Survey later reconstructed the path of the avalanche and estimated that at the outset some two million cubic yards (1.5 million cubic metres) of ice broke away from the mountain. By the time it reached Ranrahirca, the mass had been increased by water, rock and mud to seven million cubic yards (five million cubic metres), a totally irresistible force accompanied by a terrifying roaring sound.

There was no time for the people of Ranrahirca — a town of about 2 000 souls — to do anything. The awful mass swept over them, obliterating the town and its people. Fewer than 100, on the edges of the town, survived. The avalanche continued for a further mile (1.5km), reaching the Santa River and climbing 100 feet (30m) up its far bank before losing its momentum. When it stopped, its leading edge was nearly a mile (1.5km) wide and 45 feet (13m) deep.

This avalanche buried nine villages as well as the town of Ranrahirca. About 4 000 people were lost beneath it plus some 10 000 head of cattle and sheep.

Turtle Mountain

One of the worst rock avalanches in North America occurred at Turtle Mountain in Alberta, Canada, on 29 April 1903. An estimated 80 million tons of limestone became detached from the mountain, possibly weakened by the effects of coal mining, and fell towards the small town of Frank, 3 000 feet below. By the time it stopped, the rock covered more than one square mile (2.5 sq km) and was on average 65 feet (20m) deep. The entrance to the coalmine at the foot of the mountain was sealed by the fall. The miners inside chose not to try to reopen the entrance but to dig out another way where the rock was less thick. After 12 hours desperate work they succeeded, and emerged to a landscape very different from the one they had last seen.

The rockfall killed 70 people and moved the Oldham River bodily 400 feet (125m) across the valley.

Nevada de Huascarán, 1970

31 May 1970

Huascarán strikes again

A major earthquake triggers a mud and rock avalanche to even deadlier effect than in 1962.

The 1962 avalanche from Nevada de Huascarán was bad enough, but worse was to come. After the avalanche, much of the west face of the mountain was left in a very unstable state, and it was clear that any further large-scale earth disturbances could move another vast load of material, threatening life and property once again.

On the last day of May 1970 it happened. The trigger was one of the frequent earthquakes in the area. This was a major tremor, measuring 7.9 on the Richter scale, and was later described by the US Geological Survey as 'possibly the most destructive historic earthquake in the western hemisphere.' Its epicentre was some miles off the Peruvian coast.

Severe effects

The shockwaves travelled across Peru, affecting an area 600 miles (1000km) wide. Coastal towns including Chimbote, Casma and Huarmey were severely damaged, with great loss of life. Inland, in the Rio Santa valley, the main town of the area, Huaraz, suffered very badly, many of its buildings being flattened. Half of the population of 20 000 died as a result of the earthquake.

Rescuers were unable to reach much of the affected area for several days. In mountain villages, with cold weather and little if any shelter, there was further loss of life. Many people chose to stay outside rather

than find shelter as they were terrified that another quake would strike. The total death toll from the quake is believed to be in the region of 50 000, with nearly a million people left homeless.

Rocky ridge

Fifty miles (80km) up the valley was Ranrahirca — rebuilt after the tragedy of 1962 — and higher still the town of Yungay, with a population of around 20 000, which was developing as a winter sports resort. Between Yungay and the main face of Huascarán was a substantial, rocky ridge about 650 feet (200m) high; surely this would enough to protect the town from anything falling from the great mountain?

On the day of the earthquake one of Peru's leading natural scientists, Dr Morales, was in the area with two visiting geophysicists. During the afternoon he experienced a premonition, a feeling of fear, and left hurriedly. The two others felt no such qualms and stayed behind to continue their exploratory work. Morales was right; as he reached safety the shock from the earthquake struck Huascarán, dislodging an enormous mass of rock and ice from the west face. Its extent was later estimated as 10 000 cubic yards (7600 cubic metres). As it slid rapidly down the mountain and across the valley the heat and friction generated caused the ice to melt to water, which combined with the earth and stones to form a thick mud. Within this glutinous mass were huge boulders and rocks, some as big as houses.

For the second time in eight years, Ranrahirca and all its people were buried. The speed of the avalanche, estimated at up to 250 miles per hour (400kph), gave them no chance of escape. Its front was over half a mile (900m) wide and boulders weighing more than three tons were thrown right across the valley.

No hope of rescue

This avalanche had more impetus than that of 1962, and a huge 'tongue' of mud and rock, 15 feet (4.5m) deep, carried on, right over Yungay's protective ridge, and into the town. Virtually everything was buried in a very short space of time, and for those underneath the avalanche there was no hope of rescue. The few survivors included a group who were able to reach the town's cemetery, which was on a hillock, and stayed just above the level of the awful mudslide. This group included the two visiting geophysicists; they all had to stay where they were, with the dead all around them and even under their feet,

for three days and two nights before the mud hardened sufficiently for them to move, or for rescuers to get in.

Although a vast amount of material had fallen from Huascarán, there is no guarantee that future earthquakes will not set off still more avalanches, and the advice from scientists including Dr Morales after the 1970 disaster was that Yungay and Ranrahirca should not be rebuilt on their former sites.

Felt in Lima

The 1970 earthquake was felt over a wide area of Peru, including the capital, Lima, where there was some damage but few casualties. A horse-race meeting was in progress at the time of the quake, and many hundreds of spectators ran out onto the course, believing they would be safer in the open than in or around the grandstands.

Earthquakes

Earthquakes are among the most frequently recorded major natural events on earth. There are many thousands of minor tremors each year, and about 20 major shocks. These shocks almost all occur along the 'fault lines' between the great 'plates' which, it is now known, make up the earth's crust.

There are six major plates plus a number of smaller ones. The plates, which float on the layer of semi-molten rock known as the asthenosphere, are roughly 60 miles (100km) thick and move against each other at about four inches (10cm) each year. Earthquakes happen when the plates either collide head-on or grind laterally into each other. Occasional 'rogue' earthquakes occur away from plate boundaries.

The force released by plate collisions is immense, and it is little wonder that, when the earth itself can rise or fall many feet during an earthquake, buildings on the surface collapse. Earthquake prediction and building technology to minimise damage have both improved greatly in recent years, but many earthquakes occur in places where these techniques are not practised.

Of themselves, earthquakes cause relatively few deaths. The enormous casualty figures that are related in the following pages mostly came about through collapsing buildings burying people, through fire and landslide and through the major waves associated with the earth's movement, which cause severe flooding. These waves, known as tsunamis, are also dealt with in a separate section of the book.

Seismology — the study of the earth's plates and of earthquakes — is still a relatively young science. In past eras, scientific explanations for disasters such as earthquakes were rejected in favour of a strong belief that man was being punished by merciless gods. Contemporary accounts of the earliest quake dealt with here, in AD893, talk of 'a strong earthquake due to the wrath of God' and of the city 'resembling an open-mouthed hell.' Despite the scientific knowledge that we now have, for those caught up in a major quake, the description still seems very apt.

In this section, 14 earthquakes covering a period of 1100 years are looked at in some detail, and others are covered more briefly. It is impossible to say how many people have been killed in earthquakes in the period of recorded history. It certainly runs into many millions. Since 1970 alone, at least 400 000 have died, and the number could be much higher — accurate figures are still difficult to obtain.

The story will continue. Our earth is constantly moving and evolving, and we have inevitably to suffer the consequences.

Earthquake severity measurement

Modified Mercalli intensity scale (1956 Revision)

Intensity value	Description
I	Not felt; marginal and long-period effects of large earthquakes.
II	Felt by persons at rest, on upper floors or favourably placed.
III	Felt indoors; hanging objects swing; vibration like passing of light trucks; duration estimated; may not be recognized as an earthquake.
IV	Hanging objects swing; vibration like passing of heavy trucks, or sensation of a jolt like a heavy ball striking the walls; standing cars rock; windows, dishes, doors rattle; glasses clink; crockery clashes; in the upper range of IV, wooden walls and frames creak.
V	Felt outdoors; direction estimated; sleepers wakened; liquids disturbed, some spilled; small unstable objects displaced or upset; doors swing, close, open; shutters, pictures move; pendulum clocks stop, start, change rate.
VI	Felt by all; many frightened and run outdoors; persons walk unsteadily; windows, dishes, glassware break; knick-knacks, books, etc fall off shelves; pictures off walls; furniture moves or overturns; weak plaster and masonry D crack; small bells ring (church, school); trees, bushes shake visibly, or heard to rustle.
VII	Difficult to stand; noticed by drivers; hanging objects quiver; furniture breaks; damage to masonry D, including cracks; weak chimneys broken at roof line; fall of plaster, loose bricks, stones, tiles, cornices, also unbraced parapets and architectural ornaments; some cracks in masonry C; waves on ponds, water turbid with mud; small slides and caving in along sand or gravel banks; large bells ring; concrete irrigation ditches damaged.
VIII	Steering of cars affected; damage to masonry C and partial collapse; some damage to masonry B; none to masonry A; fall of stucco and some masonry walls; twisting, fall of chimneys, factory stacks, monuments, towers, elevated tanks; frame houses move on foundations if not bolted down; loose panel walls thrown out; decayed piling broken off; branches broken from trees; changes in flow or temperature of springs and wells; cracks in wet ground and on steep slopes.
IX	General panic; masonry D destroyed; masonry C heavily damaged, sometimes with complete collapse; masonry B seriously damaged; general damage to foundations; frame structures, if not bolted, shift off foundations; frames racked; serious damage to reservoirs; underground pipes break; conspicuous cracks in ground; in alluviated areas sand and mud ejected, earthquake fountains, sand craters.
X	Most masonry and frame structures destroyed with their foundations; some well-built wooden structures and bridges destroyed; serious damage to dams, dikes, embankments; large landslides; water thrown on banks of canals, rivers, lakes, etc; sand and mud shifted horizontally on beaches and flat land; rails bent slightly.
XI	Rails bent greatly; underground pipelines completely out of service.
XII	Damage nearly total; large rock masses displaced; lines of sight and level distorted; objects thrown into the air.

Note

Masonry A	Good workmanship, mortar and design; reinforced, especially laterally, and bound together by using steel, concrete, etc; designed to resist lateral forces.
Masonry B	Good workmanship and mortar; reinforced, but not designed in detail to resist lateral forces.
Masonry C	Ordinary workmanship and mortar; no extreme weakness like failing to tie in at corners, but neither reinforced nor designed against horizontal forces.
Masonry D	Weak materials, such as adobe; poor mortar; low standards of workmanship; weak horizontally.

Major earthquakes

All magnitudes on the Richter scale.

Location	Year	Mag-nitude	Deaths	Location	Year	Mag-nitude	Deaths
Erzincan (Turkey)	1992	6.7	2 000	Anchorage (USA)	1964	8.5	131
Uttar Pradesh (India)	1991	6.1	1 000	NW Iran	1962	7.1	12 000
Costa Rica/Panama	1991	7.5	80	Agadir (Morocco)	1960	5.7	12 000
Georgia	1991	7.2	100	Erzincan (Turkey)	1939	7.9	23 000
Afghanistan	1991	6.8	1 000	Chillan (Chile)	1939	7.8	30 000
Pakistan	1991	6.8	300	Quetta (India)	1935	7.5	60 000
Cabanatuan City	1990	7.7	1 653	Gansu (China)	1932	7.6	70 000
NW Iran	1990	7.3	40 000	Nan-shan (China)	1927	8.3	200 000
N Peru	1990	5.8	200	Tokyo (Japan)	1923	8.3	143 000
Romania	1990	6.6	70	Kansu (China)	1920	8.6	200 000
Philippines	1990	7.7	1 600	Avezzano (Italy)	1915	7.5	30 000
San Francisco	1989	6.9	100	Messina (Italy)	1908	7.5	58 000
Armenia	1988	6.9	50 000	Valparaiso (Chile)	1906	8.6	20 000
SW China	1988	7.6	1 000	San Francisco (USA)	1906	8.3	500
Nepal/India	1988	6.9	900	Ecuador/Colombia	1868	*	70 000
Mexico City	1985	8.1	7 200	Calabria (Italy)	1783	*	50 000
N Yemen	1982	6.0	2 800	Lisbon (Portugal)	1755	*	70 000
S Italy	1980	7.2	4 500	Calcutta (India)	1737	*	300 000
El Asnam (Algeria)	1980	7.3	5 000	Hokkaido (Japan)	1730	*	137 000
NE Iran	1978	7.7	25 000	Catania (Italy)	1693	*	60 000
Tang-shan (China)	1976	8.3	242 000	Caucasia	1667	*	80 000
Guatemala City	1976	7.5	22 778	Shenshi (China)	1556	*	830 000
Kashmir	1974	6.3	5 200	Chihli (China)	1290	*	100 000
Managua (Nicaragua)	1972	6.2	5 000	Silicia (Asia Minor)	1268	*	60 000
S Iran	1972	6.9	5 000	Corinth (Greece)	856	*	45 000
Chimbote (Peru)	1970	7.7	66 000	Antioch (Turkey)	526	*	250 000
NE Iran	1968	7.4	11 600				

*Magnitude not available

The Richter Scale

The method popularly used to measure the severity of earthquakes was devised by Charles Richter, a professor of seismology at the California Institute of Technology, in 1935. The scale is not linear but logarithmic, so that each unit represents a 10-fold increase in ground movement and a 32-fold increase in energy. For example, an earthquate of Richter magnitude 7 would have 10 times the earth shaking and release 32 times as much energy as an earthquate of magnitude 6.

Richter's scale has been refined by the Japanese seismologist Hiroo Kanamori, giving more sensitive recordings for the very largest quakes. An 'earthquake intensity scale', with values from one to 12, was devised by an Italian seismologist, Giuseppe Mercalli, in 1902 and later modified by the Americans Harry Wood and Frank Neumann. It too is still used today (see p38).

Dvin

27 March 893

The capital city of ancient Armenia is struck

One of the first such disasters of which we have an account.

The earthquake that struck Dvin, at the time the capital city of Armenia, in March 893 is one of the first of which detailed accounts are available. It was recorded by two historians, Artsruni and Ovanes, and was clearly seen as an event of some significance even in this area, one of the world's great earthquake centres.

The causes of earthquakes were not, of course, understood at the time, and all such natural disasters were thought to be the result of divine intervention, brought about by man's sinful behaviour offending God. Artsruni says: 'In Armenia in the second year of the rule of Smbat I [this equates to AD893] there was a strong earthquake due to the wrath of God ... there was underground shaking and movement of the earth, weakening the solid boundaries of hell itself, inhaling the wrath of the winds and dark waters.'

Open-mouthed hell

He goes on with more vivid prose to make the novel suggestion that the quake had 'moved the solid and weightless gravity to the surface so that hills were moved upwards' and quotes one mountain, Norabhur, as an example. He continues: 'The city resembled an open-mouthed hell, attracting people to their doom ... their homes became their graves.' This seems an excellent description of a city struck by major tremors in which large fissures opened.

According to the other historian, Ovanes, the earthquake happened at night 'accompanied by shakings, howling and terror ... the city of Dvin was destroyed down to its foundations.' He records that the palace of the rulers was shattered 'along with the homes of warriors' and that everything was 'instantly converted to a wasteland'.

Strong aftershocks

Dvin was built on a hill, on loamy soil, so fissuring is very likely to have occurred. It is known that there were many aftershocks, causing further damage and loss of life. Accurate casualty figures are, not unnaturally, unavailable, but it is thought that as many as 20 000 people may have perished. Ovanes says that 'innumerable bodies lay buried in the ruins.' Working on such records as are available, Soviet seismologists have dated the quake to 27 March 893 and believe that, by equivalent modern standards, this earthquake would have had a Richter scale reading of at least 8.

Notable victim
Artsruni records that among the victims of the Dvin earthquake was the principal church leader of the area, Bishop Grigor Rshtunishki, who died, along with his retinue, while at prayer, probably trying to placate the same God who was thought to have caused the devastation.

Eastern Mediterranean

20 May 1202

Did a million die?

Devastation over an unusually wide area from a large, shallow earthquake.

The earthquake of May 1202 that shook a very large area around the eastern Mediterranean is very well recorded. It must have become, rapidly for the time, a very notable event, for among those who wrote of it was the English historian Ralph of Coggeshall (d.1228), who says that the cities of Acre and Tyre were 'overthrown.'

These cities, on the Mediterranean coast of what is now Lebanon, were among the places worst affected by the earthquake, but it was reported from Armenia to Libya and from Sicily to Iran. In Syria, Lebanon, Cyprus, Libya and Egypt there was very severe damage. Acre and Tyre were virtually destroyed, as was the town of Safad, inland from them, and Bedegene, where 'everything was swallowed up' according to Arabic accounts of the disaster.

Collapsing mosques

Nablus, thought to have been near the epicentre of the quake, also suffered very badly, and strong tremors were felt in Damascus where, as in many others places, mosques collapsed, causing great terror amongst the population. There was heavy loss of life in Tripoli, where the old castle of Arqa was ruined.

The earthquake was felt through Egypt from Qus to Alexandria, and there was a long tremor reported from Cairo, where 'sleeping people jumped from their beds in fear.' The quake was of unusual severity for Egypt. Cyprus also suffered badly, with many buildings destroyed and considerable loss of life. Although the quake clearly destroyed many buildings, in some reports of the disaster this may have become confused with damage already caused by Saladin's attacking hordes only 12 years earlier.

Famine and epidemic

Modern seismologists studying the quake believe it to have been relatively shallow but spread over an unusually wide area, and with a Richter scale reading of probably about 7.6 — not one of the largest earthquakes by any means. Despite this, the cumulative effect was clearly catastrophic. There were strong aftershocks for several days following the major tremor.

Arabic reports speak of a million people having died. There is, of course, no way this figure can be checked. Abd al-Latif, one of the principal historians of the period, records 110 000 deaths in Cairo alone, and says that the main aftershock — which may have been almost as powerful as the principal tremor — caused the deaths of 30 000 in Nablus. However, it is known that in many places the earthquake was followed by famine and epidemics of disease, and the death toll would have been greatly increased in this way. We shall never know if this was the worst disaster ever in terms of lives lost, but it was certainly among the worst.

Rhubarb pickers

The ancient city of Baalbek was also very largely destroyed, and here it was recorded that rockfalls from above the town killed 200 people who were gathering rhubarb.

Shenshi

23 January 1556

Colossal death toll in China

If figures are accurate, this could be the worst ever natural disaster.

The earthquake which struck China in January 1556 was felt over a very large area of that great country, but its effects were seemingly most devastating in the province called Shenshi (or Shansi). The main tremor occurred at night, and many thousands of people were killed when their flimsy houses collapsed around them.

It is also recorded that thousands of peasants were, at the time, living in caves hollowed out of the cliffs. These cliffs were of loess, a soft silty material. When the earthquake struck, the whole hollow structure naturally collapsed, burying all those inside.

The earthquake is recorded as being felt in 212 districts of China, and as causing damage and death on a large scale in 100 of these. By modern standards it was most probably over 8 on the Richter scale. The death toll is given as 830 000. Even in medieval times, the Chinese were usually quite accurate with these figures, so we may well be dealing here with the worst natural disaster known to us.

Anatolia

17 August 1668

A year of major tremors

Asia Minor suffers badly over a period of months.

There were shocks and tremors throughout the summer of 1668 in the region known as Anatolia (largely today part of Turkey). The activity reached a peak in mid-August. On the afternoon of 12 August, violent shocks were felt from Istanbul to Izmir, and a number of people were killed. A further strong tremor was felt on 15 August, when the castle in Ankara was shattered and further deaths were reported.

The major shock, however, happened on 17 August. In Ankara a series of violent jolts at intervals of three to four minutes rocked the city. Cliffs above it broke up, sending large quantities of rocks and debris crashing down. The town of Bolu, north of Ankara, was almost totally destroyed, with 2 000 deaths reported.

Hacihamza was also razed to the ground, only its fort remaining standing. In Amasya, the historic 15th century mosque of Sultan Bayazid suffered severe damage, and the town of Tokat was also very badly damaged.

Total deaths from these quakes are believed to have been around 8 000. The main tremor was probably equivalent to Richter scale 8; by the end of August more than 200 aftershocks had been reported.

Some historic earthquakes

1580–1897

Major events worldwide

A catalogue of shocks and tremors affecting many countries.

Earthquakes are major events and as such are well recorded throughout history. A number of quakes, significant for different reasons, are gathered together here in a compendium of catastrophe which serves to show how restless the earth is. Few countries are exempt. Britain records a considerable number of earth tremors each year, though they rarely cause significant damage or death. There was a sizeable tremor on 6 April 1580, with its epicentre in the Straits of Dover. It caused widespread damage in south-east England, with castles and churches suffering as well as ordinary houses, and in France and Belgium. There are no accurate figures for casualties but a number of people died.

The coastal town of Port Royal in Jamaica was built on a somewhat dubious foundation of gravel and sand. On 7 June 1692 a substantial earth tremor severely disturbed the landform here, and most of the buildings of Port Royal slid into the sea. They have formed a fascinating study for marine archaeologists in recent years. It is believed that 2 000 people died in this strange disaster.

Sicily and India

Sicily has been seriously affected by earthquakes a number of times, as well as having an active volcano, Mount Etna, to deal with. In January 1693 there was a very substantial quake affecting the island. The death toll is estimated at up to 60 000.

Many towns and the city of Catania were virtually destroyed.

The earthquake of 11 October 1737 which had its epicentre in the Bay of Bengal is only one of a number of large-scale natural disasters to have struck that area over the centuries. There are few details, but such reference as is made leads to the conclusion that it was a major tremor with severe flooding and tsunami effect following it. The death toll was possibly as high as 300 000.

The Lisbon earthquake of 1755 is fully described in a separate article. Later in the 18th century, the Calabria region of Italy was severely affected by earth tremors. In February and March 1783 six substantial shocks hit the area. Contemporary accounts record that nearly 200 towns and villages were affected. A commission was set up to study the effects of this earthquake, and its report, which goes into considerable detail, is still regarded as an important piece of seismological work. The death toll from these tremors was around 50 000.

American quakes

The Mississippi/Missouri area is known more for major floods than for earthquakes, but in 1811 and 1812 there was a series of tremors affecting the area and causing considerable damage. There were three main shocks, on 16 December 1811, 23 January and 7 February 1812, centred on Missouri and Arkansas, but recorded as far away as Washington DC and Pittsburgh.

Few people died but over a wide area the landscape changed dramatically. Forests were destroyed, large ravines opened up, the great Mississippi itself changed course for a time, and Redfoot Lake was formed. The town of New Madrid was destroyed later on through river erosion resulting from these quakes.

Landforms were also distorted and changed after a major earthquake in India on 16 June 1819. This must have been a quake of unusual severity; centred on the Rann of Kutch area, it was felt 1 000 miles away. A large area of land sank beneath the sea, and the remarkable landscape feature known as the Allah Bund (a classic fault scarp) was raised up. Thousands of people are known to have died.

More investigations

Scientific investigation of natural phenomena was developing rapidly in the 19th century. During one of his pioneering voyages to the Pacific, as a result of which he published his highly controversial theory of natural selection and evolution, Charles Darwin had the opportunity to see for himself the damage caused by a severe earthquake affecting Chile. The quake struck on 20 February 1835 and caused considerable uplift of coastal areas, as well as many deaths and the destruction of towns and villages. Darwin witnessed the tsunami that followed the quake.

Another well-studied earthquake happened in Italy on 16 December 1857. Centred on the Bay of Naples, it caused a great deal of damage despite only being of about force 6.5 Richter. Several villages and small towns were wiped out, and about 12 000 people were killed. This quake was meticulously studied by the pioneer seismologist Robert Mallet, whose careful recording of the effects led to proper scientific conclusions as to the depth of the earthquake's focus.

Precursor to 1906

The line of collision known as the San Andreas Fault, in California, has been responsible for a number of major earthquakes, including the one which severely

affected San Francisco in 1906. There was a precursor to that event on 26 March 1872 when a major quake was felt, with its epicentre under the Owens Valley. There were substantial landscape changes, with new ravines appearing and other ground uplifted, but the area was lightly populated at the time, so only about 60 people died.

It was a different story in Japan 19 years later when an earthquake of about 7.9 Richter struck the provinces of Mino and Owari. The quake affected a vast area extending to over 300 000 square miles (800 000 sq km); over 120 000 houses were destroyed or seriously damaged and more than 7 000 people died. There was considerable land movement along a 70-mile (110km) fault running up Honshu, Japan's principal island.

We close the 19th century (apart from the 1893 Kuchan earthquake, recorded separately) in Assam, where the quake of 12 June 1893 created a severe undulating motion in the earth affecting an area of 30 000 square miles (75 000 sq km). This was one of the first quakes to be picked up by the new sensitive seismographs at major research centres. With an equivalent magnitude of 8.7 Richter, it was a very severe disturbance. Many thousands of buildings were destroyed, but the death toll was relatively light at 1 500.

Dragons' heads

The first known instrument for measuring earthquakes was made about AD130 by a Chinese astronomer, Chang Heng. It was a bronze dome with a carefully balanced inverted pendulum inside it. Around the rim of the pendulum were eight carved dragons' heads, each with a bronze ball balanced on the tongue. Below each dragon was a bronze toad, mouth agape. Any significant tremor would dislodge the ball from the dragon's mouth into that of the toad below, giving an approximate direction for the quake. The dragon and toad are the Chinese symbols for heaven and earth respectively.

The destruction of Lisbon

1 November 1755

An All Saints Day disaster

A great city is devastated by earthquake and tsunami.

By the mid-18th century, Lisbon was at the centre of a considerable Portuguese empire, with possessions in Africa, South America and the Far East. It was a city of some 275 000 people with a major port on the estuary of the Tagus River and had many fine buildings including the royal palace and a splendid new opera house.

Earth tremors were not unusual in Portugal, but there was no reason for the people to fear a major disturbance as they went to Mass on All Saints Day in the great cathedral and the many churches in the city. At 9:30am it must have seemed as though the wrath of God had descended upon them: for several minutes the earth shook with a loud sound like thunder. The noise of falling buildings added to the uproar.

Fire and flood

After a pause there was a second tremor, then a third. By this time a dense cloud of smoke had risen, darkening the city and alarming the survivors even further. This was bad enough, but there was worse to follow. Fires broke out in many parts of the city, destroying buildings that had survived the earthquake, and shortly afterwards people in the harbour area were terrified to see the waters rush out, exposing the seabed for over half a mile offshore. This phenomenon has become well-known in earthquakes affecting coastal areas.

Those watching this awful unnatural scene had worse to face, however. The retreating waters stopped, turned around and raced back to shore with exceptional force as a vast wave. The Lisbon wave was said to be 50 feet (15m) high when it smashed into the waterfront area of the city, destroying everything in its path and drowning hundreds if not thousands of people who had not the slightest hope of escape.

Candide's story

The great writer Voltaire used the Lisbon earthquake as the basis for a scene from *Candide*. His description is by no means overstated: '. . . they felt the earth tremble beneath them. The sea boiled up in the harbour and broke the ships which lay at anchor. Whirlwinds of flame and ashes covered the streets and squares. Houses came crashing down. Thirty thousand men, women and children were crushed under the ruins . . . the terrified Candide stood trembling with fear and confusion. "If this is the best of all possible worlds" he said to himself, "what can the rest be like?"'

Although there is no exact measurement for it, this was clearly a very substantial earthquake. Its shock waves were felt as far away as Scotland, where water levels on major lochs rose and fell by several feet. The same happened in Switzerland, and on the canals of the Netherlands, the disturbance was great enough to cause large barges to snap their anchor cables. Considerable damage was caused to towns and cities in North Africa, particularly around the town of Fez in Morocco, where death and destruction on a large scale was reported. A tsunami wave crossed the Atlantic and struck the islands of the Lesser

Antilles, reaching over 20 feet (6m) high in places.

Following the main tremors came a whole series of aftershocks lasting for many months. It is estimated that there were as many as 500 of these shocks, keeping the Portuguese people in a state of fear and alarm. In July 1756 the British Ambassador in Lisbon received a letter from his counterpart in Madrid asking: 'Will your disturbed earth never be quiet?'

Palace destroyed

In Lisbon, the effects were catastrophic. Of the 20 000 or so houses in the city, less than 3 000 were left standing. The palace and the opera house were both destroyed by fire. Churches and other public buildings were flattened, and warehouses full of fine goods were burnt to the ground, ruining their owners. The city had virtually to be rebuilt from scratch. Many people were burned alive. Numbers of dead were never accurately recorded, but it is though that Voltaire's figure is some way out and that at least 60 000 people failed to survive the disaster — over a fifth of the entire population. Large numbers died in churches where they were attending Mass. Lisbon's great cathedral was reduced to a ruin, and hundreds died there when huge pillars and sections of roof fell on them.

As it happened on a Sunday, and All Saints Day at that, questions were raised as to how a merciful God could have allowed such a thing to happen, killing so many innocent people, including children.

Many pamphlets, tracts and even books on the subject were produced. The priests, naturally, were telling their congregations that God was angry with them for their sinful lives — Lisbon had been a rich city of many pleasures, Candide's 'the best of all possible worlds' — and that they must repent.

The earthquake was extensively studied by scientists, who tried to point out — without total success — that earthquakes were natural phenomena. In *Candide*, Voltaire has the character Pangloss pontificating on the subject, saying 'the earthquake is nothing new. The town of Lima in America experienced the same shock last year. The same causes produce the same effects. There is certainly a vein of sulphur running under the earth from Lima to Lisbon'.

Lisbon has suffered a number of tremors in the past 240 years, but none nearly as severe as the quake which caused such fearful damage on All Saints Day 1755.

A government inquiry

At the time of the disaster the Marques de Pombal was one of the chief ministers in the Portuguese government. A pragmatic man with an interest in science, he is said to have replied when asked by the distraught King José I what to do: 'Bury the dead and feed the living'. Pombal arranged for a questionnaire to be sent to every town and village in Portugal to try to find out when the quake was felt, how strong it was, and what damage was caused. This was one of the first systematic inquiries into a major earthquake.

Kuchan

17 November 1893

A city torn apart

A violent earthquake shatters buildings and destroys whole forests.

The city of Kuchan in the region of Western Turkmenia was hit by an earthquake of exceptional force at about 3pm on 17 November 1893. Working on the damage created, seismologists equate it to Richter force 9. The quake was followed by powerful aftershocks. A contemporary account records that 'Almost the whole night tremors occurred one after another, reaching 70 in a 24-hour period.'

Virtually no buildings in Kuchan were left intact — 'torn apart' is the term used in the same report. Streets were deep in debris, and the area's fine vineyards were ruined, as were productive forests. It is said that: 'Forested hills were simply taken apart and rolled downward. Only a third of one of these hills remained.' The valley of the Garmab River was split by deep fissures, and over a large area the soil 'looked as if shaken by a sieve.'

This was clearly a quake of great severity. The city walls came crashing down as did its mosques, and the palace of the ruler, Il'khan Kuchan. According to local reports, at least 18 000 people died, including all of the 11 wives of the Il'khan.

Messina

28 December 1908

Sicily's capital ravaged

Shock waves and floods devastate the island.

A violent tremor, with vibrations lasting nearly a minute, multiple aftershocks, and a strong tsunami, struck the island of Sicily in the Mediterranean between Christmas 1908 and the New Year. The coastal landscape was greatly altered, with both upward and downward displacement of several feet (up to 1m) in a number of places including Reggio.

Messina, the island's capital, was particularly badly affected. The strong tremor, approximating to Richter 7.5, caused immense damage to buildings and streets.

Other towns and villages on the island were also badly damaged.

It was a terrible disaster, happening at the Christmas period, a time of celebration and religious festivals on the island. The loss of life was very great; it is estimated that 58 000 people died as a result of this, the worst earthquake disaster in the Mediterranean in modern times.

Kansu

Another December earthquake struck the Kansu district of China nine days before Christmas in 1920. Estimated at Richter 8.6, it caused great earth disturbance and there were many landslips. Ten cities or large towns were severely affected, and the loss of life was put at 200 000.

San Francisco

18 April 1906

A famous event

Earthquake and fire destroy a large part of the Californian city.

California is classic 'earthquake country'. It lies on the long San Andreas Fault, a geological boundary between two of the earth's tectonic plates, which are estimated to be moving past each other at a rate of about 2.5 inches (7cm) each year. With such movement taking place, it is hardly surprising that disturbances occur regularly in the area.

There are records of earthquakes in the area in 1800 and in 1857, the latter causing horizontal earth movements of as much as 30 feet (9m) in places. Another quake in 1872 caused considerable damage and is thought to have killed around 60 people. At the time, the towns and cities of the area were still growing. By the end of the 19th century both Los Angeles and San Francisco were large conurbations, and both were well aware of the earthquake risk. From the pattern of known disturbances over the past century, if there was to be a major quake, it seemed likely to be in the San Francisco area. And so it turned out.

Three shocks

The quake started early in the morning of 18 April 1906 and would have recorded probably 8.3 on the Richter scale. One report speaks of 'a grinding and creaking sound and a roaring in the street'. There were three main shocks, of which the third was much the worst. The line of the disturbance seems to have been from San Francisco Bay southwards across the city. It passed through the 'downtown' area, where tenements stood on reclaimed marshland: no match for an earthquake, and the houses collapsed rapidly. Nor did more modern buildings fare much better. The City Hall, only recently completed and lavishly fitted out, had cost more than five million dollars and was said to be shock-proof. After the earthquake all that was left was the outline of its tower. But, as with many similar instances, the greater part of the damage was caused not by the quake itself but by the resultant fires, which were far beyond the ability of the embryonic fire service to control. They had only 38 horse-drawn fire engines.

Wine and sewage

Extraordinary measures were resorted to. Restaurant owners used wine to try to put fires out. In some areas, the fire service tried to create firebreaks by dynamiting buildings, but they lacked expertise and many of these buildings blew outwards, merely adding to the fire damage. Even sewage was used in a desperate attempt to limit the extent of the flames.

The fire burned for three days, laying waste a large part of the city, from lowly tenements to the palatial houses of the wealthy on Nob Hill. Over 28 000 buildings were destroyed. Some buildings did survive, while others were bodily moved on their foundations, remaining upright but in a dangerously unstable condition.

The loss of life was surprisingly light. Most people were able to escape before the fire took hold, and the death toll was 500 — 0.2 per cent of the city's population. The figure includes a number of people shot for looting. In the aftermath of the quake, the city was placed under martial law while order was restored, and anybody found guilty of looting was severely punished. The earthquake left 200 000 people homeless. Many of them took such refuge as they could in Golden Gate Park, and it is reported that 23 babies were born there. Among the survivors was the great operatic tenor Enrico Caruso, in town to sing *Carmen*. He vowed never to return, and he never did.

World Fair

A major rebuilding programme started immediately, with central government help. Many of the new buildings were designed to resist future quakes. Within four years, Congress had approved the choice of San Francisco as the site of a World Fair to mark the opening of the Panama Canal. By then virtually no trace of the 1906 earthquake remained.

However, the city is well aware that another major earthquake could happen at any time. There was a fairly severe shock in 1989 (see box) but if there is a pattern to them, the next really big one would be due early in the 21st century. One possible early clue to activity being studied by scientists is 'doming' of the land in the affected area. This is reported to have happened in Japan in 1923, and is occurring now in Southern California. In some places the land level has lifted by up to a foot, a clear indication that far below the surface, there is great seismological activity. Buildings are stronger and rescue services much more sophisticated these days, but nothing can adequately prepare for a really big earthquake, and fire remains a major hazard.

The October 1989 quake

San Francisco was struck by a moderately severe earth tremor on 18 October 1989. The tremor, which recorded a maximum 6.9 on the Richter scale, caused considerable damage and killed 275 people, some of whom were gruesomely crushed in their cars when the top deck of a two-level freeway gave way, falling on to the roadway below. Major damage was limited, but it served as yet another warning of the city's vulnerability.

San Francisco after the 1906 earthquake.

Tokyo/Yokohama

1 September 1923

Japan's greatest single catastrophe

A severe earthquake and major fire takes the lives of over 140 000 people.

The earthquake of 1 September 1923 was one of the most severe of this century, recording 8.3 on the Richter scale. Its epicentre was in Sagami Bay, just offshore from Tokyo, Japan's largest city, and its port, Yokohama. Measurements taken after the quake showed the level of disturbance: the floor of the bay had risen by 800 feet in one place and fallen by 1 500 feet in another.

In Japanese folklore, the first day of September is traditionally a day for unpleasant things to happen, but the people in Tokyo and Yokohama could scarcely have foreseen the disaster that was to befall them. The main shock happened at midday, and was so great that seismograph needles in the area were sent off the scale. In terms of the damage caused, the quake could not have happened at a worse time.

Fires from braziers

Around midday, in the Japan of the 1920s, charcoal braziers would be lit in hundreds of thousands of homes to prepare a meal. The shock overturned these braziers, instantly starting fires and trapping people inside their homes. In Yokohama, oil escaped from burst tanks and poured down drainage canals, catching fire as it did so and trapping thousands more people.

The earth shook violently for over five minutes, with great holes appearing in the streets and buildings leaning over at drunken angles. Tokyo's tallest building, the Twelve Storey Tower, split in two and collapsed, but in general the fire did more structural damage than the quake itself — Japanese buildings are light with paper panels partly because of the continual threat from earthquakes; paper and wood is naturally much less harmful than falling masonry.

Nonetheless, there was terrible loss of life. A party of 200 children on an excursion train trip were buried alive under a falling embankment. Another train, at the village of Nebukawa, fell over a 150-foot cliff into the sea, drowning all those aboard except one fortunate survivor. The American Hospital in Yokohama collapsed down a cliff with all its patients and staff inside. Hundreds of people tried to escape in small boats, only to be drowned by aftershock waves or caught in burning oil slicks. The liner *Empress of Australia* picked up several thousand people before moving out into the open sea to ride out the storm.

Hotel survives

One building which did survive the quake and fire largely intact was the Imperial Hotel, designed by the American architect Frank Lloyd Wright with shallow foundations on the theory that it would 'float' above the worst effects of the earthquake. It appeared that his thinking was vindicated, but unfortunately what was successful in one way was less successful in others; the building gradually sank into the soft ground, and was demolished in 1968.

Vast numbers of people made their way to an open area in the grounds of a large clothing depot during the afternoon, thinking they would be safer there. But they were horribly trapped when one of a number of 'fire tornadoes' that were criss-crossing the city swept into the area, either burning people alive or choking them with dense fumes of carbon monoxide. With the water mains all dislocated, there was no chance of fighting any of these fires. Eyewitness reports say that whole groups of people were flung up into the air, coming down charred beyond recognition. It is estimated that 40 000 people died in this one area of Honjo alone.

No water

When it was all over, 300 000 buildings — 60 per cent of Tokyo and 80 per cent of Yokohama — had been flattened by quake or fire. Almost every major building in Tokyo was lost including 17 libraries, 151 Shinto shrines and 630 Buddhist temples. In Yokohama, the fine long pier, used by vessels from all over the world, was shattered; and the beautiful Daijingu shrine, a place of pilgrimage and peace, was reduced to charred debris. A statue of a prominent Yokohama citizen, Li Kamon-no-Kami, was turned through 90 degrees but left unharmed.

In the hours after the quake, many survivors wandered about in a dazed condition, with placards round their necks giving the names of lost relatives. Lack of potable drinking water was a severe problem in the days after the quake and there was further loss of life from injuries, disease and dehydration. A week later there were still over 25 000 people living out in the open. Large-scale evacuation then started so that clearing up and rebuilding could begin, and by the end of September over two million people had left Tokyo and Yokohama for temporary homes elsewhere.

It was Japan's greatest single catastrophe, with a total loss of 143 000 souls. Japan registers several hundred tremors every year, most of them minor, and the country is now a world leader in building design for earthquake survival. Contingency plans for cities such as Tokyo include trained 'disaster teams', ten days supply of drinking water in tanks designed to resist shocks, and large emergency stores of food and blankets. Despite this, another earthquake with the same severity as the 1923 tremor would still cause major damage to any of Japan's densely peopled conurbations (Tokyo and Yokohama have a combined population of about 15 million).

An amazing escape

One woman had an extraordinary escape during the earthquake. She was taking a bath on the second floor of the Grand Hotel when the building shook and started to collapse. However, the complicated mass of piping supported the bath, which dropped very gradually to ground level, with the woman still safely inside it — and most of the water as well!

Agadir

29 February 1960

Major earthquake hits Morocco

A coastal town suffers as tremors and tidal waves strike.

In 1960, Agadir was a busy centre for business and tourism, a Southern Moroccan town of about 50 000 people. Although earth tremors are not especially unusual in the area, major shocks are rare, and Agadir had no reason to believe it was about to suffer such a catastrophe. The last major quake in the area was in 1731.

The earthquake occurred during the night of 29 February. The first big shock caused severe damage in and around the town. Photographs exist of the Hotel Saada, an almost new building of four storeys built for the growing tourist trade. Before the quake it stands proudly, a symbol of modern Morocco; afterwards, all that can be seen is a squashed heap of rubble, less than the height of one of its storeys.

Tidal wave

The earthquake was followed, as is often the case in coastal areas, by a violently powerful tsunami which carried inland for a quarter of a mile (400m), submerging buildings, cars and streets and drowning many people. The national militia headquarters collapsed, and many serving members of the Royal Moroccan Army died. The main hospital in Agadir was badly damaged, but the staff managed to rescue most of the patients.

At the time there was a French naval base at Agadir, and it found itself the centre of relief operations. Ships of the French Navy arrived, bringing medical teams, rescue workers and supplies of food and clothing. French Air Force planes brought tools and lifting equipment, to try to locate and free people trapped by masonry and other debris.

Strong oscillations

This was not a particularly severe tremor, measured on the Richter scale (only 5.7). But earthquakes do not necessarily have to have a high reading to be damaging. Seismologists in Paris said that the oscillations in Agadir were greater than those recorded during the Lisbon earthquake in 1755, another example of a coastal city suffering from both tremor and tidal wave. The casualty figures in Agadir were revised upwards several times in the days after the quake, finally reaching a figure of about 12 000 dead and many thousands more injured, homeless or both.

It was a dreadful tragedy for the town to suffer. Aid was offered by many countries including Britain, the USA, Germany, Spain and Portugal as well as France. Agadir took many years to recover from the Leap Year earthquake of 1960. It is now again a fine city and resort, no doubt hoping that it is spared from earthquakes for another 230 years.

Push and shove

There are two main types of shock waves from an earthquake. They are called P and S (for primary and secondary) but have also been neatly described as 'push and shove'. The P wave travels very rapidly and in a relatively straight line. The S wave, which follows, travels much less fast, and moves from side to side. Both waves can cause tremendous damage.

Alaska

27 March 1964

The Good Friday earthquake

The state's economy is ruined as a major earth tremor and tidal wave causes widespread devastation.

The earthquake that struck Alaska on Good Friday 1964 was one of the most severe shocks ever recorded. It was a complex tremor and straightforward readings were difficult, but it seems to have peaked at about 8.4 on the Richter scale. It registered even higher on the scale devised by the Japanese seismologist Keiti Aki, which bases its measurements on the 'seismic moment' — the amount of slippage over the entire fault surface.

Alaska is the USA's largest and most remote state. Despite covering over 500 000 square miles (nearly 1 500 000 sq km) it has a population of under half a million and few large towns. It contains much virgin forest and tundra and holds North America's highest peak, Mount McKinley (20 320 ft/6 194m). There are several active volcanoes including Mt Katmai, a protected 'national monument'. The state is on the Pacific Rim fault line, one of the earth's major earthquake zones.

The major shock was felt at 5:36pm. The epicentre was in Prince William Sound, 80 miles (130km) east of the town of Anchorage. The shock was felt over a radius of 1 000 miles (1 600km) and seismologists later estimated that perhaps as much as 100 000 square miles (250 000 sq km) of the earth's surface had moved either upward or downward.

Streets tilted

Anchorage (the largest town in Alaska, with a population of about 100 000) was very badly damaged. In some areas, the slippage was so bad that streets were left with one side as much as 11 feet (3.3m) higher than the other. There was similar damage in Port Richardson and other smaller towns. The central business area of Anchorage was declared a write-off. Fortunately, as it was the Easter holiday and outside normal working hours, few offices were occupied, or the loss of life might have been much higher. As it was, over 1 000 homes were completely destroyed.

An eye-witness described how he felt the shockwaves and ran outside, watching in horror as great fissures opened in the earth, and his house groaned under unimaginable forces before it crashed down. He was himself swept away by a landslip into a newly-created ravine and was lucky to escape. All services in Anchorage were cut off and emergency provision had to be made for power, fuel, drinking water and waste disposal. A mass inoculation programme was put into effect to ward off diseases such as typhoid.

Valdez, on the coast, was almost completely destroyed, with 26 people reported dead. The population of about 1 000 were moved 100 miles to a safer location. Kodiak Island, south-west of Anchorage, also suffered grievously. Of the island's population of 2 500, 70 per cent were killed either by the quake or the huge tsunami waves which followed it.

Wave damage

These waves were a major feature of the Alaskan earthquake. They raced southward down the coast as far as California, and right across the Pacific to New Zealand and Japan. There was considerable damage in British Columbia, Canada's westernmost state, and in the Pacific states of the USA, with a number of people drowned. Twelve died in Crescent City, California, when waves crashed over the seafront business area, and four children sleeping on a beach in Oregon were swept out to sea and lost. The waves reached 20 feet (6m) high in a number of places.

Considering the severity of the earthquake, the loss of life was light, with fewer than 200 people killed. But the damage to property and commerce was enormous, and Alaska's economy was very seriously affected. The state was declared a disaster area and President Johnson promised federal aid. The tsunami wave devastated the fishing industry, one of the state's mainstays, and there were serious forest fires affecting the logging trade. Docks, canneries, and wood processing plants were destroyed in coastal towns.

Restoring services

It was estimated that at least $30 million was needed just to restore basic services. Property damage was put at over $350 million. Three-quarters of the state's businesses were affected in some way and the loss for 1964 alone was put at $750 million. A nationally coordinated aid programme was immediately put into effect. Alaska was fortunate at least in having the backing of a wealthy and powerful government to start the restoration of its shattered economy.

There were several sharp aftershocks in the days after the main quake. On Monday 30 March a shock registering 7.3 Richter shook the area, but without causing too much further damage, and on 3 April the alarmed citizens of Anchorage felt another tremor, though again little fresh damage was caused. It was a reminder that an earthquake is not a single event; in this case, the fault slippage could have been from 30–60 miles (50–100km) below the earth's surface, and there is always a 'settling-down' period when less violent aftershocks occur.

Detailed study

The 1964 Alaskan earthquake was the subject of detailed research by scientists and seismologists. Work went on for several years and in 1973 the US National Academy of Sciences produced an eight-volume report running to 4 700 pages. It led to considerable improvements and refinements in the way earthquakes are predicted and in designing buildings to minimize damage.

Friuli

Italy, 6 May 1976

The end of a way of life

Towns in Northern Italy are destroyed by severe shocks.

The earthquake of May 1976 saw the end not just of fine old towns and villages in Northern Italy but also possibly of a way of life. The destruction was so severe, and the consequences so long-lasting, that many people left the area never to return.

Earthquakes in this area are the result of pressures accumulating through the northward movement of rocks under the Adriatic Sea thrusting against the Alpine strata. As with Lisbon in 1755, the result is liable to be a large number of small shocks as well as major disturbances. This pattern disrupted life in the Gemona area of Northern Italy after the main quake, hampering attempts at restoring the area to normality.

Castle destroyed

The main shock happened on the evening of 6 May 1976. Registering 6.0 on the Richter scale, its epicentre was near Udine, the largest town of the area known as Friuli. Smaller towns and villages such as Gemona and Maiano were, however, worse affected: four-fifths of all the houses in Gemona were destroyed, along with the town's medieval castle. The shock was felt over a very wide area, from Yugoslavia to Belgium. In Venice electricity was cut off, but there was little structural damage.

In the Friuli region, over 50 000 people were made homeless — a third of the total population — and when all the wreckage and rubble had been cleared, the death toll from the earthquake reached 939. Survivors had to find such temporary accommodation as they could, in tented villages or even empty railway coaches. The Italian Government promised aid but it was slow to arrive. To add to the problems, in the months after the main tremor there were dozens of minor aftershocks.

As the summer drew towards its end, many hundreds were still living in tents or other temporary shelter. The unsettled earth had not yet finished with Friuli, however. The disturbances of the previous months culminated in two severe aftershocks on 12 September. Houses damaged in May collapsed, and such new buildings as had been started also fell. Roads and railways were blocked by landslides.

Autumn had arrived early, with unusually low temperatures and a persistent cold rain. The mood of the people turned to despair. They had stayed with their shattered homes through the summer, but the thought of a long winter without proper homes was too much. More than two-thirds of the population of Gemona, Maiano and the other villages left. They were given accommodation in holiday apartments and chalets on the Adriatic coast.

By April 1977 prefabricated houses had been erected in the Friuli villages, and some of the people returned, but many had decided to make their life elsewhere, even overseas in countries such as the USA with strong Italian communities. The once close-knit life of Friuli was shattered, just as their homes had been on that awful May night.

> **The Skopje quake**
> Across the Adriatic Sea from Italy, the town of Skopje in Yugoslavia was severely damaged on 26 July 1963 by an earthquake of similar magnitude to the Friuli shock. Over 15 000 houses were destroyed and about 1 000 people lost their lives.

Tang-shan

China, 28 July 1976

The greatest modern earthquake disaster

A city of a million people is reduced to rubble in a few minutes.

Tang-shan is one of those cases where the full human toll may never be known. It is generally accepted as being the worst disaster of modern times with an earthquake as its root cause, but the Chinese authorities have released widely contradictory figures at different times.

The major shock was recorded worldwide. Instruments at the US Geological Survey centre in California had it reaching a maximum of 8.3 on the Richter scale — an exceptionally severe disturbance. Its centre could be traced to the area of Tang-shan, an industrial and mining city some 85 miles southeast of Beijing. The city had a population before the quake of around one million, and Tang-shan District, which includes much excellent agricultural land, held about six million.

The main shock, which occurred at 3:45am local time, lasted a full two minutes and caused immense destruction in the city. Out of 680 000 buildings, 650 000 were destroyed or suffered serious damage. Factories and water towers collapsed. Over 100 road bridges and many rail bridges fell, and 330 reservoirs were damaged in some way. All of the city's basic systems — water, electricity, sewage and communications — were crippled. To quote a Chinese report: 'In a matter of seconds a flourishing industrial city was reduced to rubble.'

Aftershocks continued for some time, one of them, at 8pm the same evening,

registering 7.1, which is quite exceptional. This shock caused the destruction of a major hydroelectric generating plant 12 miles (20km) from Tang-shan. The severity of the situation was compounded by the fact that Tang-shan had many miles of mining tunnels beneath it. These collapsed, not only worsening the damage on the surface but trapping 10 000 miners who were on night shift.

Enormous resources

Once the scale of the disaster became apparent, the Chinese government poured enormous resources into the Tang-shan area. Immediate aid included 140 medical teams, 650 vehicles and 28 000 soldiers. In the following weeks, 30 000 'technical staff' (rescue workers and other specialists) were sent in, and an almost unbelievable 52 000 workers arrived to repair the shattered road and rail system, which was all reopened by 10 August.

The aid almost overwhelmed Tang-shan. In the days immediately after the quake, because the roads were so badly affected, enormous traffic jams built up around the city, and were not eased until 30 July, when a proper transport system was worked out. Rescue operations were highly successful — over 80 per cent of those found buried were brought out alive, as were many of the miners trapped underground, though hundreds still perished. The last survivor to be brought out was a miner, rescued 181 hours after the quake.

The medical teams at the disaster scene numbered many thousands. They had to well over half a million people needed medical aid of some sort, 360 000 of them in Tang-shan itself.

Amended figures

Accurate estimates of the numbers of dead and injured were hard to obtain. At first sources in China (though not the official government information service) said that 650 000 people had died. This figure was later amended to 750 000, and a large number were said to have been injured. A figure of 655 237 dead was published in January 1977, but in a later report, in November 1979, the New China News Agency gave the Tang-shan death toll as 242 000.

A book about the disaster, written by members of the Chinese Seismological Service and published in English in 1988, gives amazingly precise figures. It says 242 419 died (135 919 in Tang-shan city) and 164 581 suffered serious injury. The book contains much fascinating detail about the earthquake and the way it was dealt with, and we have no reason to doubt its veracity.

After the earthquake, virtually nothing remained of the city of Tang-shan, and there must have been equally severe devastation in surrounding towns and villages. Peter Griffiths, a reporter on *The Times*, reached the area a year after the quake, and described what he saw in graphic terms: 'The transformation from rural near-normality to scenes of urban destruction is swift and shocking. One minute the train is speeding by waving fields of wheat, the next it is crawling through a desert of rubble stretching as far as the eye can see'.

City rebuilt

A rebuilding programme was carefully worked out, and construction started in 1979, though the vast amount of earthquake debris was not finally removed until 1981. By October 1985, 95 per cent of the people of Tang-shan had moved into new houses. The industries resumed production, and Tang-shan is today again a thriving city of over a million people. The great disaster of July 1976 is not forgotten, but Tang-shan looks to the future.

Animal warnings

Chinese seismologists have developed many ways of predicting major earthquakes. They are now looking at animal behaviour patterns. In the days before the Tang-shan quake, there were many reports of strange behaviour. Chickens ran about, clucking incessantly and refusing to eat, frogs stopped their night-time croaking, and goldfish jumped out of bowls. Such behaviour, indicating alarm, has also been reported from other parts of the world.

*Chinese workers start the job of rebuilding near **Tang-shan**.*

Mexico City
19 September 1985

The city centre resonates and falls

Although the earthquake epicentre was 250 miles (400km) away, its worst effects were felt in Mexico City.

A combination of unfortunate circumstances led to the severe damage and loss of life experienced in Mexico City in September 1985. The earthquake was a big one, measuring 8.1 on the Richter scale. It was felt from Texas to Guatemala, a distance of 1300 miles (2000km). Anything over 8 is likely to cause massive damage, but the epicentre of the quake was 250 miles (400km) south-west of Mexico City, on the Pacific coast. Coastal regions suffered, but not on the scale of the capital city. Acapulco, the popular tourist resort on the coast, reported only minor damage.

Mexico City is one of the largest conurbations in the world, with a population approaching 19 million. The central part of the city is built on the long dried-up bed of an old lake. Over the past 100 years, the water table here has dropped as water has been extracted, and the surface has subsided by about 25 feet (8m), leaving the former bed of the lake part-hollow, and akin to a drum in that it has a natural resonance. This resonance can be measured, and approximates to a 'beat' every two seconds.

The main quake happened at 7:19am on 19 September; the seismic waves radiated out also with a resonance of one beat every two seconds. Meeting the lake bed, a 'bounce' effect was set up, which was transmitted through the surface and into build-ings. The third linking factor was that this part of the city held a number of apartment blocks, offices and government buildings of around 10 to 12 storeys. Such buildings also have a resonance of two seconds.

Dancing buildings

The combination was disastrous. Survivors described how buildings 'swayed as if they were dancing' — a very apt description indeed. Inevitably, many fell, trapping hundreds of people under the masonry. In the suburbs the damage was much lighter, but in the city centre a major catastrophe had occurred. More than 250 large buildings including hospitals were either totally destroyed or seriously damaged. Power lines, water mains and other services were cut. There was a fire at the central telecommunications tower, cutting international telephone and telex lines. Many people were trapped in the underground railway system for hours. They were actually safer than people on the surface — earthquakes rarely cause underground damage. But the main concern was for people buried in the collapsed buildings.

The Mexican government declared a state of emergency. Aid arrived from many countries. Specialist teams from the USA and Europe brought thermal image cameras, cutting tools and dogs trained to sniff out people buried under avalanches. Searchers worked round the clock as long as hope lasted. On 26 September, from the collapsed ruin of the Juarez Hospital, where hundreds died, a young woman and her tiny premature baby were brought out alive. Later that day a nurse, Angela Mendez, was also rescued, after a tunnel 40 feet (12m) long had been cut through debris.

Demolition teams

On 29 September, the Health Ministry, seriously concerned about the spread of disease, ordered that all collapsed buildings should be fumigated, and demolition teams moved in. A major inoculation programme against typhoid and tetanus was also started. The human problem was daunting in its scale. Up to a million people were surviving in tents or other temporary shelters, or in the open, without proper food or running water.

Many people spent days searching for missing relatives without success. There was no time to wait for organized funerals. As soon as bodies were identified, they were buried in mass graves. Appeals were broadcast on radio and television for people to come and identify bodies. This was partially successful, but those still unidentified after a few days were carefully photographed and then buried.

Ships lost

The exact death toll is not known. The Mexican authorities, naturally anxious to play down the scale of the disaster, issued a figure of 5 000. Rescue services and aid agencies put the total at not less than 10 000 and perhaps as many as 20 000. Even the latter number would be only 0.1 per cent of Mexico City's total population. Hundreds more died in outlying districts and in the coastal regions. A number of ships were lost at sea as great waves developed. On the evening of 20 September there was a further major shock, which caused more damage.

A rebuilding programme got under way with little delay, but the earthquake compounded Mexico's already serious economic difficulties, despite emergency assistance from the International Monetary Fund. The effects of the 1985 earthquake will be felt for many years yet.

> **Babies survive**
> More than 50 small babies were rescued in the days after the quake. Their survival was put down to the simplicity of their existence, with a total lack of psychological stress, making them unaware of the seriousness of their situation. Their main problem was dehydration. The last survivors to be found, ten days after the main quake, were two babies.

Armenia

7 December 1988

A major Soviet disaster

Great loss of life as several towns in Armenia are flattened.

The earthquake which struck Armenia, in the south-west of the former Soviet Union, at 8:48am GMT on 7 December 1988 was not by any means one of the largest, in world terms. It measured 6.9 on the Richter scale, and in seismological terms does not classify as a major event, for which a reading of at least 7 is needed. However, it was undoubtedly a major human catastrophe, with enormous loss of life as a city and several towns and villages were very severely damaged.

It should be said, to put things in perspective, that an earthquake registering 6.9 is still equivalent to the simultaneous detonation of 100 hydrogen bombs. Little wonder that the effect was so devastating. The quake was most seriously felt in the city of Leninakan on the Turkish border (population about 250 000) and the town of Spitak (pop. 16 000). It was reported that three-quarters of Leninakan, Armenia's second city, lay in ruins, and that Spitak was almost completely destroyed.

In both places, apartment blocks were reduced to rubble and all services were disrupted. Many schools were destroyed, and early reports spoke of hundreds of children among the dead and dying. That this was a major disaster became apparent when an initial figure of 50 000 deaths was given.

Specialist teams

A major relief effort began immediately after the earthquake with specialist teams of rescue workers and doctors flying in from Moscow and other main Soviet cities. Casualties were flown out by helicopter to unaffected towns such as Yerevan where emergency medical centres were set up. There was an urgent need for temporary shelter, blankets and clothing, and supplies were coordinated by the Soviet Red Cross. Thousands of Soviet citizens answered broadcast calls for blood by becoming donors at special centres set up at hospitals, universities and other centres.

The Soviet president, Mikhail Gorbachev, who was on an official visit to the USA, left immediately when told of the disaster, cancelling proposed calls in Britain so that he could travel to the disaster area. He found scenes of ruin and desolation as survivors struggled to find what shelter they could from bitter winter weather, with overnight temperatures as low as minus 20°C. Over two million people were homeless.

International aid was offered from many countries. Specialist teams went from Britain with thermal search equipment to help look for survivors trapped under fallen buildings, and aid workers from the Red Cross and other charities were also soon involved. On the first day of an appeal being opened, the London branch of the Moscow Narodny Bank received donations totalling nearly £200 000 as well as practical offers of help.

Large fissures

As searches in the affected area continued, it became clear that initial casualty figures would have to be revised upwards. A local spokesman said that 'in the Spitak region, which had a total population of 55 000, there is almost no-one left alive' and Leninakan was described as 'looking like a scene from a war film'. It was said that the death toll could reach 100 000, making this one of the worst earthquake disasters of the century. It seemed that the quake opened large fissures in the earth and that the tremors had been exceptionally violent, with whole buildings disappearing into the chasms opened up and others simply shaken to pieces.

Four days after the earthquake, there was further tragedy when an Ilyushin-76 military transport aircraft carrying servicemen coming to help rescue efforts collided with a helicopter on approach to Leninakan. All 78 people on the transport plane and the helicopter crew of four were killed. On the same day, however, 200 workers were found alive in the basement area of a factory which had collapsed. The underground part of the building had survived almost intact.

The tragedy brought warring people in neighbouring Soviet republics together, their friction forgotten. There has been long-standing conflict between Christian Armenia and Muslim Azerbaijan, but the latter state freely opened its borders to Armenian refugees, who came in thousands to find shelter, temporary accommodation and support. According to Radio Moscow, 'this awful event has ended hostility between the two republics'. The peace turned out to be only temporary.

Turkey escapes

As is usual with earthquakes, there were a number of aftershocks, the strongest measuring 5.8 Richter, but so much damage had been done by the first major tremor that the aftershocks caused relatively little new damage. While Armenia struggled to come to terms with the disaster, across the border in Turkey there was relief that so little damage had been caused. Only four deaths were reported, showing the intense, local nature of the quake.

When Mr Gorbachev visited the area he was faced by angry people demanding to know why warning of the earthquake had not been given. Unfortunately, it is still not possible to give proper, accurate warning of major quakes. Periodic trends can be discerned in areas such as Armenia, which lies in the 'collision zone' between two tectonic plates, the Anatolian, moving north, and the Eurasian, moving south, but genuine forecasting is still impossible. Until it is, people living in zones of major earthquake activity will continue to live with the ever-present danger of a tragedy such as that in Armenia.

Earlier quake

This was not the first severe earthquake to affect the town of Leninakan. On 22 October 1926 the area was hit by three substantial tremors, the strongest equivalent to a reading of 8 on the Richter scale. Over 4 000 buildings in Leninakan — 40 per cent of the total — were destroyed, at least 400 people died, and over 50 000 were left homeless. There was also great damage in the surrounding areas.

North-west Iran

21 June 1990

The country's worst earthquake

Severe tremors in the area bordering the Caspian Sea kill many thousands.

Much of Iran lies within a recognised earthquake zone. The area is on the Turkish–Aegean tectonic plate, which pushed up the Elbruz mountain range in past millennia. Its highest peak, Demavend, reaches 18 400 feet (5600m). Just after midnight on 21 June 1990 — the summer solstice in the northern hemisphere — there was a major tremor registering 7.3 on the Richter scale.

The earthquake's epicentre was under the Caspian Sea, a few miles off the coast near the Iranian border with Azerbaijan. The worst affected areas were the coastal province of Gilan and an inland region, Zanjan. Damage extended over a wide area and the towns affected included Qazvin, the medieval capital of Persia, which gave its name to the Caspian, the largest inland sea in the world..

In Rasht, the provincial capital of Gilan, a city of about 300 000 people on the Caspian coast, whole apartment blocks collapsed. Buildings destroyed included the historic town hall, built by Russians 200 years ago. In Zanjan, the colourfully-named Valley of Assassins was badly affected. The towns of Manjil, Loushan and Roudbar-e-Alamut, with a combined population of 100 000, lost 70 per cent of their buildings. The tremor was felt in the Iranian capital Tehran, 250 miles (400km) to the south-east, and in Sanandaj, near the Iran/Iraq border in the west of the country.

Figures revised

First estimates put the number of dead at up to 10 000, but this figure was quickly revised as rescue teams reached more and more communities and found them devastated. A week after the quake, a figure of about 40 000 dead was being suggested, with 250 000 injured and 500 000 homeless, making it, in human terms, Iran's worst earthquake disaster. Accurate figures will probably never be available as many bodies were buried very quickly once found, in mass graves, to try to prevent the spread of disease.

The death toll could have been even higher had it not been for two factors. One was the hot summer weather, in which many people sleep in the open. This reduced the number of casualties from falling debris. The other factor reflects the rapid spread of technology even into quite remote regions such as this. Large numbers of people were watching a World Cup soccer match between Brazil and Scotland on television at a time when normally they might have been asleep, and were thus able to take action very quickly instead of being trapped or buried as they slept.

At first, the Iranian government denied there was a need for outside help. Many countries offered help, but for several days, until the full scale of the tragedy became apparent, it was declined. Then, as casualty figures climbed, there was a change of heart. The Iranians contacted the UN Disaster Relief Organization and asked for help.

International effort

A major international rescue and relief effort was rapidly under way. Appeals were opened in many countries, and the Red

Crescent swiftly organized an airlift of thousands of tents and blankets for temporary shelter, together with rice, tea, sugar and other supplies. Casualties were airlifted out to Tehran and other larger towns and cities, to relieve overburdened hospitals in the affected area.

Ironically, expertise acquired by Iranian forces and medical teams during the long war with Iraq was put to good use in the earthquake zone. Outside help was also offered, with experts from Switzerland, France and Britain flying in. France's Minister for Aid, M. Bernard Kouchner, went to Tehran himself to help organise the relief effort. At times like this, political differences are put aside and countries such as the USA, which had severed diplomatic ties with Iran, freely offered humanitarian assistance. President Bush sent a message of sympathy to his Iranian counterpart, President Hojatolislam Rafsanjani.

Villages wiped out

The rescue teams were able to reach towns and larger villages in the area without much difficulty, but they faced a tougher job in getting through to literally hundreds of small villages in the mountains, many of which, from such reports as were available, seemed to have been virtually wiped out. Houses in these villages are still built of baked mud, and collapse quickly when tremors strike. They are, on the other hand, easily rebuilt.

In the days after the main tremor, there were many aftershocks in the area, causing further damage. Earthquake specialists warned that this could be the beginning of a period of high activity in the region. Examination of past records of tremors indicated a 20-year cycle at regular intervals. Time will tell whether they are right; meanwhile, the people of Gilan and Zanjan are rebuilding their shattered towns, and their lives.

Another severe earthquake

There was another major tremor in Iran in September 1978, registering 7.7 on the Richter scale. The city of Tabas was very seriously damaged, and it was estimated that up to 25 000 people had died in the eastern part of the country.

Erzincan

13 March 1992

A city is devastated

Turkey's year of disasters continues with more death and destruction.

On the evening of Friday 13 March 1992 — a day traditionally associated with bad luck in the West — an earth tremor registering 6.7 on the Richter scale struck eastern Turkey. It affected a large area, with damage reported from many villages and towns, but by far the most serious effects were on the city of Erzincan.

With a population of around 100 000, Erzincan is 3 000 feet (900m) above sea level. It is in a known earthquake zone, and because of this, buildings of more than three storeys are officially banned. However, enforcement of the regulations has been lax and many buildings of five and six storeys were badly damaged or destroyed in the quake.

The tremor struck as families were sitting down to the evening meal that breaks the daily fast during Ramadan. The winter had lingered long in Turkey, and nighttime temperatures were well below freezing, adding to the problems of people trapped beneath debris. One survivor described how there was 'a great roaring sound' and the earth 'shook and then shook again'.

State of emergency

The Turkish government, already shaken by the serious avalanches of February and the pit disaster just 10 days before the earthquake, declared an official state of emergency and rushed aid to the stricken city. The Turkish Red Crescent sent aircraft and lorries with thousands of tents and blankets, a mobile hospital, food and supplies of blood. International aid came from Britain, France and Switzerland with trained disaster rescue teams and medical staff. Help also arrived from the USA and Russia.

Dramatic rescue

People watching on Turkish television saw a dramatic moment captured on film as a reporter shouted into a damaged building and was answered by a voice saying that 20 people were alive. They were all rescued safely.

There were many deaths in the Hotel Uratru in Erzincan, one of the large buildings which collapsed, and in two mosques which were full of people at evening prayer. The deputy governor of Erzincan province was at prayer at his home after breaking his fast. 'As I turned towards Mecca' he said, 'the ground began to collapse under me. I thought the Day of Judgement had arrived.'

The total death toll was expected to rise to over 2 000. Three days after the main tremor, a severe aftershock measuring 6.4 Richter struck the area, causing further damage and disruption. Despite the cold weather, many survivors were sleeping out of doors to reduce the risks of being trapped in buildings.

Unlucky city
Erzincan suffered from a previous severe earthquake in 1939. On that occasion 30 000 people were killed and the city was very badly damaged. There was another earthquake disaster in Turkey in 1983 when over 1 300 people were killed in Erzurum by a shock measuring 7.1 on the Richter scale.

Environmental disasters

The consequences of man's actions, particularly in the field of industrial production, on the world's environment have only begun to be properly appreciated during the past 40 years. During that time a number of environmental disasters have occurred, and a selection is described here.

Before World War II there undoubtedly were environmental disasters, but they were either of smaller scale or less well documented. Control of production, effluent and waste disposal was minimal in industries such as coal mining, textiles and chemicals. When 'health checks' on fresh waters began to be carried out, many were found to be either dead or badly polluted.

This section concentrates largely on individual incidents. Very large scale problems such as acid rain, the destruction of the world's rain forests and global warming have not been tackled here. These problems are still the subject of intense debate among environmental scientists and cannot adequately be dealt with in the short space allocated to each incident in this book.

What we have here is quite bad enough — a chapter of accidents indeed, and a warning that we often get into areas of probable pollution impact before properly understanding what we are about. Huge oil tankers sailed the world's seas at a time when there was only scant knowledge of how to deal with the results of a major spill: we have had to learn from experience, and wildlife in particular has suffered grievously as a result.

The appalling human tragedies of Minamata, Seveso and Bhopal show that we still have much to learn in keeping industrial processes involving toxic or inflammable materials under control. The Spanish 'olive oil' case shows only too clearly what the results can be when profit is the driving force.

Three incidents from the former Soviet Union are included. In two of them, Kyshtym and Sverdlovsk, the full facts will probably never be known. How many other such incidents have been hushed up despite serious consequences? The third, Chernobyl, could not be kept quiet. The effects of the world's most serious accident to a nuclear plant (so far) will continue to be assessed for decades to come.

Ten of the incidents described here have occurred in the 15 years before this book was written. It remains to be seen whether the next 15 years will produce 10 more, or 100, or whether lessons really have been learned. We meddle with the environment, quite literally, at our peril.

Minamata

Japan, 1950s

Disaster comes to a fishing community

Mercury poisoning from a chemical plant affects thousands.

Minamata is a fishing village on the island of Kyushu, the southern part of Japan. It was a quiet, pleasant place until the Chiso Chemical Company established a plant there in the early 1950s for the manufacture of plastics. Before many years had passed, Minamata was to give its name to a disease that attacks the brain cells and has no hope of cure or even alleviation.

Among the earliest signs of trouble were village cats acting in a very strange manner. Some were seen to jump into the water and drown while others ran around in a crazy fashion. Nobody thought that whatever was affecting the cats of Minamata could affect the people too, but by 1953 cases began to be reported.

Mental disorders

The symptoms included convulsions, muscular spasms, blindness (temporary and permanent), impaired speech and, most tragically of all, deformities and mental disorders amongst babies born in the area. Scientific testing established the source of the problem as a poison formed by a compound of mercury and methyl, and the source of the poison as infected fish from the bay: the staple diet for both the villagers and their cats.

Suspicion fell on the Chiso plant. If the company had discharged mercury along with its other wastes into the bay, this mercury could have combined with methyl formed when micro-organisms in the water broke down organic waste (a normal process) to make the deadly cocktail. Chiso denied all responsibility, and refused to allow any scientific testing of its effluent, and the Japanese government backed the company.

The number of cases grew steadily, and so did the public outcry, but it was not until the mid 1960s that either Chiso or the Japanese government acknowledged that the plastics plant was the source of the problem. The plant closed in 1966, and after a long legal battle, Chiso had to pay out millions of yen in compensation. At least 150 people died of the poisoning, and hundreds of others were affected.

Contaminated tuna

The Minamata case alerted other countries to the danger of mercury getting into the food chain: it was used in pesticides and also occurred in factory effluents, as at Minamata. Unacceptably high levels of methyl mercury were found in the seas around Sweden and Norway, and in the USA all canned tuna was withdrawn from sale when samples were found to be contaminated.

In 1972, over 90 nations signed an agreement banning the dumping of mercury (and other harmful wastes) into the sea; but for the people of Minamata the problems continue. Affected children and adults have to be cared for, and women are afraid to have more children in case the babies are born deformed.

Mad Hatters

The expression 'mad as a hatter' is common; a character called the Mad Hatter appears in Lewis Carroll's *Alice in Wonderland*. Like so many similar phrases, there is some basis in fact. In the 19th century, a compound of mercury was used in millinery and there were well reported cases of hat workers exhibiting, though in a milder form, some of the symptoms later seen at Minamata.

Kyshtym

USSR, February 1958

A mysterious radiation escape

*Another Soviet incident which
has never been fully explained.*

It seems certain that something happened
in the Kyshtym area, in the Russian Urals,
early in 1958. Nuclear material, possibly
from a large underground waste store, appears to have escaped in substantial quantities, and affected a large number of
people with radiation sickness. One report
talks of over a thousand cases of severe
burns. As was usual with events which the
Soviet government did not wish to see pub-
licized, the facts are difficult to establish.

There were many nuclear establish-
ments in the area around the town of Kyshtym, and it is believed that a major waste
depository was established there by the
early 1950s. From reports which have appeared recently, and witnesses who have
broken their silence, it seems that an
escape occurred early in 1958. It may have
been through waste material overheating
underground, causing a large explosion; it
may have been through an accident at one
of the nuclear plants; it may have been
through contaminated water supplies affecting towns and villages.

Nothing spared

The Soviet pursuit of nuclear weapons su-
premacy in the years after World War II
took little account of human safety. This is
confirmed by Professor Mikhail Klochko,
who sought political asylum in Canada in
1961. He said that: 'To achieve the goal of
making the bomb in the shortest time, the
authorities spared neither material ex-
pense nor human life.' He reported that

one of his colleagues from the Urals had
told him: 'You cannot imagine the colossal
death rate — each time I visit the plant I
find the cemetery has doubled in size.'

One of the most important plants was
called Kyshtym 40. It produced weapons-
grade plutonium and had a reprocessing
plant, and it was the site of a major waste
storage facility. If there was to be a serious
accident, this was a very likely place. The
problem is that reports are sketchy and to
some extent contradictory. In 1979, a report prepared by scientists at the US nuclear research centre at Oak Ridge,
Tennessee, concluded: 'A major airborne
release occurred in the winter of 1957–8
. . . the most likely cause was the chemical
explosion of high-level radioactive wastes
associated with a military plutonium production site.'

Further evidence comes with the disap-
pearance from later maps of a considerable number of small towns and villages in
the Kyshtym area, and downwind of it, and
reports that road signs warned drivers not
to stop, and to keep their windows closed.
The full truth may never be known, but it
seems clear that a human tragedy of large
proportions occurred at Kyshtym.

The Love Canal affair

The Soviet Union is not alone in initiating
industrial disasters. A notable case
happened at Love Canal, not far from the
Niagara Falls in New York State, in the late
1940s and early 1950s, though the effects
were not fully realized until many years
later. Drums containing hazardous and
highly toxic chemical waste were regularly
dumped in the area, and over a period of
time, began to leak. A large area of
countryside was contaminated and several
hundred homes had to be evacuated. The
affair caused a national scandal.

Torrey Canyon

18 March 1967

The first big oil spill

The environmental impact of supertankers losing their cargo begins to be felt.

Before the *Torrey Canyon* ran aground, oil spills from tankers were not regarded as a major environmental threat. The events of March 1967 changed that. At 118 285 tons, *Torrey Canyon* was at the time the 13th largest vessel afloat; today there are many bulk carriers more than twice her size.

Torrey Canyon was owned by the Barracuda Tanker Company of Bermuda, a subsidiary of Union Oil, Los Angeles. She flew the Liberian flag, had an Italian crew and on her last fateful voyage was under charter to BP, sailing from the Persian Gulf with a full load of crude oil for the BP refinery at Milford Haven in South Wales. Up to its final stages, the voyage was uneventful.

The master, Captain Pastrengo Rugiati, was a very experienced officer, but he was under some pressure to make port; the ship's agents in Milford Haven had advised him that unless he could catch the evening tide on the 18th, he would have to wait until the 24th to dock. Six days wasted would be expensive.

Heading for the rocks

The first indication of trouble came when the chief officer picked up a radar reflection of land at 6:30am on 18 March. He was expecting an echo marking the Scilly Isles, but to starboard; this reflection was to port. He altered course to pass west of the islands, the normal passage, but for some reason Captain Rugiati countermanded the order, bringing the ship back to her previous heading. He also put the vessel on automatic pilot, whereas in such a situation it would be more normal to take over manual control. The ship was steering straight for the Seven Stones rocks. The lightship there saw the danger and fired warning rockets, but it was too late, and at 9:15am the *Torrey Canyon* struck the Pollard Rock, westernmost of the Seven Stones, at 16 knots.

During the next few days, several attempts were made to pull the tanker off the rocks, without success. During this period an explosion in the engine room killed a crewman; as a result, the vessel was abandoned. Final attempts were made over Easter weekend (25–6 March) but the vessel was jammed fast, and on the evening of Easter Sunday the *Torrey Canyon* broke in two.

Major spill

Oil had been leaking from her since she ran aground but a major spill now resulted. With over 100 000 tons aboard, disastrous pollution seemed inevitable. A vast oil slick 35 miles (55km) long and 15 miles (24km) wide developed, drifting towards the coast. Over 50 000 tons of oil escaped, fouling most of the coast of Cornwall, much of Brittany and parts of the Channel islands — all popular holiday areas. Many thousands of birds and marine animals died — 8 000 oil-covered birds were recovered from Cornish beaches alone — and tourism was badly affected. It took three years for the fishing industry of the area to begin recovering.

At the time, little was known about ways of minimizing the effects of such a major oil spill on the environment. Desperate efforts were made to contain the oil, and to stop it drifting onto beaches. Detergent was used to treat the slick, but later studies found that the detergent caused more damage to marine life than the oil. In recent years techniques have been developed including the use of foam, flexible barrages to prevent the oil reaching the shore and guide it out to sea where it can eventually disperse, and the use of 'vacuum cleaner' barges to suck up the oil from the sea. Eventually, the British government ordered Navy strike aircraft to bomb the wreck, to fire the remaining oil. This was partially successful.

In the aftermath of the *Torrey Canyon* disaster, the British government was much criticized for failing to foresee that such a thing could happen; even if foresight had been there, the means of dealing with an oil spill of perhaps 100 000 tons were not. The previous largest oil spill in British waters was less than a tenth of that amount.

Oiled birds

Although the oil from the Torrey Canyon had a dreadful effect on the environment, lessons were learned which were applied to later disasters, particularly about the way to treat oiled seabirds. There are now a number of specialist centres in Britain ready to deal with oiled birds. Repeated washing with warmed vegetable oils breaks down the crude oil and cleans the bird's feathers and plumage. A period of recuperation is then needed for the bird's own natural oils to re-establish themselves before controlled release into the wild can take place.

*Seen from Penzance, smoke from the **Torrey Canyon** after it was bombed by the Royal Navy.*

Seveso

Italy, 10 July 1976

A deadly chemical cloud

*Dioxin affects a wide area in
Northern Italy.*

In the years since World War II there have
been a considerable number of incidents
involving escapes of chemicals from manufacturing plants. Some, including the
best-known and those with most widespread or tragic effects, are detailed in
these pages. Others have been 'hushed up'
or have happened in areas such as the
Soviet Union or China where release of
information has, in the past, been strictly
controlled. All of these incidents have
added to the global pollution load, and
have caused human tragedy and suffering.

Seveso was one of the worst of these
incidents, partly because the chemicals
which escaped were being used to make a
powerful herbicide, which itself is harmful
to the environment. So one wrong was
compounded by another, and people and
animals suffered grievously as a result.

Chemical cocktail

The Seveso explosion occurred just after
noon on Saturday 10 July 1976 at the plant
operated by ICMESA in the town, which is
not far from the major industrial city of
Milan. The explosion forced open a valve
and allowed a chemical cocktail to escape
into the atmosphere and fall slowly onto
Seveso and the surrounding area. The
cloud contained dioxin, one of the deadli-
est of all poisons. To their considerable
discredit, the ICMESA company did not
disclose the make-up of the chemicals in
the cloud for nine days, and a further five
days elapsed before a company doctor advised that evacuation of the worst affected

areas was the best course. By then it was too
late.

The toxic cloud had its most serious effects over an area of about 300 hectares.
Within this area were the houses of some
6 000 people together with market gardens, fields of grain and some grazing
land. Within two days, many people felt ill
and had symptoms of diarrhoea, vomiting,
severe headaches and sores on their bodies. Thousands of birds were found dead,
as were hundreds of animals including
cats, dogs and rabbits.

Overloaded doctors contacted public
health officials for clues as to the nature of
the poison, but since ICMESA had not
given any detail, saying merely that the
cloud might possibly have had herbicidal
material in it, analysis was impossible.
Once the company (and its parent company, Givaudan, a Swiss conglomerate)
had admitted that dioxin was involved,
proper action could be taken.

Evacuation zone

Public health officials divided the affected
area into two zones. The worst infected
area was named Zone A. It covered about
100 hectares (250 acres), taking in the
homes of 750 people. This area was
completely evacuated, fenced off with
barbed wire, and guarded by troops,
largely to stop people from trying to return
to recover their possessions.

In the outer Zone B, less stringent precautions were taken. The people living in
this zone, totalling about 5 000, were allowed to remain in their homes, but many
children were evacuated during the daytime period to reduce the risks to them,
and no visitors were allowed lest they take
the contamination out with them.

The government and scientists tried
hard to find ways of restoring the worst

affected area so that people could return, but the dioxin contamination was too severe. It was present on plants, trees, grass, and road surfaces, and had penetrated clothing and household effects. It seemed impossible to find a solution, and this inner area has still not recovered. All the topsoil was removed and buried in a deep sealed pit, but it was impossible to remove every trace of the poison.

There was further concern as it became clear that the effects had spread, possibly through dioxin getting into watercourses. Traces have been found in Milan, and the full effects may take many more years to work through food chains and water tables.

As for the people of Seveso, the worst symptoms appeared to clear up fairly quickly, but longer-term effects have made themselves apparent, and there may be other problems still to come. Many people, particularly children, have suffered from chloracne, an unpleasant disfiguring skin disease. Blood tests have shown markedly reduced white blood cell levels; one consequence of this could be a high level of leukaemia in later life.

Seveso is a sad story. So far only a small number of people can be said to have died as a direct result of the release of dioxin, but the number will undoubtedly grow, and as with many incidents of this kind, the longer-term consequences both for life and for the surrounding environment may turn out to be far more serious than was originally thought to be the case.

An English escape

Two years before the incident at Seveso, there was a serious incident at a large chemical works operated by the Nypro company (owned jointly by the National Coal Board and the Dutch State Mining Company) at Flixborough, on the River Humber in Eastern England. The plant produced caprolactam, used in the manufacture of nylon. During the process, cyclohexane — toxic, inflammable and explosive — is produced, and very precise control must be exercised.

On 1 June 1974, something went wrong, possibly a leak from a gas pipe which led to a fire. The cyclohexane went up in a massive explosion, which led to further explosions and a raging fire. The plant was extensively damaged, and surrounding houses were also affected. 29 people died either directly from the explosion or from the fire that followed it. It was the UK's worst industrial disaster for many years. The only crumb of comfort that can be drawn is that it happened on a Saturday, when relatively few people were working at the site. The death toll on a weekday would inevitably have been far higher.

Amoco Cadiz

Northwestern France, 16 March 1978

A vast oil spill causes catastrophic damage

Another tanker runs aground, seriously affecting large stretches of the French coastline.

The *Amoco Cadiz* case has some similarities with the *Torrey Canyon*: both ships flew under the Liberian flag, and both were crewed by Italians. However, *Amoco Cadiz*, built in Spain in 1974, was one of the new breed of 'supertankers'; at 228 513 dead-weight tons she was more than twice the size of the *Torrey Canyon*, and she carried nearly a quarter of a million tons of crude oil in her vast tanks.

In February 1978, she set out from the Gulf for Rotterdam, fully loaded with Iranian crude oil. She went round the Cape of Good Hope (ships of this size are too big to use the Suez Canal) and sailed up the Atlantic to reach Europe. By now it was mid-March and the equinoctial gales were beginning to blow. Early in the morning of 16 March she entered the 'traffic separation scheme' off Ushant. She had to alter course to get into the correct north-bound 'lane', and then at 9:45am disaster struck: the ship's steering gear failed completely.

Radio warning

Captain Bardari responded by sending a radio warning to all vessels in the area. A German salvage tug, the *Pacific*, heard the warning and radioed the *Amoco Cadiz* offering assistance. Before he could accept that assistance, Captain Bardari had to contact a representative of his ship's owners, and that meant locating someone in Chicago, where it was the middle of the night. At

3:45pm Captain Bardari got through to the operations manager in Chicago; approval for a tow was immediately given. But the tanker was too big, and the towing chain snapped.

Running aground

Desperate measures were now called for. The tug tried to secure a stern line. The tanker dropped her anchors. It was all to no avail, and just after 9pm she grounded on rocks off the Brittany coast. The captain cut all power immediately, to reduce the risk of fire, but the worst was to come, as the vast cargo of oil began to spill out.

The total spill was 223 000 tonnes, four times as much as escaped from the *Torrey Canyon*. There was very serious pollution of nearly 200 miles of the French coastline, exacerbated by changes in the wind direction. Marine and bird life was terribly affected, and the tourist industry suffered disastrously for a full year, despite intense efforts to minimise the damage. The livelihood of hundreds of Breton fishermen was wrecked. Yet the grim 'record' established by the *Amoco Cadiz* was to last only a little over a year, when it was broken following the collision between the *Aegean Captain* and the *Atlantic Empress*.

Blowout off California

Between the *Torrey Canyon* and *Amoco Cadiz* incidents, there was a serious oil spill off the Californian coast. In January 1969 a deep oil well 'blew out', releasing 250 000 gallons of crude oil over a period of 12 days before the well could be plugged. The slick grew to 200 miles (320km) in length, and the coast of California, with its many holiday resorts, was affected as far south as the border with Mexico.

The Sverdlovsk anthrax release

USSR, April 1979

A disaster that never happened?

The full facts of the incident will probably never be known.

The Sverdlovsk anthrax incident is a classic Soviet case of disinformation, rumour, contradictory stories and half-truths. It seems certain that something happened in Sverdlovsk, a large city in the Urals area, but whether the resultant deaths are to be measured in dozens, hundreds or thousands, we may never know.

The Soviet authorities have admitted that there was an outbreak of anthrax poisoning in the Sverdlovsk area in the spring of 1979. The official cause was given as contaminated cattle feed, and reports released in 1986 spoke of 96 cases of affected people, of whom 64 died. This would still make it the worst human anthrax tragedy of the 20th century. Suspicion lingers, however, that both the cause and the scale of the disaster were different.

Strict censorship

An investigation by the US Defense Intelligence Agency (DIA) in 1980 concluded that an explosion had occurred at the Microbiology and Virology Institute in Sverdlovsk, a military facility, and that as much as 22 lb (10 kg) of dry anthrax spores was released into the atmosphere, contaminating an area with a radius of several miles. The number of deaths was put at '1 000 or more', and the report says that 'strict censorship served to neutralize early panic and limit the fears of the Sverdlovsk population'.

The Soviet authorities reacted indignantly when they heard of this report, with its implication that they had secretly been working on germ warfare at Sverdlovsk, in contravention of international treaties. Internationally respected scientists also found the DIA account less than credible. Dr Vivian Wyatt of the University of Bradford said that 'The story of a germ warfare disaster does not ring true . . . it isn't likely that the Russians would risk playing around with anthrax near a vital military town'. An American professor, Donald Ellis, was actually in Sverdlovsk with his family in April 1979 and encountered no restrictions on his movement, nor did he notice any panic in the town.

The US government set up a special group of experts to try to piece together, as far as they could, what actually happened in Sverdlovsk. Their conclusion was that there was a large airborne release of spores, probably from a military compound, which infected the local meat supply. However, they did admit to a chance of 'about ten per cent' that the Societ account was correct. The main difficulty, as with many other incidents in the pre-glasnost USSR, lies in establishing which reports to believe.

Scottish experiments

Anthrax has been used in germ warfare experiments for some time. During World War II, Gruinard, an island off the north-west coast of Scotland, was infected with anthrax in an experiment to assess how deadly the spores were on sheep, and by extrapolation on people. It was to be 50 years before the island was subjected to intensive chemical cleaning and declared safe. It was then returned to the descendants of its previous owner.

The Aegean Captain/Atlantic Empress collision

Caribbean, 19 July 1979

Two vast ships collide

The second largest vessel ever lost at sea and the greatest oil spill.

The chapter of accidents leading to the collision between two loaded vessels with a combined deadweight of half a million tons is shocking to relate. As far as can be discovered, neither vessel was keeping an adequate radar lookout.

The *Aegean Captain*, a supertanker of 210 257 tons deadweight, was loaded with Venezuelan crude oil and was bound for Singapore. Although flying the Liberian flag, she operated out of Piraeus, the port for Athens, and most of her crew were Greek. The *Atlantic Empress* was an even bigger vessel, of 292 666 tons deadweight, and also had a largely Greek crew. She flew the Greek flag. She was bound from the Persian Gulf for the port of Beaumont in Texas.

Heavy squall

The collision occurred north-east of the island of Little Tobago, and the trouble started when the weather deteriorated into a heavy squall of rain at about 6:35 in the evening, just as it was getting dark, which it does very quickly in these latitudes. Visibility was down to about a mile. The chief officer on the *Aegean Captain* said at the inquiry into the disaster that he saw no other vessel on his radar; as the *Atlantic Empress* was lost, the situation on board cannot be established with any accuracy, but no avoiding action was taken on either vessel until visual sighting took place, by which time, at a distance of under a mile

and at a combined speed of some 30 knots, it was far too late.

The *Aegean Captain's* bow struck the *Atlantic Empress* on her port side at 7:05pm. Fire started on both ships. On the *Aegean Captain*, an orderly evacuation took place, all of the crew getting away safely with the unfortunate exception of an electrician, who drowned.

No drills

On the *Atlantic Empress*, things were more chaotic. Discipline on board was lax, and no emergency drills had been held for months. Efforts to launch the lifeboats were only partly successful, as their release mechanism had not been properly maintained. It is not surprising that 26 of the 42 people on board lost their lives.

The release of oil from the *Aegean Captain* was fortunately light — 14 000 tons, some of which caught fire. The ship was towed to Curaçao where the rest of her cargo was successfully discharged. The *Atlantic Empress*, however, lost 279 000 tons of crude oil. The effect on marine life is still being measured.

Mighty collision

The collision described here does not take the record for greatest combined weight of vessels. That belongs to the sister ships *Venoil* and *Venpet*, belonging to the Bethlehem Steel Company, which collided off southern Africa on 16 December 1977. Both were of over 330 000 tons deadweight. *Venoil* was loaded with crude oil; *Venpet* was in ballast. Some 26 000 tons of crude was lost, but much of the oil burned off. No lives were lost.

Bhopal

India, 3 December 1984

An appalling human tragedy

*A large-scale toxic gas leak
causes death and injury on
a massive scale.*

Bhopal was one of the worst industrial/environmental disasters of the 20th century. It was tragic because of the numbers affected and because a company which at first had seemed to be bringing prosperity and jobs to a poor area turned into destroyers of the people.

The Union Carbide Corporation opened its Bhopal plant in 1980. The opening was greatly welcomed locally, as it brought 800 new jobs into the area. Bhopal is the capital of the state of Madhya Pradesh in central India, an industrial city with a population of about 750 000. The plant, located near to the railway station and surrounded by the densely-packed housing of the Jayaprakashnagar area, was to produce pesticides for agricultural use, one of the principal chemicals in the process being methyl isocyanate (MIC for short). Union Carbide, who had a similar plant in West Virginia, USA, set up an Indian subsidiary to operate the plant. It was soon apparent that there were problems at the Bhopal plant. There were stories of leaks and of poor or disregarded safety procedures as early as 1982. An internal report, made public after the accident, talks of valve problems and of 'major concern' over workers being exposed to toxic material.

Gas escape

The accident that was to have such devastating consequences happened at night, at about 1am on 3 December 1984, when there were few staff on duty. It seems that the tanks holding the MIC — which is highly volatile — were contaminated by water. Pressure built up. When MIC reaches a temperature of 38°C it vaporizes. Despite various safety devices, this happened at Bhopal, and about 45 tons of highly toxic gas escaped before the leak was discovered and plugged.

The gas spread over the houses as people slept. The pungent, acrid smell woke many up, possibly saving their lives. Others, whose small houses were almost literally turned into gas chambers, died in their sleep. The gas affected their respiratory tracts and their eyes. Hundreds died from pulmonary oedema (fluid accumulating in the lungs) and some from poisoning by cyanide, seemingly a by-product of the MIC reacting with water and the atmosphere. Still others died from accidents caused by their partial or total blindness as they rushed in panic into the streets trying to escape the deadly fumes. Not surprisingly, in the dark and with choking lungs, there was considerable panic and confusion. Hospitals and rescue services were simply overwhelmed by the numbers affected. Small children and old people had the least resistance to the gas, and many hundreds of each died.

Crisis point

The cloud of gas, being heavier than air, sank to the ground and drifted at or near ground level. When this was realised, vast numbers of people tried to get to the higher parts of the city and its surrounds to escape. The situation reached crisis point, and for some time all movement of vehicles, trains and aircraft into or out of the town, other than those carrying vital medical supplies, was stopped.

Union Carbide reacted promptly, sending specialist teams from the USA. When its chairman, Warren Anderson, arrived in Bhopal, he was arrested and charged with causing death by negligence. After an appeal, he was released on bail. The plant was initially closed, but the company then announced that production would resume on 16 December to use up the remaining 16 tons of MIC, this being the safest way to deal with it.

Not unnaturally, further panic followed this announcement, and an estimated 150 000 people left the city, to temporary camps or to other towns and villages. The area round the plant was strangely quiet when 'Operation Faith' as it became known got under way, with elaborate and very visible safety measures in place. Fortunately, there were no problems, and when the MIC had all been used up, the factory was closed. After further investigations, the plant in West Virginia was also closed.

Mass burials

Figures are difficult to arrive at — in the days after the escape, there were mass burials and cremations in order to try to prevent the spread of disease. Many thousands of head of cattle, vital to the local agriculture, were also burnt after they had succumbed to the gas. Human deaths continued for many weeks. The best estimates indicate that at least 2 500 people died and that perhaps as many as 200 000 were affected in some way.

Acting on behalf of the bereaved and injured, the Indian government filed claims for compensation against Union Carbide in India and in the USA. There was anger in Bhopal when 'ambulance-chasers' — US lawyers specializing in such cases — arrived shortly after the incident. But in fact damages awarded by US courts are likely to be much higher than those awarded in India, so it was perhaps better for claims to be heard there, even though the complainants would have to trust the lawyers. The cases have dragged on ever since and many are still not settled.

Saving sight

The inquiry into the escape found that many people in Bhopal were unaware that potentially lethal chemicals were in use at the Union Carbide plant. There were no local emergency procedures for use in a large-scale escape. Doctors had little or no knowledge of the effects of MIC and how to treat victims; despite this, the sight of thousands was saved by prompt action. Most of those affected recovered from their blindness, but thousands of people suffered long-term damage to their eyes and lungs and continue to be troubled by eye irritation and breathing problems.

Bhopal is a desperate indictment of the situation in many of the world's poorer countries. Inward investment is eagerly sought, and large plants bringing many jobs are welcomed, especially in cases such as this where the product, pesticides, was also vital to agricultural development. But too often, as in Bhopal, such plants are placed far too close to conurbations of packed, crowded houses, safety regulations are ineffective, and workers are not fully aware of what they are handling or the dangers that can develop. Ignorance and tragedy are never very far apart. When they come together, as in Bhopal, the effects can be disastrous almost beyond comprehension.

No warning?
At Union Carbide's West Virginia plant, workers and people living nearby were given warnings that in the event of a large-scale leak of toxic material they should stay indoors and keep a wet towel over their faces. It seems that no such warning was given in Bhopal, possibly because of the sheer density of housing, and the people were totally unprepared for such an eventuality.

Spanish cooking oil tragedy

1981–9

A major public health scandal

Hundreds die and thousands are affected by adulterated oil.

In the spring of 1981, people in Madrid and elsewhere in central Spain began to feel ill: very ill indeed, with awful stomach cramps, breathing problems and weight loss. For a while, doctors were baffled. Then, as the number of similar cases rose through the hundreds into the thousands, a clear link was established: the use of a brand of cooking oil supplied by a certain company, or by street traders. It was to become one of the worst public health disasters of modern times, and a scandal which dragged on for years.

Before long, deaths began to be reported. The toll rose steadily, and indeed went on rising for several years as the after-effects of the adulterated oil proved fatal to elderly or weak people. There were soon demands for investigations and for those responsible to be brought to justice. A judicial inquiry which began in late 1981 dragged on for years and although a number of government ministers gave evidence, no officials were charged.

Rape-seed oil

Eventually, 38 people were brought to trial. Two of the principal accused, San Sebastian industrialist Juan Manuel Bengoechea and his brother Fernando, ran an oil importing firm called Rapsa. They were accused of selling a rape-seed oil, of a quality only suited for industrial use, to a Madrid company called Raelca for use as oil for human consumption. Two other brothers, Ramón and Elias Ferrero, who ran Raelca, were among those charged.

By the time the trial opened, at the end of March 1987, the death toll had risen to nearly 600 and a further 25 000 people had been seriously affected. The oil that caused the problems was sold by Raelca, believing it to be fit for human use. They said that the oil they bought from Rapsa was labelled 'vegetable oil'. The four men also faced fraud charges.

Bullet-proof screens

The 38 accused were placed behind bullet-proof screens at the trial, which went on, with a number of breaks, for over a year. More than 2 000 witnesses were called and there were frequent demonstrations outside the courtroom, formerly one of the pavilions at the Madrid Trade Fair and refurbished for the trial at a cost of £2 million.

The trial ended in June 1988, but the verdicts were not announced until nearly a year later. Juan Manuel Bengoechea was sentenced to 20 years imprisonment and Ramón Ferrero to 12 years. Eleven others received shorter sentences, but were immediately released on parole, and 25 people were acquitted.

The cause
In giving its verdict, the court acknowledged that the toxic element present in the oil was never located in laboratory tests, but placed the blame for the deaths and injuries on anilides present in the rape-seed oil, thus confirming the view of the eminent British epidemiologist Sir Richard Doll. An alternative theory that pesticides were to blame was flatly rejected.

Chernobyl

26 April 1986

The worst nuclear incident so far

A reactor explodes causing death and widespread contamination across much of Europe.

The nuclear complex at Chernobyl, some 80 miles (130km) north of Kiev in the Ukraine, is one of the largest in the world — a 'nuclear city' with thousands of workers. The power station where the explosion occurred used a type of reactor called RBMK-1000, a design only found in the former Soviet Union. The reactor, which is water-cooled, has a graphite core with more than 1 500 cylindrical channels for fuel rods. The heat produced by the nuclear reaction boils water held in the core to generate steam which drives the power turbines. There are a considerable number of these reactors in the Soviet countries and as far as is known there were no serious accidents before Chernobyl.

In April 1986, staff at Chernobyl discussed the possibility of producing electricity by allowing the turbines to freewheel with the normal supply of steam from the reactors cut off. This experiment was never authorized, but on 25 April staff decided to carry it out anyway. The power supply to reactor no 4 was steadily reduced through the day, the emergency cooling system was disconnected and other safety mechanisms were turned off.

Disastrous consequences

At about 1:30am on 26 April (8:30pm GMT 25 April) preparations were complete, the steam supply was shut off and the turbine slowed down. The consequences were disastrous. As the flow of water coolant to the reactor decreased, there was a rapid rise in both temperature and power production. The reactor went out of control before any preventative action could be taken. Fuel rods began to break up, heating the remaining water to steam in a few seconds. The massive build-up of pressure which resulted could only have one outcome. A huge explosion rocked the plant, blowing the building's protective roofing away as if it was paper. A further reaction and explosion followed, releasing carbon monoxide and hydrogen, which ignited. At this point the reactor shut itself down.

A very significant amount of radioactive material had been blasted high into the air. Pieces of fuel rod landed in several places up to half a mile (1km) away, starting more fires and leading to a sharp rise in radioactivity, well beyond permitted levels. Workers and firemen displayed great bravery as they fought, successfully, to stop the fire spreading to Chernobyl's three other reactors. Several were killed at the time or died later of radioactive poisoning.

The incident was not announced to the outside world for three days. The 'nuclear cloud' had meantime drifted on the wind over Scandinavia, on across Britain and then back over Europe. Governments in many countries seemed uncertain as to what action to take, and several issued reassuring statements that were not based on fact. In some places (Poland was one) children were dosed with iodine to counteract radioactive poisoning. Livestock was badly affected in a number of areas, the most tragic perhaps being the case of the Lapps in northern Scandinavia, most of whose reindeer, their staple food and bartering tool, had to be slaughtered.

Desperate measures

At Chernobyl, desperate measures were introduced to put out the fire in the reactor core. Water could not be used; it would react with the graphite to create clouds of radioactive steam. Instead, helicopters dropped loads of sand, clay and lead on the reactor. This extinguished the fire, but the core went on producing radioactive material for over a week. It was later entombed in a 'sarcophagus' of concrete.

Scientists from the International Atomic Energy Authority in Vienna and specialist medical teams from several countries including Britain and the USA went to the Kiev area to give what assistance they could. Casualties seemed surprisingly light: the official figures stated that 31 people had died and a further 80 were seriously burned or contaminated. There were however some hundreds more affected by radiation sickness to a greater or lesser degree, so the final toll may still be rising.

Large-scale evacuation

The authorities organized a large-scale evacuation of an area around Chernobyl with a radius of 20 miles (32km). Well over 100 000 people were bussed to towns further away and rehoused. The area immediately round the plant was subjected to intensive cleaning activity, with soil excavated and buried elsewhere or incinerated and buildings treated with a special polymer to reduce the build-up of dust. This work continues.

The longer-term effects of the disaster are still a matter of prediction. High radioactivity levels were being found in upland areas of Britain, and elsewhere in Europe, five years after the explosion, and farmers had to be compensated for the loss of saleable livestock. It has been said that there will be deaths from cancer for decades to come.

Following the break-up of the Soviet Union, responsibility for Chernobyl passed to the Ukraine. On the sixth anniversary of the disaster, in April 1992, the country's environment minister, Yuri Shcherbak, said it could not cope, and appealed for international help. He said it might cost up to £1.5 billion to repair and strengthen the concrete sarcophagus in which reactor 4 was buried, which had become dangerously cracked. There was still 'a serious risk' of further radiation escapes.

Ukrainian authorities estimated that up to 1992, between 6 000 and 8 000 people had died from causes linked to radiation, and the number would continue growing for many years yet. Health minister Yuri Spizhenko said 'Chernobyl will acquire an even bigger ecological, psychological and material scale in future'. There are now chronic environmental problems throughout the Ukraine including serious industrial pollution.

Following Chernobyl, the RBMK-100 design was modified, and stricter regulations were introduced at Soviet nuclear plants. Despite this, there was great concern in 1992 about possible radiation escapes from nuclear power plants near St Petersburg (formerly Leningrad). The Chernobyl station director, Viktor Bryukhanov, and five others, were convicted of carrying out unauthorized experiments and thereby endangering public safety. The name Chernobyl, unknown outside Soviet countries before April 1986, has passed into common usage as a reference-point. As long as there are nuclear power plants, another Chernobyl is always possible.

> **The nuclear argument**
> The disaster at Chernobyl sharpened the long-standing debate about the value and safety of nuclear power generation. Anti-nuclear campaigners argued that Chernobyl was an accident waiting to happen, and that previous incidents at Windscale in England and Three Mile Island in the USA were forewarnings that were ignored. The pro-nuclear lobby said that Western design was far superior and that such an incident could not happen here. The debate continues, and nuclear power still makes a significant contribution to generation in many countries.

See illustration on following page.

*Aerial view of the **Chernobyl** nuclear power plant after the explosion.*

Exxon Valdez

Alaska, 24 March 1989

The greatest oil spill in US waters

An environmental disaster arouses international outrage.

The stranding of the tanker *Exxon Valdez* in Prince William Sound, Alaska, in March 1989 generated enormous amounts of publicity worldwide. There was public outrage in the USA and elsewhere that such a thing could have happened in an area seen as a 'clean' environment, and the Exxon company, held directly responsible, suffered a public relations disaster as well as being held liable for covering the substantial costs of the clean-up operation.

The oil terminal in Prince William Sound was constructed after Alyeska, the consortium of eight oil companies extracting oil from the difficult North Slope Field in Alaska, failed to gain permission to transport the oil across Canada by pipeline. They decided in 1973 to build the terminal, where the oil would be loaded onto VLCCs (very large crude carriers) for onward transport to refineries in the US. Before the terminal was built, there was little evidence of man in Prince William Sound. Ice-bound for several months in the winter, it is home to a variety of arctic wildlife.

Young captain

The tanker *Exxon Valdez* was built in 1986 and was equipped with every modern aid. Displacing 211 469 tons deadweight, she had a crew of 20, with a very young master. Captain Joseph Hazelwood was only 32 at the time of the incident, but already had ten years of experience. He had made many successful trips into and out of the Valdez terminal (after which his ship was named).

The *Exxon Valdez* was due to sail at 9pm on 24 March 1989, and right on time she left her berth with her pilot, Ed Murphy, on the bridge to take her through the Valdez Narrows and Valdez Arm, a difficult run of some 20 miles (32km). This was successfully accomplished and Murphy disembarked off Rocky Point at 11:25pm. Captain Hazelwood then found his course blocked by ice in the form of small bergs or 'growlers' (so called because of the noise they make) and received permission from the Vessel Traffic Control Centre on shore to change course.

It was from this point that things began to go wrong. The captain handed command to the third mate, Greg Cousins, telling him to take the ship between Busby Island and Bligh Reef, a narrow passage but without undue difficulty. The light on Busby Island was passed at 11:55pm and five minutes later the helmsmen changed watch — Cousins had agreed to be relieved later on. A change of course was ordered at midnight but, from evidence on the ship's recorder chart, nothing happened until a minute later. As it turned out, this delay was fatal to the vessel.

Nearing the reef

At two minutes past midnight Cousins could see from the radar that the ship had barely altered course. He ordered the rudder angle increased to 20°, and two minutes after that ordered hard right rudder, which took the ship onto a bearing of 247°. Kagan, the helmsman, however, had been told that the bearing required would be 'between 235° and 245°', so he checked the turn. Cousins realised that the ship was dangerously near the reef and buzzed the captain, saying 'I think we are in serious trouble'. As he did so, the *Exxon Valdez* struck Bligh Reef and stuck fast. Captain

Hazelwood told the shore station 'Evidently we're losing some oil and we're going to be here a while.'

'Some oil' was an understatement. The spill reached about 11 000 000 gallons, and an area of 500 square miles (1 300 sq km) was polluted. Over 800 miles (1 300 km) of coastline was affected, with oil reaching up to 100 yards (90m) above the tideline. Attempts at cleaning it up were hampered by the remoteness of the site and its difficult weather — the ground is unfrozen for only a few short summer months.

There was also a delay in starting the clean-up due to the vessel needed being temporarily out of service. Two days after the spill, the weather, calm until then, turned stormy enough to rip off part of the roof of the terminal building at Valdez airport. In the next two weeks only about 20 per cent of the spilled oil was recovered or controlled and the slick had drifted up to 70 miles (115km).

Tremendous efforts were made, and the damage was minimized as far as possible, but up to 30 000 seabirds may have died along with many otters and other mammals. The problems continue as the food-chain remains affected. Prince William Sound is an important stopover and feeding place for millions of migratory birds, and if the fish they eat are contaminated, the birds may well die. That dead bird could be eaten by a larger bird or a mamal such as an otter, and so the chain goes on. The incident raises serious questions as to whether large-scale industrial facilities should be sited in such remote and environmentally sensitive places.

Not guilty

Captain Hazelwood faced charges of criminal negligence and mischief in the US courts, but was acquitted. The view was however expressed that the accident would not have happened had he stayed on the bridge. Hazelwood preferred, he said, a 'hands-off' approach, trusting his officers to take command of the ship. On 24 March 1989 he made a tragic misjudgement.

Kuwait burns

February 1991

Hundreds of wells are set alight

In the aftermath of the Gulf War, Kuwait suffers serious pollution.

The brief Gulf War in early 1991 was relayed around the world on television as it happened. Pictures were instantly available of almost every aspect of the operation. The only place without coverage was Kuwait City itself, invaded by Iraqi forces in August 1990. As the overwhelming weight and firepower of the Allied forces forced the Iraqis out of Kuwait, they reacted by trying to destroy the small state's most precious asset, its oil, in two ways.

Firstly, oil was released from holding tanks and refineries directly into the Gulf. At first it seemed that a pollution incident of horrifying proportions was developing. However, although the oil slick covered a very large area of sea — up to 350 square miles — the coverage seemed to be patchy and the oil thin. Earlier estimates that as much as 460 million gallons of oil had been released were revised downwards to nearer 50 million gallons. This was still a serious spill, affecting coastal areas and marine life, but international agencies reacted promptly, sending expert teams to begin a clean-up operation.

Blotting out the sun

Kuwait has seven major oilfields with 950 wells. When pictures of the freed city were relayed out, it was seen to be blanketed by dense black clouds, blotting out the sun even at midday. The retreating Iraqi forces had adopted a 'scorched earth' policy, setting fire to hundreds of oil wells. Two serious problems were created.

The first was air pollution. With more smoke billowing out every day, the city continued to be covered by thick clouds, and suffered from sooty deposits as well. People went around with their faces covered to try to avoid breathing in the worst of the polluted air. Oil fires on this scale had not happened before, and there is no way of assessing the long-term impact on both personal health and the environment, not just in the Kuwait area but elsewhere, as the clouds drifted into the atmosphere, adding to its increasing load of pollutants.

Capping the wells

The second, and immediate, problem was putting the fires out so that normal life could resume and oil production, on which Kuwait depends, could be restarted. The fires varied in size and character and the teams of specialist firefighters brought in from many different parts of the world to tackle them found that each one had to be assessed individually. Some could be 'capped' and put out quite easily, while others resisted every effort.

By early 1992, all the burning wells had been capped and were cooling prior to repair before production was restarted. It was an extraordinary operation using a mixture of sophisticated technology, experience gathered over decades in other oilfields around the world, and bravery in tackling the flames.

Economic loss

As well as the environmental damage, Kuwait suffered serious economic losses from the war. Before August 1990, Kuwait produced about 1.5 million barrels of oil a day. It has almost 10 per cent of the world's reserves. Income was lost for up to two years, and to that had to be added a possible $100 billion for rebuilding.

Famine

Famine — starvation and death due to insufficient food — has been recorded since the earliest times. There are several instances in the Bible and other sacred literature. The cause was generally a crop failure due either to lack of rain or too much of it. Sometimes plagues of pests such as locusts were responsible. Whatever the cause, the effect was disastrous. Populations were decimated. International aid was not available, and if people could not fend for themselves, they died. It was, as with other natural disasters, an act of God.

The increasing sophistication of agricultural techniques has not prevented famine. India suffered many times, and a number of such cases are recorded in this section, as is the Irish potato blight famine of the mid-19th century, a human tragedy on a tremendous scale which bled that country of people by death and emigration as the survivors tried to find a better life in another land.

After a century in which famine seemed to be decreasing, we now find it occurring on a vast scale in many parts of the world. Rapidly increasing populations in Africa depend on regular harvests to survive, and in recent years the harvest has been very uncertain as intense drought has affected many areas. The pictures brought back, both still and moving, have led to major international aid efforts being mounted, but famine continues particularly in the countries bordering the Sahara Desert. Three examples are looked at here.

The underlying cause may well be changes in the global climatic pattern which are still not fully understood. Combine this with the almost continual state of unrest in many of these poor African countries, and a too-rapid jump from nomadic self-sufficiency to Western capitalism, and you have a good recipe for disaster.

As this introduction is written, in early 1992, there is famine on some scale in almost every continent, from Albania to Zimbabwe. The countries of the former mighty Soviet Union are not immune, and relief food supplies have had to be sent to Russia. Agronomists and nutritionists repeatedly assure us that the world can easily feed itself, but evidence to the contrary is, sadly, only too readily found. In the crowded countries of Asia and Africa in particular, there is a perilously thin line between sufficiency and starvation.

India
1769–1943

Repeated sufferings

*Drought and starvation
continue through peace and war.*

The people of India have faced drought and famine many times. There are reports of large-scale famine in Kashmir in the 10th century and in several parts of this huge and densely populated country in the 17th century, during the last years of the Mogul empire.

India then became a British colony, but the new masters could do little about the vagaries of weather and harvest, and famine still occurred. One of the most serious famines was in 1769–70 when the rains in Bihar and Bengal failed almost totally. Millions of starving people made their way to Calcutta seeking food, presaging similar scenes in Africa in recent years. It is thought that up to 10 million people may have died in this famine.

Hastings' granary

There was further famine in the early 1780s, after which the then governor-general, Warren Hastings, ordered the construction of a vast grain store at Patna in Bihar. Over its door was the inscription 'Built for the perpetual prevention of famine in these provinces.' The granary was never properly supplied, and famine continued.

The Indian people suffered repeatedly in the 19th century through the British government's policy of unrestricted trade. There was no attempt to control prices in order to regulate supplies to badly affected areas, nor any check on export of grain from these areas. The result was widespread suffering. A particularly severe famine occurred in the Orissa region in 1866–7 when again grain was not supplied to the areas which needed it most desperately, and millions more died of starvation.

After this, there was at last a change of policy. When the next famine threatened, in Bihar in the 1870s, grain was sent there without restriction. By now railways were spreading across India, making transport of supplies easier, and the government introduced a 'famine code' so that food and grain could be moved to affected areas before the situation reached crisis level. This system worked for the next 70 years.

Invasion fears

The last major famine in India was at least indirectly the result of war. When the Japanese invaded Burma in 1942, there was a real concern that India might be their next target. Alarmed, the government removed large amounts of rice and grain from stores in Bengal, but a cyclone battered the area in October, severely damaging the year's crop. The price soared to a level which ordinary people could not afford, and by spring 1943 there was widespread famine in the area. Hampered by the war, relief was slow and the situation did not improve until the following year, by which time it is estimated that 3 000 000 people may have died through starvation and the rapid spread of cholera and malaria.

Impeached by his peers
Warren Hastings, governor-general of Bengal in the 1780s, was later to gain notoriety through being impeached at the bar of the House of Lords for supposed fraudulent and inhumane conduct during his years in India. The proceedings opened in February 1788 and lasted seven years, but he was eventually acquitted.

The Irish potato famine
1845–8

A population starves

Repeated failure of their principal crop leaves the people of Ireland in a desperate plight.

In the first half of the 19th century, the population of Ireland rose steadily. Away from the towns and cities, the people lived out a crofting existence, in poor dwellings and with an acre or so of ground on which they grew potatoes. Most had a 'house cow' which provided milk, some of which was turned into buttermilk; this, mixed with the potato, was the staple diet. Any other livestock reared, or cereal crop raised, had to be sold each year to pay rents to the landlords, few of whom lived anywhere near this source of income.

It was a poor existence but a reasonably settled one until 1844: unbeknown to the people of Ireland, a blight that began to affect the potato crop in North America that summer would lay waste their land and lead to a million and a half of them dying from starvation or fever.

There was regular traffic across the Atlantic, and the spores responsible for the blight must have come across by ship early in 1845. Sporadic outbreaks of blight were reported, then more and more. Its rapid spread was aided by a very rainy August; the blight was caused by a parasitic fungus which flourished in wet weather. Much of the crop was destroyed, leaving the people with the thinnest of subsistence diets. Worse, however, was to follow.

The crop fails

In 1846 virtually the entire potato crop in Ireland failed. At that time the whole of Ireland was part of the United Kingdom, and the London government's response to the crisis was to provide work for Irishmen on such tasks as road and canal construction, so that they would have money to revive the Irish economy and to buy food for their families. This policy was a total failure. The workmen were paid only a pittance and there was in any case little food available: it had been a poor year throughout Europe for harvests, and the price of grain rose steeply, far above what the people of Ireland could afford.

Families were seen desperately scavenging in fields and hedgerows, looking for anything they could use as nourishment. Nettles, plant roots, bracken, even grass was tried. Others resorted to the workhouses, those grim repositories of lean succour, which were soon full to overflowing.

As so often happens, disaster visited upon disaster. The winter of 1846–7 was exceptionally cold. Ireland normally enjoys mild winters, protected by the seas around it from severe cold, but that winter snow lay on the ground for weeks at a time and thousands of people, already weakened by malnutrition, died of cold or fever. With no income, families were unable to pay rent, and many were evicted, causing further suffering. Still the government failed to provide proper assistance. Soup kitchens were set up, but the food had to be paid for locally, and the Irish economy had collapsed; there was simply no money available. The Chancellor of the Exchequer, Charles Wood (later Viscount Halifax) urged local officials, from the comfort of his London home, to go 'to the verge of the law, and a little beyond if necessary' to deal with the situation. Many did, causing yet further suffering.

Disease spreads

In 1847, there was no blight, but with so many people dead or dying, only a fraction of the normal sowing had taken place, and in 1848 the crop failed again. Disease spread rapidly, with the people having little resistance. Typhoid and cholera killed many thousands. It was 1849 before anything like a reasonable potato crop was again harvested in Ireland, and by then the population was decimated. Many who survived were forced to emigrate, a further million leaving the country in this fashion.

Anyone who could find the money for the passage left for the 'promised land' of North America. Many thousands died on the journey, often undertaken in terrible conditions in leaking, grossly overcrowded ships with poor provisions. At least 20 000 Irish people are thought to have died at sea in that period.

Those that did reach America safely were kept in quarantine, on Grosse Island in the St Lawrence River or Staten Island off New York, before being allowed in. So many came that the immigration authorities were overwhelmed. Disease was inevitably introduced and there were over 1 000 deaths from typhoid in New York alone in 1847. One of those who did successfully make a new life was the grandfather of Henry Ford, the motor magnate.

The memory of the potato famine remains strong in Ireland, and the bitterness towards the English government (as it was seen) persists. Ireland is still a troubled country today.

An eyewitness acount

A report in *The Times* from an Irish rural magistrate, Nicholas Cummins, in early 1847, gave a starkly graphic description of conditions for the desperate people. In a hut he found: 'Six famished and ghastly skeletons . . . huddled in a corner, their sole covering what seemed a ragged horsecloth. I approached with horror, and found by a low moaning they were alive — they were in fever, four children, a woman and what had once been a man. In a few minutes I was surrounded by 200 such phantoms, such frightful spectres as no words can describe'.

Biafra
1967–70

The first major African relief operation

Internal strife in Nigeria leads to widespread starvation for the Ibo people.

Before mid 1968, the name Biafra was little known to the outside world. In June of that year a small group of British journalists flew to Nigeria to report on the war between the federal army and the small breakaway would-be state in the east of the country. The photographs and stories they brought back focussed world attention on the plight of 8 000 000 people.

The story begins in 1967 when Colonel Emeka Ojukwu declared that Biafra was to secede from Nigeria. The background is that the Ibo tribe, who held the land known as Biafra, were becoming increasingly dissatisfied with their lot within Nigeria. Outnumbered in parliament and opposed to many of the policies of the government, they reached the point where secession seemed the best option. It was a decision that would lead to tragedy and suffering on a massive scale.

Missionary friends

The Nigerian government attempted to impose a blockade on the Ibos in Biafra. The federal army was sent in, and the Ibos had to retreat to a small area, in the process losing much of their productive agricultural land. They had been largely self-sufficient until that point but cut off from the land that had supported them, they found increasing difficulty in feeding themselves.

Before world attention was focused on the Biafrans' plight, most major governments supported the Nigerians in their efforts to overturn this troublesome revolution. The Biafrans found friends among Catholic missionaries, who chartered aircraft to fly from the offshore island of São Tomé loaded with food for the starving people.

When reports appeared in the western press starkly outlining the true situation, with photographs — all too familiar to us now, but a great shock at the time — of children with swollen bellies and emaciated limbs begging for food, attitudes began to change. There were demonstrations in Britain and other European countries including Belgium, Holland and Germany. In the USA, Senator Edward Kennedy, who was chairman of the Senate Sub-Committee on Refugee Peoples, led a strong movement urging the US government to change its stance and help the people of Biafra. The United Nations supported his call.

The first really large-scale international relief operation into Africa began. With charities such as the Red Cross and Christian Aid doing much to maintain public support, up to 40 flights a day were organized, taking food and clothing into Biafra. The relief workers too were shocked at what they found. Accurate figures will never be available, but it seems certain that at least a million people died of starvation or disease in Biafra's short lifetime. It was tragedy on a scale that, sadly, was to be repeated in Africa all too regularly in the years that followed.

End of a rebellion
Biafra's brave attempt at independence lasted only until 1970. Early in that year Colonel Ojukwu abandoned his attempt to keep the Nigerian forces out, and fled the country. Biafra was slowly, and not without difficulty, reintegrated into Nigeria.

The Sahel

1969–74

Another African tragedy

The people on the western fringes of the Sahara desert are severely affected by drought.

Like Biafra, the Sahel area of Western Africa was hardly known to the outside world until 1973, when reports of a disastrous drought and crop failure began to appear. Improvements in lighter, hand-held television cameras and the spread of communications satellites meant that for the first time filming could take place in such areas, with the pictures reaching the world within hours instead of weeks or months as previously. This was the first time the plight of the people of areas such as the Sahel had been brought to the notice of people in developed countries through television, and it brought a powerful and positive response.

The Sahel (the name is Arabic, and means 'shore land') extends west to east, on the southern fringes of the Sahara, across six countries — Senegal, Mauritania, Mali, Upper Volta, Niger and Chad.

Summer rains

The normal pattern in these areas is for rain to fall in the summer. The people sow crops such as millet and sorghum, which grow very rapidly and are cultivated. Grass also springs up, supporting the cattle herded by the nomadic peoples such as the Tuareg. The cattle then fertilize the ground ready for the next crop. The rains also replenish the deep wells scattered at oases throughout the area. After independence, cattle herd sizes were increased, leading to overgrazing of the limited grassland. New wells were sunk, but they disrupted the supply to the older wells. The traditional barter system was replaced by an economy based on money, which the tribesmen did not understand.

The situation, already deteriorating, was brought to the point of crisis by a severe drought which started in 1969. For four years the people struggled on with little outside help, until large-scale relief programmes began to be instigated in the mid 1970s. By then the rains had returned, but it is estimated (reliable figures will never be available) that over 1 000 000 people died either from starvation or diseases such as tuberculosis and typhoid. Millions of head of cattle were lost, and the Sahel people have had to rebuild herds almost from scratch.

The emphasis now is on sustaining, and very gradually improving, the traditional way of life. As has been shown, to introduce too many changes too rapidly is disastrous, and it only takes a natural problem such as the failure of the rains — which might have been survived in the past — to create an unmanageable crisis.

A unique way of life

The Tuareg people live in extended family groups, herding as much livestock as they need to survive each year, to provide for their own requirements and with a little over to barter for goods. A family of six will ideally have one or two camels, for transport, three or four cows and perhaps eight sheep. They move around, cropping the grass and continually fertilizing the soil with the animals' dung. Water is drawn from wells at oases. This way of life has persisted for centuries, but as modern life encroaches ever further, it is under great threat.

Ethiopia

1984–5

The 'Live Aid' operation

The world's conscience is stirred by a nation's plight.

Ethiopia covers an area of 470 000 square miles (1 225 000 sq km) in eastern Africa, stretching from its central and western highlands down to the Red Sea. It is bordered on the west by Sudan and on the south and east by Kenya, Somalia and Djibouti. Its population of around 50 million have an average life expectancy of only 48 years.

Following the overthrow of the last Emperor, Haile Selassie, in 1974, a left-wing military regime took over, but despite receiving help from the USSR and Cuba, the country has faced continual internal unrest since then, with active guerilla movements in the provinces of Eritrea and Tigré. The economy relies to a considerable extent on the annual rains, and when these fail, as they did in the early 1980s, disaster quickly follows.

Harrowing pictures

There was virtually no rain in 1982, 1983 or 1984. By late 1984 a number of African countries were facing drought and famine, with perhaps as many as 150 million people living at starvation level. The world's attention focused on Ethiopia after a BBC crew visited the country in October 1984 and brought back harrowing pictures of emaciated children dying in the vast camps outside towns such as Makalle and Korem.

'Live Aid' concerts

After the film had been broadcast, a major international relief effort got under way.

The Band Aid record 'Feed the World — Do they know it's Christmas?' had reached number one in the charts, and the following summer dozens of leading performers gave their services free for the Live Aid concerts. Large sums of money were raised and the following spring the momentum continued with the *Run For The World* appeal, when charity runs were organised in countries throughout the world.

Although large amounts of food and other supplies were now available, there were very serious problems in distribution. It was difficult to reach the affected areas, and guerilla fighters often blocked supplies. Food accumulated at ports and distribution depots in Ethiopia when it was desperately needed in the interior. The situation improved only slowly, and not before hundreds of thousands of people had died of starvation. Accurate figures are impossible to obtain, but in Ethiopia and neighbouring countries one estimate put the number of dead, many of them children, as high as 5 000 000.

The rains returned in 1985 but failed again in 1987 and 1990. Meanwhile, fighting continued in Eritrea and Tigré. Ethiopia's future, and that of its people, remains very uncertain.

Chinese famine
There was a serious drought in northern China in the 1870s. After three years without proper rain, famine was widespread. The Chinese authorities shipped grain and other supplies to northern ports but there was insufficient transport to take it to the worst affected areas. It is believed that over 10 million people died through this famine.

Fire

Fire has been regarded with awe, reverence and fear since the dawn of civilization. Controlled by man, it brings warmth for comfort and heat for cooking. Out of control, it brings devastation to people and property. The worst punishment that could be reserved for witches and others thought to be possessed of evil in former times was to be burnt at the stake, and death by fire is still one of the most awful of tragedies.

Seven very different fires are described here. Two destroyed great cities — London in 1666 and Chicago two centuries later. Four were terrible tragedies in a single building. The conflagration of La Compania in Santiago in 1863 killed over 2 000 women and children in a church. The Cocoanut Grove fire ravaged a Boston club where hundreds were enjoying a night out. Both seem the more awful for their circumstances.

The fire at the Iroquois Theatre takes us back to Chicago, 32 years after the blaze that devastated the city. The theatre proudly labelled itself as 'fireproof' when it was clearly not, and hundreds died when fire broke out during a pantomime performance. The Joelma Building fire of 1974 in São Paulo was a real-life version of the film *Towering Inferno*, with hundreds trapped in a high office block.

The final fire in this section is a bush blaze in Australia. Large-scale bush and forest fires occur in many parts of the world. This one was the more awful because of the evidence that it was started by the deliberate action of an arsonist: the fascination with fire turned corrupt.

Fire often attends natural disasters, and is referred to in other sections of this book — air crashes, earthquakes, environmental disasters, industrial accidents, rail and road disasters, marine tragedies, volcanoes, all have had their effects amplified by fire. There is even a sporting tragedy involving fire, at Bradford in 1985.

Fire is one of the four great elements. We cannot live without it. The technology of fire control and prevention has advanced rapidly in recent years, but fire very often reminds us of its awesome destructive powers, and we lose the sense of respect accorded the bright dancing flames by our distant ancestors at our peril.

The Great Fire of London

2–6 September 1666

The capital city destroyed

A world-famous event, the fire had an innocuous beginning.

In the mid-17th century, London, like most large towns and cities of the time, was full of houses constructed largely of timber, packed tightly together, many of them coated with pitch for weatherproofing. In other words, it was a colossal fire hazard. There were no firefighting services as such, and once a large-scale fire started it would be almost impossible to put it out.

The 1666 fire is very well documented. Its starting point has been precisely identified as a baker's shop in Pudding Lane, a narrow alley in the congested area between London Bridge and the Tower of London. Early in the morning of Sunday 2 September, one of the baker's servants alerted his master to the fire. No effort seems to have been made to put it out: the baker and his family escaped by climbing through an upper window onto the next-door roof, but his maid would not follow, and she died in the flames, the fire's first victim. The fire spread rapidly, and it soon reached Thames Street, a riverside area with wharves and warehouses full of inflammable material — hemp, pitch and oil.

Here the fire really took hold, and by daylight it had got as far as London Bridge, where it destroyed the pumps that controlled much of London's water supply, thus making the task of firefighting even more difficult. As higher buildings such as churches caught fire, material from their roofs fell onto surrounding houses and shops, setting them alight.

The flames continued burning, and spreading, for two days, steadily engulfing the old city. According to the diarist Samuel Pepys, the lead on the roof of St Paul's Cathedral melted 'like snow before the sun'. In all, 85 churches, including St Paul's itself, were destroyed or seriously damaged.

Firefighting king

The heart of the city, including the fine medieval halls of the great livery companies, was not immune. Every effort was made to contain the fire, but it was a slow process. Even King Charles II himself joined the firefighters, taking his turn in the long lines of men and women with buckets, his clothes 'smoke-grimed and ash-covered, wet and filthy' according to a contemporary account.

The fire burned itself out on Thursday 6 September. Only eight people are known to have died, but most of the city was in ruins. Over 13 000 houses were destroyed, 100 000 people were homeless and hundreds of businesses faced bankruptcy. It was a disaster from which London took a long time to recover.

An opportunity missed

After the fire, the great architect Sir Christopher Wren produced a plan for rebuilding London on a grand and spacious scale, with broad streets and fine buildings, largely of brick and stone. His plan was only partially carried out: many churches including St Paul's were rebuilt to his design, but speed took precedence over space, and houses (though of better materials and limited in height) rapidly went up on the same crowded street plan as before.

La Compania

Santiago, 8 December 1863

Unimaginable scenes of horror

A dreadful death toll as a Jesuit church blazes, trapping women and children at prayer.

The Feast of the Immaculate Conception is a very important event in the Jesuit calendar, and the intensely religious peoples of South America have long celebrated such occasions with fervour. Preparations are detailed and carried out with loving care. Such was the case in December 1863 in the city of Santiago, the capital of Chile.

La Compania was a superb 17th century church, one of the finest in all of South America. For the festival the interior was decorated as lavishly as could be arranged, and it is said that there were 20 000 coloured lamps hung in groups on every ledge and in every small niche. Every afternoon it took several hours to light all the lamps before the evening service, when the church would be packed with a congregation of almost 3 000 people, most of them women, either standing, kneeling or squatting on small mats they brought with them — there were no chairs or pews.

Such an illumination

On 8 December more lamps than ever had been lit. It seems this was, in part at least, to combat a remark made by a Papal Nuncio visiting from Rome, who said that the lighting in the Holy City was far finer than in Santiago. One of the local priests, Father Ugarto, responded by saying 'I will give him such an illumination as the world has never seen'. His words were to come true in the most ghastly manner.

The service was due to begin at 7pm. As before, the church was full. On the high altar was a statue of the Virgin Mary, the centrepiece of the celebrations. Her feet were set upon a crescent moon (in the manner of Murillo's famous painting), this moon being made from canvas and wood, with lamps inside it. As the final lamps were lit, the moon caught light. In a few minutes the flames had spread through the church.

There was little chance of escape: only the main door was open and not unnaturally panic ensued. People outside, within a few yards of the church, were helpless onlookers as the crowded building echoed to the screams of the dying. An eyewitness account vividly portrays the nightmare: 'Women were seen to undergo a transformation as though by an optical illusion, first dazzlingly bright, then horribly lean and shrunk up, then black statues rigidly fixed in a writhing attitude'.

As the flames spread, the priests hurried to the sacristy — literally a place of sanctuary on that terrible evening — and shut the door firmly behind them. They later said this was to safeguard the church's priceless silver and other valuables, but it meant that a possible escape route was closed.

Within half an hour the horror was over. Some 2 500 women and children had died. Many of the victims were under the age of 20; hundreds were servants. This is still the greatest toll of lives for fire in a single building. La Compania was never rebuilt.

Priests blamed

Bereaved families, particularly fathers and husbands, bitterly blamed the priests — who had made good their own escape — for the catastrophe. When some of the clergy returned to La Compania to try to say Mass for the dead, they were driven off by men beating them with muskets.

The destruction of Chicago

8 October 1871

Flames sweep through an American city

The terrible fire said to have been started by Mrs O'Leary's cow.

During the 19th century Chicago grew rapidly, and by 1871 it was an important commercial and industrial centre, handling substantial amounts of grain, with its own stock market, and a major railroad terminus. The population had grown to around 330 000. In one day a third of them were made homeless by a fire started, like so many, by a small, simple accident.

The fire certainly started in a barn belonging to the O'Leary family, in DeKoven Street in the southwest of the city, at about 9:30pm. Popular legend has it that Mrs O'Leary's cow kicked a lighted kerosene lamp over, setting fire to a pile of hay or perhaps wood shavings. The lady herself (who happily survived the fire) denied the tale.

Whatever the initial spark, the fire spread quickly. A strong westerly breeze was blowing, fanning the flames. There had been no rain for over a month, and many of the buildings were of timber. The fire had plenty to feed on: along its course as the wind drove it towards the city centre were yards holding wood and coal, grain stores, distilleries and other places loaded with inflammables.

Natural barrier

By midnight the fire had reached the river, a natural barrier, but ineffective on this occasion. The wind took blazing pieces of wood across and the fire continued on its way into the heart of the city. The account in the *Chicago Daily Tribune* described how the flames would 'hurl themselves bodily several hundred feet and kindle new buildings. The whole air was filled with glowing cinders, looking like an illuminated snowstorm. Fantastic fires of red, blue and green played along the cornices of buildings'.

The First National Bank was built to be fireproof; but the heat was so intense that its iron framework expanded, breaking the exterior walls, which fell. Every large hotel in the city was either destroyed or seriously damaged, as were all the banks, every theatre, the grand Opera House and the City Hall. The fire only stopped when it reached the shores of Lake Michigan. An area of over three square miles was devastated, and nearly 100 000 people were homeless after that awful night.

As the flames subsided, the city took toll. More than 250 people were dead. A total of 18 000 buildings had been utterly destroyed. The value of the property lost was calculated at nearly 200 million dollars — a massive amount 120 years ago. Chicago would rise again — upwards, for this was where skyscrapers were first built — but the night of 8 October 1871 will never be forgotten.

The mansion that survived

When the citizens of Chicago surveyed their wrecked city, they found Mahlon Ogden's house still, astonishingly, largely intact in the middle of an area of almost total devastation. Seeing the flames approaching, the family hung every available carpet, blanket and sheet over the exterior and roof, soaking them continually with water, and even with cider, to fend off the fire. This desperate measure worked, and the house survived. So too, ironically, did the O'Leary house: the wind took the flames from the barn in the opposite direction.

Iroquois Theatre

30 December 1903

A new 'fireproof' theatre is gutted

Hundreds die as flames sweep the overcrowded building.

As the people of Chicago rebuilt their city after the terrible fire of 1871, they must have hoped that such a disaster would never visit them again. New buildings were designed to have greater fire-resistance and public buildings in particular were given what were thought to be adequate exits in case of emergency.

The Iroquois Theatre, an elegant building in the heart of the city, was ready for opening in November 1903. It had a capacity of 1 600 and the proprietors were looking forward to full houses over the Christmas period for the lavish production of the pantomime *Mr Bluebeard,* a big hit in London the previous year. To reassure its patrons, and with 1871 clearly in mind, the theatre went so far as to advertise itself as being 'absolutely fireproof'.

Above capacity

Mr Bluebeard did indeed draw packed houses; so much so that it seems extra people were let in on occasion, above the theatre's safe capacity. Such seems to have been the case at the afternoon matinée on 30 December 1903; there were people standing at the back and even in the gangways and there may have been as many as 2 000 present.

With the best will in the world, any theatre at that time must have been a fire hazard. Wood and painted canvas was used for scenery, and the seats and drapery were of inflammable material. During the performance, it seems that one of the stage lights blew out and sparked, setting fire to gauze draperies being used for a 'moonlit' effect. The fire spread quickly across the stage and towards the auditorium.

The performers and stagehands fled through the stage door to safety, but panic broke out in the auditorium as flames licked towards the seats. A desperate struggle to get out led to the gangways and exits becoming hopelessly jammed with people. Although there were fire exits, they led into narrow alleyways where there was further bad crushing. All the exits from the upper floors, the balcony and gallery led into one passage.

Bootmarked faces

Those still inside and unable to get out were overcome by fire and dense smoke from the upholstery and fittings. The fire services were soon on the scene and the fire was put out quite quickly, but the damage had been done. More than 200 people died in the theatre itself and a further 400 in the stampede for the exits. Some were found with boot marks on their faces where they had been trampled upon.

The tragedy, happening in the Christmas-New Year period, shocked America, and was widely reported in Europe as well. Examination of the theatre found the 'fireproof' claim to be unsubstantiated: there were many shortcomings. Other theatres across the USA were inspected, and over 50 were closed as being unsafe.

> **Safety curtain**
> All theatres where live performances are staged have a fireproof 'safety curtain' which can be lowered should fire break out in the high-risk stage or backstage areas. The safety curtain at the Iroquois was lowered, but not before flames had already escaped from the stage area and begun to eat into the seating and fittings.

Cocoanut Grove

28 November 1942

A packed Boston night club blazes

A wartime night out ends in tragedy with many hundreds dead or badly injured.

The Cocoanut Grove night club in Boston, Massachusetts, was opened in the late 1920s and rapidly became very popular. Downstairs was the Melody Lounge, redecorated in 1941 with simulated leather chairs, artificial palm trees and swathes of silk adorning the ceiling. Upstairs was a smaller room with a revolving stage on which the nightly floorshow was staged.

On 28 November 1942 the club was packed. There were servicemen on leave from Europe with their wives and girl-friends and a considerable number of out-of-town visitors who had been at an American Football game in which the un-fancied Holy Cross team beat Boston 55–12. Celebrations were in order. The exact number inside the club has never been established, but it was not far short of 1 000 when the bandleader, Micky Alpert, started playing *The Star-Spangled Banner* to announce the beginning of the cabaret.

Terrible firetrap

The cause of the fire has been established. At about 10pm, a young waiter, Stephen Tomaszewski (who was in fact underage for night work) was sent over to a corner table to replace a light bulb. He climbed on a chair and lit a match to give himself extra light. Somehow, one of the decorative 'palm' trees caught fire, and within seconds a major blaze had started.

Cocoanut Grove was a terrible firetrap, with its plastic upholstery and walls, which either burned with an intense heat or gave off choking clouds of toxic smoke. Although there were a number of exits, they were not clearly indicated, and the only obvious way out was a revolving door at the front of the Melody Lounge. Desperate scenes ensued as people fought to get out amid rising panic. The main entrance could have been reached, if anyone had realised, by going up a flight of steps to another door in Piedmont Street. But all those inside the club could see was apparently blank walls. Survivors described how a young naval officer was seen trying to keep people calm and get some order into the rush for the revolving door. He had little chance under the circumstances, and was later found among the dead, his uniform torn to ribbons.

Onto the roof

A young dancer, Marshall Cook, saved 35 people, mostly artistes, by finding a way out onto the building's roof from where a ladder gave them an escape from the spreading flames. Inside, many were less fortunate. Although firemen arrived rapidly, they could not get into the building for the press of people. The floor of the Melody Lounge gave way, pitching people into the darkness of the basement area. Many asphyxiated or were crushed. When rescuers did get inside, the scenes that met them were horrible, with twisted bodies piled six deep.

If people inside had realised that there were other exits many could have been saved — but in intense heat and blinding smoke it is difficult to behave logically. One exit door, which should have opened under pressure, was found to be bolted.

Firemen worked through the night, bringing the fire under control, locating bodies and taking them out, and rescuing survivors. Hospitals, overwhelmed with the injured, many badly cut by glass or burned, had to plead for blood and plasma to be released from war emergency supplies. Many of the dead were so badly burned as to make identification very difficult.

Scapegoats sought

The final toll was 474 dead and many more with serious burns. It was an awful tragedy, and as often happens, scapegoats were sought. It was found that the city regulations covering the use of materials for decoration in clubs were inadequate, as were the requirements for sprinklers and the labelling of exits. The city's building commissioner, Mr Mooney, was indicted as was a senior policeman, Captain Bucigross. They got off relatively lightly, but one of the club's owners, Barnett Welansky, was convicted of reckless operations and fail-

ing to supply adequate firefighting equipment. He was jailed for 12 years.

The official inquiry published its report in November 1943. Its findings were predictable. The club had been overcrowded beyond reasonable limits, exits should have been much more clearly marked, and much loss of life was due to panic when people could not see a way out. Cocoanut Grove was a wartime tragedy that was not brought about by any action of war.

The Club Cinq-Sept

A similar disaster happened at the Club Cinq-Sept (Club Five-Seven) near Grenoble in southern France, a popular night spot in a forested area. On the night of 1 November 1970 a fire started, probably through someone simply dropping a lighted match. As with Cocoanut Grove, the building was alight in seconds. The main exit, a turnstile, jammed; other exits had no signs or were blocked. Safety regulations had been ignored, and 146 young people died.

Cocoanut Grove *night club, where the revolving doors increased the death toll.*

Joelma Building

1 February 1974

An office block inferno

A multi-storey building in Brazil turns into a death-trap.

The Joelma Building tragedy is a real-life parallel to the dramatic film *The Towering Inferno,* in which the upper floors of a multi-storey building are engulfed in flames, making rescue exceptionally difficult. The horrifying situation of finding yourself trapped by fire with no apparent means of escape came true in Brazil in early 1974.

São Paulo, Brazil's largest city, grew very rapidly in the 1960s and 1970s to a population of over 8 000 000. The city was a commercial and industrial centre and there was much new building to cope with the expansion. The lower six floors of the Joelma Building were a multi-storey car park, with offices, including the headquarters of the Crefisul Bank, on a further 14 storeys above. About 600 people worked in the building, and on the morning of 1 February 1974, customers present pushed the figure to nearly 700 at the time that fire broke out on the 11th floor.

Thousands of sightseers

It was quickly clear that a major blaze was under way. At the time São Paulo had fewer than 20 fire stations (Chicago, a city of comparable size, has 300) and the firefighters' task, already almost impossible, was made even harder by the thousands of people who flocked to the scene to watch the fire, jamming nearby streets with their cars. Inside the building, horrific scenes were developing.

People ran screaming from offices with their hair and clothes on fire, desperately trying to get down the stairways. A porter saw several people trampled to death. Others crawled out onto window ledges and clung there, shouting for help. The fire brigade's tallest extending ladders only reached halfway up the building, and those on the upper floors were helpless.

Little comfort

The fire services did everything they could. Ropes were shot from nearby buildings and one firemen, Sergeant José Rufino, rescued 18 people in this way, going back and forth to get them one by one. A large notice was made saying to the trapped people 'Courage, we are with you', but this can have been of little comfort to anyone on a narrow window ledge with fire behind.

When the fire was brought under control, the task of removing bodies began. Identification was difficult, but the final toll was put at 227, with a further 250 seriously injured or burned. The city's fire chief was dismissed, as a scapegoat, and the director of public safety, General Vota Melo, admitted that the city 'lacks the equipment to cope with a fire of this magnitude'. São Paulo now has a population of over 10 000 000; Joelma could happen again here, or in any one of dozens of large cities the world over, and rescue would be equally difficult.

Fire in Las Vegas
There was another terrible fire, at the MGM Grand Hotel, Las Vegas, on 21 November 1980. The fire started in one of the kitchens and spread rapidly. It knocked out electrical circuits very rapidly, so fire alarms did not sound. Guests were rescued by helicopter, winch and across scaffolding to nearby buildings, but 84 still died and over 600 were injured.

Two Australian States burn

February 1983

Bush fires sweep Victoria and South Australia

Drought is followed by terrible fires causing death and vast amounts of damage.

Bush fires are a regular occurrence in Australia. In most instances, the fires can be confined to a relatively small area and kept away from houses or other buildings. Sometimes, however, fires rage out of control, and a terrifying scenario develops where escape becomes almost impossible.

There were severe fires in 1939, when 71 people are known to have died. In the early 1980s, many places in south-eastern Australia were suffering the effects of the worst droughts of the century. In some areas, no rain had fallen for four years. The whole of Victoria and South Australia was dry. Then, in mid-February, with the daytime temperatures peaking at over 100 °F, the fires started.

Charged with arson

There were so many fires that it is impossible to say which was the first, or how they all began. Some certainly appear to have been started deliberately, and a young man of 19 was arrested near Adelaide and charged with arson. Whatever the cause, the fires, fanned by northerly winds, rapidly swept across vast areas of dry bush, engulfing not just the countryside but whole communities. Firefighting services performed heroics but for several days were unable to do more than contain the blaze wherever they could.

Small towns were severely affected. In direct line of fire, and without large-scale firefighting services, there was little such places could do. The town of Cockatoo was completely destroyed, and about 30 people died there. Coastal communities including Airleys Inlet, Upper Beaconsfield and Anglesea were burned out, as were Naringal and Framlingham inland. Eye-witnesses described how huge incandescent fireballs roared through towns making a noise like trains, consuming everything in their path. Eucalyptus trees were exploding with flame as the heat reached them.

As the fire took hold, thousands of people were evacuated from their homes, often having to leave with little chance of taking anything with them. Servicemen and volunteers joined the regular firemen in trying to stop the awful spread of the flames. Victoria and South Australia were both declared disaster zones by the Australian government. In Victoria, over 500 farms were severely affected, with many thousands of head of sheep and cattle dead. Seven towns in the state had been destroyed, at least 2 000 homes were razed, and more than 10 000 people were homeless. Over a thousand square miles of the state were devastated.

Devastated farmland

The situation in South Australia was if anything even worse. The damage here extended to over 2 000 square miles as the fires charred a path 75 wide through the state. Freeways were cut, and people trying to flee their homes were trapped in their cars. Vast areas of farmland were devastated, and it was estimated that the state had lost over 200 000 head of sheep and more than 6 000 cattle. Cleland Conservation Park, eight miles (13km) southeast of Adelaide, was destroyed.

Other areas affected include Clare Valley, 90 miles north of Adelaide, one of Australia's main wine-growing centres, and the winter sports resort of Mount Buffalo. On Tuesday 22 February, when the exhausted fire services at last believed the situation was under control, lightning set off a further series of fires in Victoria, and thousands of acres of state forest in the Grampians were destroyed. Fortunately, the thunderstorms were accompanied by heavy rain, which damped down most of the fires, and this time there was no damage to property or loss of life.

Saved by a tunnel

There are often stories of miraculous escapes in disasters like this. One story which emerged was of 83 people in the small town of McMahon's Creek, near Melbourne. With the flames rapidly approaching, they grabbed what food, clothing and bedding they could and took shelter in a floodwater tunnel at the Yarra Dam. The tunnel was 100 feet long, five feet high and only three feet wide, but everybody managed to get in. Flames approached to within 300 yards of the tunnel before a change of wind direction took them away. After a cramped and uncomfortable 24 hour stay in their strange refuge, all 83 emerged safely. They included three pregnant women, a baby of just a year old, and a woman of 70.

At Mount Macedon, an elderly couple fled their burning house in their nightwear, turned the garden hose full on their car and then got into the car themselves. They stayed there throughout the night with flames surrounding the car and although the paintwork was scorched, they survived.

The final death toll from these awful fires was put at 77, including 12 firefighters. The loss of property and possessions was incalculable. In Victoria alone a conservative estimate put the figure at $A200 million. The homeless had to rebuild their lives knowing that the danger of bush fires was never far away in the summer heat of southern Australia.

Ironic name
At the height of the blaze, the state capital of South Australia, Adelaide, was blanketed by smoke and ash. It gave a grimly ironic twist to 16 February, innocently recorded in diaries as the religious festival of Ash Wednesday.

Floods

It is not surprising that water can be so destructive. This vital element, without which life cannot exist, is very heavy and carries great force. One cubic foot of water weighs 62 pounds (25kg), and if you filled an average house with water, it would weigh about 400 tons. Any flood can cause enormous damage.

Floods are the subject of some of the oldest and most enduring of human stories. This book does not generally cover the legends of prehistory, but in the case of Noah's Flood an exception has been made. Not only is this a universal story, repeated in one form or another in the writings of many religions besides Christianity, the story told in the Bible has been shown by archaeologists to have some origin in fact.

When the sea turns savage and drowns the land, all that can be done is to try to minimise the effect. The low-lying areas around the southern North Sea have always been prone to flooding, and even with modern defence walls, inundations such as the disastrous flood of 1953, re-counted here, still happen.

The world's great rivers are nearly all liable to widespread flooding from time to time. These inundations can drown vast areas of land and take many weeks to subside. Little wonder that the Yellow River became known over the centuries as 'China's Sorrow'. It has taken untold thousands of lives and caused immense damage to property and land. The paradox is that these same rivers bring the fertility and agricultural richness which has provided the basis of life for the peoples of their flood-plains.

The other principal type of flood covered here is the sudden flash flood caused by torrential rainfall. Whether in Lynmouth, Florence or Colorado, the effects of millions of tons of water thundering down a restricted space are catastrophic. Solid stone buildings are swept away like toys and, in the case of Florence, priceless art treasures received the same lack of respect as anything else in the water's path.

There are also two examples of floods originating at dams. In one, a large earth dam gave way, causing terrible damage and loss of life in Johnstown, Pennsylvania. In the other, a large landslip caused the waters to overflow the Vaiont Dam in Italy, with equally disastrous results.

River and sea defences are repeatedly rebuilt and strengthened, but the mighty waters continue to overturn man's efforts, and the toll from damaging floods is certain to continue in the future.

Noah's flood

Prehistory: possibly around 4000BC

The story of the Ark

The great Biblical disaster has some basis in fact.

'And the waters prevailed exceedingly upon the earth, and all the highest hills, that were under the whole heaven, were covered'. So runs the graphic description in the Bible of what has come to be known as Noah's Flood, a story that has persisted down the ages. It tells of God's wrath being visited upon the earth in the form of terrible rains and floods that lasted for many days and nights, from which Noah, his family and the pairs of animals only escaped by sailing in their Ark until the waters went down, when they were left dry upon Mount Ararat.

Such a story could easily have arisen from a civilization whose knowledge of the physical world was limited to their own surrounding area; and in ancient Mesopotamia (modern Iraq) this was the case. The valleys of the Tigris and Euphrates Rivers were the centres of considerable early civilizations, and excavation has revealed that there was indeed a major inundation of the area in ancient times.

inundated area measured 400 by 100 miles (640 by 160 km), which is certainly large enough to be the compass of a cohesive civilization of the time. The habitable land lay between the mountains and the desert, in the fertile river valleys, and if all this land were inundated, it would seem to the people that their world had been drowned.

Those few who survived, and particularly their descendants, would naturally mark the event in literature and legend, and if one man managed to get his whole family and their livestock to safety in a boat, he could well become the hero of the epic. It is not too fanciful to suggest that as the origin for the great Bible story.

The cause of such a disaster is a matter for speculation. One theory that has been put forward is that an intense cyclone, or a tsunami perhaps resulting from an earthquake, drove a huge mass of water up the enclosed Persian Gulf and into the river valleys. As the Bible says, 'all the foundations of the great deep were broken up'. There could also have been associated violent storms with torrential rainfall, or this could have been another event which became linked with the flood as generations passed the story down.

Thick sediment

Whilst working on the site of the city of Ur, the birthplace of Abraham, in 1930, the great archaeologist Sir Leonard Woolley uncovered evidence of a devastating flood. The layer of sediment left behind was 8 ft (over 2m) thick, and below this sediment were traces of occupation, indicating that a natural disaster had happened.

Further work, both here and elsewhere in the area, led to the conclusion that the

A global story
There are stories of great floods in the folklore and legends of cultures and peoples worldwide, with the broad outline agreeing in many cases. They cannot all refer to the Mesopotamian flood, so perhaps a number of natural disasters occurred at the one time. It has been estimated that Noah's flood, or similar stories, are referred to in 80 000 books in 72 languages.

Yellow River
Prehistory–1938

'China's Sorrow'

The Huang He has caused millions of deaths over the centuries.

The Huang He, the mighty Yellow River, is the sixth longest river in the world, measuring 3 400 miles (5 500km) from its main source in Qinghai Province, west of Bayan, to its mouth at the Gulf of Po Hai on the Yellow Sea. It drains, and irrigates, an area of about 400 000 square miles (1 000 000 sq km) and is one of the great natural features of China. In places it is nearly a mile (1.2km) across.

The river gets its colloquial name from the vast amounts of yellowish 'loess' — a mixture of clay and sand — it carries down from the highlands and across the great plains of eastern China. The river is embanked for considerable distances in its lower reaches, and in places is as much as 15 feet (4.5m) above the level of the surrounding fields. Little wonder that it is prone to disastrous floods. The Yellow River has caused so many deaths, and so much suffering, over the centuries that it is also known as 'China's Sorrow'. It is believed that it has been responsible for more deaths than any other natural feature in the world. The number is incalculable but certainly runs into many millions.

Son of Heaven

Accounts of flooding are recorded in China's long history for at least 4 000 years. It is said that in about 2300BC there was a flood which lasted for 13 years. The people began to wonder if their country would be submerged for all time but Yu, the Son of Heaven, brought the waters under control; for this mighty work he was created Emperor of China.

River defences in the form of substantial banks or 'levees' were being built 2 500 years ago, but the great river regularly burst through them, causing death and destruction and bringing havoc to the agrarian economy. Nature always gives as much as she takes away, and the silty mud left behind after major floods is an excellent natural fertilizer.

One of the most disastrous floods of recent times was in September and October 1887, when the river broke through the restraining levees at a bend where the current ran more rapidly, at a place called Cheng-chou, in the province of Honan. The gap rapidly widened as the swollen river rushed through, until it was over half a mile (1km) long. Further breaches happened as the heavy upland rains continued to send vast quantities of water and silt down the river.

No escape

At the height of the flood, an area of 50 000 square miles (125 000 sq km) was under water. Eleven large towns and hundreds of villages were inundated, two million people were made homeless, and at least 900 000 died. There was no escape; the area lacks high ground and the waters simply covered everything. After the flood finally subsided, thousands more people died from hunger or disease. It was a national calamity of immense proportions.

The breaches were sealed and strengthened, but the river was not to be denied, and in 1933 there was a further serious flood. Though not as extensive as the great flood of 1887, it still drowned an area of

4 500 square miles (11 250 sq km) and affected over three million people. The official death toll was given as 18 000 but the true figure may have been higher.

In April 1938, man intervened to aid the river in its destructive work. The Japanese Army was advancing across China, and Chiang Kai-shek ordered that the levee on the Huang He should be dynamited at one point, the idea being to release enough water to stop the Japanese. The Yellow River, however, had other ideas, and as with so many of man's efforts at meddling with nature, the result was utterly catastrophic — almost as bad as 1887.

River management

Seizing on this unexpected opportunity, the river covered an enormous area of flood plain. Exact figures have never been released but it is believed that up to 500 000 may have died, with millions more made homeless. It was a colossal price to pay for halting an invading army.

In 1952, Mao Tse-tung ordered a vast programme of river management to start, with the words 'Work on the Huang He must be done well!'. Dynamiting has altered the path of the river to cut out dangerous bends, levees have been greatly strengthened, and dams built to contain the water in a number of places. The Yellow River, described by one hydrological engineer as 'the greatest outdoor laboratory in the world for flood control', appears to have been subdued, if not entirely tamed.

There have been floods since then, but nothing on the scale of the great inundations of the past. Students of natural forces would, however, not be surprised if 'China's Sorrow' still had the last word.

North Sea floods through history

1099–1947

Flood disasters in Britain and the Low Countries

The North Sea has long been the source of disastrous floods, with great loss of life and damage often occurring.

Records of great floods from the North Sea go back at least as far as the 11th century, when there were several such disasters. A flood in 1099 drowned much of Eastern England and Holland, with many thousands reported dead. There were exceptional floods in the 13th century. In January 1219 a great flood drowned much of Holland and Jutland, with considerable loss of life. Norfolk suffered in November 1236, when a large number of houses were destroyed and over 100 people died. In mid-December 1287 there was a disastrous flood. Much of East Anglia was under several feet of water and over 500 people are said to have died.

The Great Drowning

Across the North Sea there was even greater damage. The Dutch had already started their long work of reclaiming land from the sea, but in 1287 the sea struck back, inundating huge areas. It is said that the whole area around the Zuiderzee was under water, and that 50 000 people died.

One of the greatest of all North Sea floods occurred in January 1362. In Holland it was known as the Grote Mandrenke (the Great Drowning). Contemporary accounts speak of as many as 100 000 deaths, but more recent study of such records as

are available puts the figure at perhaps nearer 30 000. The marshlands of Jutland and Schleswig were almost completely inundated. There was also considerable damage and loss of life in England; many church towers fell, from London to Norwich.

In November 1421 the Low Countries were again battered by wind and sea. Contemporary reports say that 70 villages disappeared after this flood and that 10 000 people died. There was a further severe flood in 1436.

The All Saints flood

A storm surge of colossal proportions struck the Low Countries on 31 October–1 November 1570 (date according to the Julian calendar). Known as the 'All Saints Flood', it inundated large areas of Amsterdam, Rotterdam, Dordrecht and many other Dutch towns and villages. The Belgian coast was also seriously affected, but this flood spared Eastern England.

At its peak the sea was 15 feet (4.5m) above normal level. Dykes were breached in many places on the afternoon of 31 October, starting along the Belgian coast. As the weather front proceeded slowly eastwards the sea pounded Holland and breaches occurred there too. Different sources give the number of people drowned as anything from 100 000 to 400 000.

The coasts of Germany and Denmark were battered by another great storm surge on 21–2 October 1634. Over 1 000 houses were destroyed and 6 000 people lost their lives. The great storm of December 1703 is dealt with in the windstorms section of this book. The next really severe flood happened in December 1717.

A Christmas flood

This was one of the greatest flood disasters since modern dyke building began. It affected not just England and Holland but also France, Belgium, Germany and Sweden, where a tidal surge swept into the streets of Gothenburg. December 1717 was a particularly bad month for storms, though mainly mild with little snow, even in Scandinavia.

The Christmas flood occurred at least partly through a clash of warm air from the south with much colder air from the north starting on 21 December. A deep depression off Norway on 24 December rushed down, fed by strong north-westerly winds, then a frontal 'wave' travelled quickly across behind it from Belgium to the Baltic. Winds are believed to have reached over 100mph (160kph) at times.

Severe coastal flooding was reported from many places. The German coast was disastrously affected and hundreds of people were drowned in their beds in the early hours of Christmas morning. In Holland there were reports of up to 2 000 people drowned and many thousands of homes inundated and severely damaged. In all, 11 000 people died in this flood, as well as perhaps as many as 100 000 cattle, and the economy of the whole area was severely disrupted for some years.

In more recent years, there were severe floods in 1825 and 1836, and a violent storm struck the area on the night of 28–9 October 1927, with a major sea surge affecting almost the whole of Britain. On 7 January 1928 a storm surge fuelled by powerful north-westerly winds drove water far up the Thames, causing serious flooding in many parts of inner London. Fourteen people were reported drowned.

There was a most unusual storm on 1–2 June 1938, a time of year not noted for gales and floods. The Met Office reported it as having 'a violence unprecedented for the time of year since systematic measurements began.' The storm was accompanied by snow even in England, and coastal flooding in many areas.

There was very extensive flooding across much of England in March 1947. Heavy snowfall was followed by a rapid thaw with rain. The water created by the snowmelt swelled rivers to many times their normal size. More and more countryside disappeared until, at the height of the flood, nearly all the land south and east of a line from the Solent to the Wash was under water. England had become a lake with islands where the higher ground stayed dry. The rainfall that March was nearly seven inches (20cm), three times the average. Happily, there were no deaths, as the waters spread slowly, but a very great deal of damage was caused.

Johnstown

USA, 31 May 1889

The day the dam broke

An earth dam bursts and inundates an industrial town.

In the late 19th century, Johnstown was an industrial town of about 8 000 people in western Pennsylvania. The disaster that overwhelmed the town stemmed from the South Fork Dam, 12 miles (20km) away to the north-east and at the time the largest earth dam in the world — 72 feet (21m) high, over 500 feet (150m) in thickness at the base, tapering to 40 feet (12m) thick at its top. The reservoir impounded by the dam was about two miles long and a mile broad (3km by 1.5km), with a capacity of 5 000 million gallons of water — the USA's largest manmade lake at the time.

The dam had been built by the state authorities in 1852 as part of a large-scale water management system which included canals, but had been made redundant by the advent of the railway. The dam was sold to fishing interests and the reservoir was a popular place for angling, but maintenance was neglected and there was local concern about the safety of the huge structure for some years before the tragedy of 1889.

On 30 May 1889 a great storm hit the area. It continued for 48 hours, flooding Johnstown and many other settlements, and placing the South Fork Dam under intolerable pressure. At 3:10 on the afternoon of 31 May, the dam broke, releasing water with a weight of approaching 20 million tons, travelling initially at a mile a minute.

Gaping hole

The break in the dam widened to a gaping hole 430 feet (130m) across, but the rushing water was slowed by the debris it collected. The valley above Johnstown narrowed significantly, and the accumulated debris almost stopped the water several times before it came on again. As the wall of water neared Johnstown, it struck the Gautier rolling mill. Its force was irresistible and huge furnaces together with boilers and drums of cable and wire were swept up by the flood. At 4:10pm, an hour after the initial break, the flood reached Johnstown.

Much of the town was wrecked, but the flood was halted by the Stone Bridge, which carried the railway line to Pittsburgh. The bridge checked the waters, held them, and then as the debris piled up around its massive piers, slowed them to a less destructive force. Unfortunately, despite all the water, this wreckage caught fire — it contained live coals, petroleum and much other inflammable material — and people who had survived the onrush of water died by fire.

The flood continued, though much abated, and when the wreckage of one building arrived in Pittsburgh, 60 miles (100km) away, the next day, rescuers found a five-month-old baby alive inside. Many others were less fortunate. Estimates of the toll vary from account to account, but it is thought as many as 3 000 may have died. This was one of the most serious flood disasters in the USA's history.

Further floods

After the 1889 flood, Johnstown was rebuilt, but despite extensive flood prevention measures, the waters continued to batter the town. The latest serious flood was in July 1977, when following another storm, several small dams upriver burst and Johnstown was again inundated. About 80 people were killed and the damage caused was put at 200 million dollars.

Mississippi River
April 1927

Millions of acres are inundated

*America's longest river floods
with disastrous effect.*

The Mississippi and its tributaries — it is said there are as many as 100 000 — form America's greatest waterway. With a total length of over 3 700 miles (6 000 km), this is the fourth longest river in the world. This vast system has always been prone to flooding and efforts to contain it date back to the early 18th century, when French settlers in the state of Louisiana (named, of course, after one of their kings) began building large earth embankments. Using a word from their own language, they called them *levées,* a name which is still used today.

By the beginning of the 20th century, the levee system extended for hundreds of miles on either side of the river and undoubtedly prevented much flooding. However, sometimes the 'Father of all Waters' (as the river was known to the Red Indians) had the last word.

Huge tide

The Mississippi system drains 1 250 000 square miles (3 000 000 sq km) and when floods occur, often in the spring, more than 60 cubic miles of water are in motion. This huge tide moves relatively slowly, at about 30 miles (50 km) each day. If the water in the main channel reaches a higher level than that of the side rivers, a 'backflow' occurs and floods result as the levees are breached.

This happened in April 1927, with disastrous results. At the height of the flood, 26 000 square miles of land was inundated and many places were under 15 feet of water. The temporary sea was more than 1 000 miles long and up to 50 miles wide.

The water was a brownish-yellow colour, from all the silt and earth that had been displaced. As the flood moved inexorably down through the southern states, there was great alarm in New Orleans, one of the places where the Mississippi meets the sea. To save the city from absolute disaster, the levees were deliberately holed and a diversion channel created to take the river to the sea.

Remarkable escapes

The flood waters did not subside for over two months. More than 600 000 people were made homeless and 313 lost their lives. There were some remarkable escapes. On the Arkansas River, a group of about 200 people trying to escape the flood were stranded on a bridge just above the level of the water for three days and nights before rescue boats arrived. Other people were rescued by a Mississippi steamboat which became known as *Noah's Ark.*

Following this great flood, which caused damage estimated at $300 million, a new system of river management was set up, including large reservoirs and spillway channels, but the Mississippi will never be completely tamed. There were further serious floods in 1937, 1973 and 1983 and research has indicated that the average volume of water passing down the river has more than doubled in the past 50 years.

The voice of God

During the 1927 floods, aircraft flew over the area broadcasting warnings and offering help. People who had rarely if ever seen an aeroplane apparently thought it was the voice of God and that the end of the world was at hand.

Lynmouth

15–16 August 1952

A Devon disaster

Swollen rivers cause severe damage to a coastal resort.

Rain can create serious flash floods. In March 1864, the 'Dale Dyke' in Yorkshire burst after torrential rain and the subsequent floods killed over 200 people, but the worst rainstorm flooding in Britain in recent years was at Lynmouth, Devon, on the night of 15–16 August 1952. Nine inches of rain (22cm) were recorded in 24 hours, greatly swelling the volume of water in the waters of the East and West Lyn Rivers, which fall 1 500 feet in under four miles (7km). As a comparison, steady rain for a similar period would probably amount to about one inch (2.5cm).

The ground was already quite seriously waterlogged, and the underlying rock structure made rapid drainage impossible. Something like 90 million tons of water had nowhere to go except down the two rivers, and it was estimated that 600 tons of water was crashing down the river gorges *each second* at the height of the storm.

Battering-ram trees

The roaring, racing waters lifted large boulders from the river bed and tumbled them downwards, turning them into projectiles capable of causing tremendous damage. Trees too were swept along, acting like battering rams on everything in their path. In the four-mile stretch between moor and coast there were 17 bridges; after the storm none was left intact. Several times the debris jammed into huge piles before the force of the water broke them free, causing more damage.

When dawn came, Lynmouth was a dreadful sight. Houses, hotels and other buildings were wrecked and tons of debris were mixed with huge quantities of mud and silt. Roads were cracked, split and scoured with deep holes. At one garage the underground petrol tanks simply disappeared, ripped from their foundations by the force of the water.

On the foreshore debris was piled 25 feet (8m) high. It was estimated that 200 000 tons of rock and other debris had been torn down and taken out to sea. Up to half a mile (800m) offshore, trees could be seen standing in the water. A noted local historian, S H Burton, said 'When I visited Lynmouth after the flood, I could not find my way about. Sea and air bombardment could not have wrought more fearful devastation.'

It is remarkable that the death toll was as low as 34, considering the violence of the storm. Nearly 100 buildings were destroyed, 28 bridges were down and well over 100 vehicles were lost. A relief fund was opened, and reached over £1 300 000. Lynmouth's defences were rebuilt and strengthened. The next great storm came on 8 October 1960 when another violent torrent roared down the rivers into the town. But the job had been well done, and the water swept through and out to sea.

Record rainfall

The record for rainfall in a 24-hour period stands at 73 inches (187 cm) recorded at Cilaos on the island of Réunion in the Indian Ocean, on 15–16 March 1952, equivalent to over 7 500 tons per acre. The record for a year is held by Cherrapunji, India, with 1041 inches (2646 cm) from 1 August 1860 to 31 July 1861.

The North Sea overflows

31 January–1 February 1953

Fens and polder are inundated

Severe gales sweep water far inland in England and Holland causing death and destruction.

The low-lying areas of Eastern England and Holland are always liable to inundation in times of very high tides. Each time it happens the sea defences are further strengthened, and for a while all seems safe. Then circumstances combine to prove once more that Nature is stronger than man.

The great flood of winter 1953 had its origins in an unusual meteorological combination. On Friday 30 January a depression near Iceland moved south-east, deepening as it travelled. Next morning winds of over 120mph (190kph) were recorded in Orkney. The track of the depression meant that winds were driving down the North Sea from the north; the normal wind direction for depressions in the area is west or south-west. This fierce wind, combined with an already high spring tide and the unusually low barometric pressure, drove a vast volume of water southwards down the narrowing North Sea. ('Spring' in this case does not refer to the season, but is derived from the Norse word 'spreng' meaning swollen.)

At Aberdeen, on the east coast of Scotland, the tide was three feet (1m) higher than normal, but little damage was caused. The River Tees, in north-east England, overflowed its banks, but the worst damage by far was further south, in the low-lying counties of Lincolnshire, Norfolk, Suffolk and Essex, and across the Channel in Holland. The Lincolnshire coastal towns of Mablethorpe and Skegness were the first to be inundated; 40 people were drowned here. By 7:30pm the seawall in north Norfolk had given way, and a further 80 were drowned in the area around King's Lynn and Hunstanton.

Holiday bungalows

Many of these were American servicemen and their families, housed in holiday bungalows which were not intended for year-round occupation and had no chance of resisting such forces. By 11pm Yarmouth was under assault, with thousands of homes flooded. The tide was growing higher all the time; there were complaints later than insufficient warning was given to Essex in particular, but the emergency services in the more northern counties were working flat out, and most telephone lines were in any case downed by the storm.

The tide swept inexorably on, causing severe damage in Harwich, Felixstowe and Clacton. Reaching the Thames Estuary it completely overwhelmed Canvey Island, most of which was reclaimed land lying below normal high-water mark. Houses were flooded almost up to roof level, and 58 people were drowned here. Several ships were sunk in the Thames, and the great surge stopped only a few inches below the top of the river embankment in central London. It was the highest tide ever recorded in the capital, and an even greater disaster was only narrowly averted. The building of the Thames Barrier at Woolwich was a direct result of this narrow escape.

On the other side of the country, the same storm was responsible for the sinking of the ferry *Princess Victoria* shortly after she left Stranraer for the short crossing to Larne, in Northern Ireland. Over 100 people were killed as the ferry foundered in huge seas.

Dykes burst

Across the Channel, in Holland, warnings had been given, but nothing could have prepared the people for the awful disaster that befell them as midnight passed and February began. In the provinces of Zeeland, South Holland and North Brabant, the painstaking work of generations in reclaiming the polders from the sea and making them fertile was undone in minutes. Dozens of dykes burst and over 400 000 acres (160 000 hectares) was inundated.The tidal wave reached 12 feet (4m) high in places, smashing into houses and carrying before it trees, debris and livestock.

Many people were in bed when the waters struck and had no chance to escape. The death toll was over 300 in England; in Holland it reached 1 800, and over 90 000 people had to be evacuated from their homes.

The aftermath of the flood was severe on both sides of the Channel. The waters went down only slowly, and many thousands of people had to be housed in temporary accommodation until their houses could be reclaimed — or rebuilt in many cases. It was less than eight years since World War II had ended, and to be subjected to a natural battering as severe as any enemy action was a desperately hard blow to have to take.

An American hero

A corporal in the US Air Force, Reis Leming, was one of many heroes of the disaster. Though a non-swimmer, he single-handedly rescued 27 people from the bungalows on South Beach in Hunstanton, repeatedly wading out through the cold water to fetch more folk to safety. He was very tall, and was able to go where shorter men might have struggled to survive. His efforts were recognized when he became the first non-British recipient of the George Medal, awarded for conspicuous gallantry in peacetime.

Canvey Island, Essex, where evacuation was compulsory before the afternoon tide.
See illustrations on following page.

A bus was used to evacuate residents from Canvey Island, Essex.

The Lord Nelson Public House in Sittingbourne, Kent, where flood waters were still 10 feet deep on 3 February.

Vaiont Dam

Italy, 9 October 1963

A valley is drowned

A major landslide causes a reservoir to overflow.

The Vaiont Dam was constructed in 1960 as part of a major scheme to generate hydro-electric power using the water of the Piave River and its tributaries in north-eastern Italy. The dam was considered a masterpiece of civil engineering. Reaching a height of 865 feet (261m), it blocked a narrow valley between high mountains, creating a reservoir capable of holding 150 000 000 cubic metres of water. The front wall of the dam had an unusual double curve, intended to give it extra strength.

Earth movements

The dam was in a difficult location. One of the mountains above it, Mount Toc, was known to be liable to earth movements, and authorization to fill the reservoir was delayed until 1962 while engineers assured themselves that the construction was safe.

The dam was well made, and it survived the disaster that was to befall the people in the valley below it almost intact; but its positioning must be questioned in view of what happened. Locals warned that there would be problems one day, and those problems arrived as the people of the Piave Valley were at home, in bed or watching television, on the evening of 9 October 1963.

Put in simple terms, a vast chunk of Mount Toc collapsed into the reservoir. The cause is known to be an earthquake inside the mountain — minor in most terms but disastrous here — which started at about 10:30pm. Half an hour later the collapse took place. Millions of tons of rock and earth crashed into the reservoir, sending the water up in a huge wave that reared over the dam and fell 900 feet (280m) into the valley below.

Wall of water

Gathering more debris as it went, this wall of water overwhelmed the villages in its path within minutes. Longarone, the principal settlement, was almost wiped out, with 80 per cent of its houses destroyed; many smaller villages suffered similar damage. The Treviso to Calalzo railway line, together with station buildings, wagons and rails, disappeared; sections of track were found miles away downstream, rolled up like coils of wire.

Work to clear the debris and look for survivors could not begin until the next morning. When they arrived, rescue services were shocked at the amount of damage. Well-made houses were smashed into fragments of stone and wood, and a sea of mud and other debris covered everything.

When searches were completed it was found that 1 190 people had lost their lives, and a valley landscape had been transformed. The Vaiont Dam still stood, but behind it was a hill, not a lake. The inquiry into the disaster criticized the electricity company, ENEL, for choosing this site for a major dam, and the civil engineers for failing to realize the inherent dangers present.

> **The Mayor's warning**
> The day before the flood, the Mayor of Erto had put up notices around the area warning people not to go too near the lake behind the dam 'owing to the fact that landslides from Mount Toc could cause dangerous waves . . . which could run dozens of metres up the shore, carrying away even the most expert swimmer.'

Florence

3–4 November 1966

A cultural heritage under attack

The River Arno floods the Italian city, damaging many priceless works of art.

There had been floods in Florence before. Fed by mountain rains or melting snows, the River Arno, which flows through the city, is liable to considerable fluctuations in level, particularly in spring and autumn. There are dams on the upper river with sluices which normally control the flow, but in autumn 1966 they were unable to cope, and Florence suffered disastrously as a result.

It had been a wet early autumn in Italy, with more rain than usual through the month of October. There was relief when November started dry, but it was no more than a brief interlude. On 3 November up to six inches (15cm) of rain fell in parts of northern Italy — a quarter of the seasonal total in under 24 hours. The Arno rose so rapidly that the dams and their sluices were unable to cope with the flow. The river rushed on, collecting debris as it hurtled down the valley towards Florence.

Goldsmiths' shops

It struck overnight on 3–4 November. There was some warning, and people did what they could to protect themselves and their possessions. Shopkeepers in particular moved as much of their stock as they could. The historic goldsmiths' shops on the famous bridge over the river, the Ponte Vecchio, were greatly at risk, and shopkeepers and staff worked through the night to remove what they could take, while the river roared beneath them.

During the night the Arno surged over its walled banks in Florence and raced through the lower parts of the old city. As it did so it broke many central heating boilers and radiators, adding to the debris a foul oily slime, which was deposited up to a foot deep in streets and houses and caused irreparable damage. It is estimated that up to half a million tons of mud and slime was dumped on Florence that night.

This was a severe human tragedy: the final count was 127 lives lost, hundreds more injured, and thousands of people with damaged homes or business premises. But perhaps even worse was the terrible damage caused to Florence's superb cultural heritage, built up over centuries. The water and slime was no respecter of art or tradition. It got everywhere — into museums, galleries, old churches — damaging or destroying rare books, paintings, statues, tapestries and artefacts that were literally priceless.

Doors of Paradise

The Crucifixion, by the 13th-century artist Cimabue, was severely damaged, much of the paint washed off and the canvas torn. Frescoes by Giotto were damaged by silt, mud and exposure to damp. Rare musical instruments at the Bardini Museum were utterly destroyed, and the 15th-century bronze doors, by Ghiberti, on the Palazzo del Duomo, praised by Michelangelo as 'the doors of Paradise', lost half of their superb bronze carved panels. The panels were later recovered, though damaged.

At the Uffizi Gallery, staff worked all morning carrying priceless paintings to the upper floors. Over 300 were saved. The curator of the Science Museum, Maria

Bonelli, was alone in the building but managed to save many rare exhibits, including Galileo's telescope.

The unique collection of books at the National Library suffered dreadfully. After the waters subsided, students formed a long human chain passing the books and manuscripts to safety. Those at the lower end of the chain had to wear gas masks, so foul was the air. Many of these books, thought at the time to have been irreparably damaged, have been saved by entirely new methods of restoration devised after the disaster: out of bad some good may come.

At the height of the flood, 80 prisoners escaped from Santa Teresa prison. Although some simply made for freedom others, shocked at the city's suffering, stayed to help and were later praised for their efforts.

Returning to normal

Over half of Florence's estimated 10 000 shops were seriously affected, their stock lost or damaged beyond redemption, and there were many cases of real hardship in the city in the winter that followed. The cleaning-up operation was carried out with great determination and by the end of 1966 all the museums and galleries had reopened with the exception of Santa Croce, as had most of the hotels and restaurants.

The work on the art treasures continued for many years. Florence is still a very beautiful city containing many magnificent treasures, but it will never forget that night in November 1966 when the Arno threatened its very heart. Defences have been strengthened, and it would take a flood of unimaginable force to overwhelm Florence today: the 1966 flood was unimaginable at the time, so the warning has been given.

A present for the river

The custom in many parts of Italy is not to have presents on Christmas Day but to exchange gifts on Twelfth Night early in January: and they come, in legend, not from Father Christmas or Santa Claus but from a good witch called La Befana. She brings sweets and toys to children who have been good, and something black (traditionally coal) for the naughty ones. On Twelfth Night 1967 the city was still recovering from the flood, and the scars, both actual and mental, were still fresh. Little surprise then that a sock several feet long was hung from the Ponte Vecchio. Filled with coal, it was labelled 'to the Arno'.

Florence, 4 November 1966.
See illustrations on following page.

Flooding in Rome and Florence. Lower photograph shows Ponte Vecchio in background.

Big Thompson River

31 July 1976

A violent flash flood

Torrential rains turn a gentle river into a raging killer.

Flash floods are a not infrequent occurrence in the canyon country of the USA. Sudden and torrential rainfall can turn dry gullies and ravines into raging torrents of water, moving with enormous force and speed, gathering large quantities of debris and causing immense destruction before being spent almost as rapidly as they arose.

This happened on the Big Thompson River in Colorado on 31 July 1976. By a meteorological freak which is still not fully understood, weather systems became almost stationary around the head of the river, and violent thunderstorms deposited nearly 10 inches (25cm) of rain on the area in only four hours, from 6:30pm to 10:30pm.

Immense force

This released about 50 million tons of water down the canyon holding the river, which rose from its normal level of two to three feet (1m) to as high as 20 feet (6m) at the peak of the flood. Not surprisingly, the force of this cataract was immense. Mature trees on the canyon sides were ripped up by their roots and boulders several feet across were loosened and joined the flood debris.

It is estimated that the rate of water flow was 200 times the normal. By the time the waters reached the canyon mouth their force was unstoppable. US Highway 34 was, in the words of one eye-witness, 'chewed into pieces of asphalt'. A two-storey hydro power station was reduced to rubble, and a large section of its major supply pipe, which was nine feet (2.5m) in diameter and weighed many tons, was swept downstream a quarter of a mile (400m) and crashed into a house.

End of the world

The water scoured the river bed, rolling silt and mud forward in a tide of ever-increasing depth, burying animals, people and cars. A CB radio enthusiast, listening in to local frequencies, heard a woman in the path of the flood cry out 'My God! It's the end of the world!'. Her car was found later completely buried, with her body inside it.

The river crosses a plain after leaving the canyon and here the flood gradually diminished, weakening until it ran out of impetus after passing through the town of Lovelace. The residents had been warned and had left their houses. There was considerable damage to property but no lives were lost in the town.

Higher up, where there was less time to give warnings, it was a different story. The sudden flood killed 145 people. Some 600 houses and other buildings were either destroyed or severely damaged, and the rebuilding costs were estimated to be over $35 million.

> **Molasses**
> Boston, Massachusetts, suffered a unique flood on 15 January 1919. A vast storage tank in the harbour area, holding over a million gallons of molasses (black treacle syrup) burst, and the molasses literally poured away, through the streets. The sticky wave reached a height of 15 feet (4.5m) and was estimated to be travelling at over 30mph (50kph). It killed 21 people, caused an enormous amount of damage, and left a dreadful cleaning-up operation to be undertaken.

Sudan

August 1988

The Nile overflows

Many thousands die or are made homeless as the area around Khartoum is inundated.

Khartoum, the capital of Sudan, is a city of about 1.5 million people, at the confluence of the Blue Nile and White Nile. The River Nile, the longest river in the world at over 4 100 miles (6 600km) continues northward through Sudan and Egypt, fertilizing the plains on either side. The Nile is vital to the economy of both countries and it is always a relief when the annual rains arrive, swelling the river.

In summer 1988 there was great concern, particularly in Egypt, at the prolonged drought in Ethiopia and Sudan. Lake Nasser, impounded by the Aswan Dam and fed by the Nile, was so low that the turbines which provide much of Egypt's electricity were only just below the water. If the water level had fallen further, serious economic problems would have resulted.

However, towards the end of July there was news that the rains had started in the highlands feeding the Blue and White Nile. The river began to rise and with it the level in Lake Nasser — the world's largest man-made lake. What was good news for Egypt was, however, turning into a disaster for its southern neighbour, Sudan.

Three feet of water

The rains continued, and the rivers went on rising. In early August they broke their banks around Khartoum and much of the city was inundated. One aid worker described it as 'like Venice without the gondolas — the centre of Khartoum is under three feet of water.' Many houses, simply constructed with baked mud walls, just fell apart, and the people inside them were drowned or left homeless. As larger areas of countryside disappeared under water, reports of casualties came in. It was clear that a disaster on a very large scale was affecting Sudan.

The Sudanese Red Crescent (a similar organization to the Red Cross) described the situation as 'catastrophic . . . entire city without electricity, water mains inoperative, most streets impassable. Minimum number 800 000 persons severely affected with 100 000 homes destroyed.' The message ended, ominously: 'Please note these figures are conservative.'

The waters continued to pour down throughout much of August, and there were reports of serious flooding over a wider area, from Geneina in western Sudan to Shoak in the east. Ironically, people surrounded by a vast flood had no access to drinking water, and diseases such as dysentery started to spread. An emergency appeal committee was set up in Britain, to coordinate the supply of food, blankets, tents and other material.

The floodwaters did not subside until September, leaving a major operation to be undertaken in rebuilding houses, shops and offices and restoring services over a large part of Sudan. The situation was not helped by the military coup of June 1989, which has led to further unrest and the suspension of normal political activity, or by the continuing periods of drought affecting this and neighbouring African countries.

No accurate casualty figures have been issued, but there were certainly many thousands of deaths and over a million people were left homeless.

Industrial disasters

Since the Industrial Revolution began in Europe, about 250 years ago, there have been extraordinary advances in production techniques and systems which have led to many industries achieving very high levels of output. This advance has not been without its human cost. Conditions in many labour-intensive industries such as textiles and mining were very poor until quite recent times, and workers were regarded by less enlightened industrialists as expendable items on the balance sheet.

Large-scale tragedies and disasters have tended to be concentrated around a small number of industries. Coal mining was hazardous from the start and with the very rapid development of deeper mines in the 19th century, miners were constantly at risk. Three of Britain's worst pit disasters are recorded here in some detail, to try to give an idea of what conditions were like. There were hundreds of pit explosions and fires between 1850 and 1950, and many thousands of men were lost.

The fourth mining-related disaster tells of the day in October 1966 when a huge waste tip slid down on to the village of Aberfan in South Wales, covering a school and burying over 100 children: a tragedy that shocked a nation and led to radical revisions in the way colliery waste was treated.

There are two examples here of hazardous cargoes exploding, devastating entire communities: Halifax, Nova Scotia in 1917, and Texas City 30 years later. The transportation and storage of toxic and hazardous materials, including nuclear waste, continues to be a source of great concern to many people today.

The North Sea could be said to be the modern equivalent of the mines in terms of the hazards present. Both are hostile and unnatural working environments, and in both there are risks. The devastating explosion on the Piper Alpha rig in July 1988 is the worst so far. Disasters caused by large-scale escapes of oil are dealt with in the environment section of the book.

The tendency in modern industry is for fewer workers and more sophisticated machinery, so are the days of very large-scale industrial tragedies coming to an end? It seems doubtful, given man's seemingly endless prediliction for creating, with every step forward in technology, an equal step forward in new potential for disaster.

The Oaks

12–18 December 1866

England's worst pit disaster

A series of explosions underground leads to the death of 361 men.

The Oaks colliery, about a mile south of the town of Barnsley, was one of the largest in the vast Yorkshire coalfield. Owned by Firth, Barber & Co, it opened in the 1840s and had three shafts which led down to a maze of nearly 50 miles (80km) of galleries and shafts between 800 and 1 000 feet (250–310m) underground.

The seams here were known from the start to be 'fiery' and prone to gas escapes and firedamp, and considerable precautions were taken including the provision of good ventilation and regular safety checks. Despite this, there was an explosion on 5 March 1847 which killed 73 miners. In the following 15 years, fires and explosions in Yorkshire pits killed nearly 400 men.

As Christmas approached each year, miners felt the need to earn as much as possible, to give their families a little extra. Each Wednesday was 'making-up day', when miners tried to produce even more coal than usual.

The first explosion

Wednesday 12 December 1866 was therefore a day of great activity at The Oaks, with over 300 shiftworkers and another 70 or so daymen and officials down the mine. At about 1:30pm there was a loud explosion. The cage in no 2 shaft had disappeared and that in no 1 was broken and disconnected from its rope. It was repaired as far as possible, and Thomas Dymond, a mineowner, went down with two others.

The rescue party found about 30 men at the foot of the shaft, all badly burned but still alive. They were sent up as quickly as possible, but most of them died from their injuries. Other than that, in the choking dust all they could find were bodies. Rescue efforts continued through the day and into the long December night, but only bodies were found. As each was brought up and identified, grieving widows and other relatives came forward to claim their menfolk. Below ground the grim work went on, and the ventilation system was restored to help the searchers.

Further tragedy

There were more deaths to come. On the Thursday morning at 9am the pit 'fired' again, killing 27 rescue workers. The tragedy was widely reported in newspapers and attracted national attention. A fund was started and by Christmas had raised over £10 000.

In the days up to Thursday 18 December there were at least 14 more explosions at The Oaks. The mine was clearly in a very unstable condition, and it was decided to fill it in. Earth and stone was tipped down the shafts for several weeks until the danger was thought to be past. The Oaks had taken the lives of 361 men and its name was to be synonymous with pit disasters for generations.

A miraculous escape

On Friday 14 December at about 4:30am the signal bell of no. 1 shaft at The Oaks was heard. A temporary cage was rigged and two men went down. They found one miner, Samuel Brown. Knocked unconscious by the second explosion, he had been in the mine nearly 24 hours when he was rescued.

The Blantyre mine explosion
22 October 1877

A Scottish tragedy

Explosion, fire and firedamp kill over 200 miners in Scotland's worst pit disaster.

In the 1870s, coal mining developed very rapidly in the area around the town of Hamilton in Scotland, a few miles south of Glasgow. The village of High Blantyre was a mining community, described at the time of the disaster as 'a maze of dirty and intricate ways and byways'. The mine was a little way south of the village. It had five pits, opened between 1872 and 1877, and in that time produced nearly 900 000 tons of coal — a very rapid rate of production.

The mine, owned by the firm of William Dixon, had very little problem with water, often a severe trial to mining operations, but was known to be very gassy. The pits were prone to 'firedamp', a highly combustible gas that was responsible for thousands of deaths in mine disasters. A few days before the explosion, one of the foremen, Joseph Gilmour, had brushed aside the concern of a miner about gas, saying 'There'll not be a man fall in this pit, I'll guarantee that.' He was to be proved tragically wrong.

Backbreaking work

On Monday 22 October 1877, the early shifts went down the mine as usual at 5:30am. There were about 235 men on the no. 3 shift. No unusual conditions were reported underground, and the men went to their backbreaking work of extracting coal in the low tunnels called 'stoopings'. At about 8:45am there was a loud explo-

sion and flames were seen emerging from two shafts, no. 3 and no. 5. The miners in no. 1 shaft felt the blast but were not affected by it.

Hearing the explosion, people hurried to the scene. Women and off-duty miners congregated at the pit, the women looking for news, the men offering their help in rescue. Soon, seven bodies were hoisted up from no. 2 shaft, but it was no. 3 that gave most concern. The mines inspector, Ralph Moore, had been sent for, and he and his assistant went down no. 3 pit at around midday.

At the South Level they found what they had most feared — roof falls and the clear smell of firedamp. The ventilation was very poor, and the main shaft was blocked by debris from the explosion. Nothing could be done until a way through could be forced, and teams worked throughout the day and into the evening, finally getting through at about 10pm. Four seriously injured miners were found and taken up: all died later. The situation in the shaft was very unsafe, with continual slippage of debris.

Difficult operation

Work continued through the night and into the next day. The weather was poor, with rain and sleet, but despite this, hundreds of sightseers arrived from Glasgow and Hamilton, and a hundred police had to be brought in to control the crowds. Meanwhile, the High Blantyre families were becoming very distressed at the delay in bringing bodies out. It was to take the rest of the week, a difficult and at times dangerous operation. The shaft had to be cleared slowly and with great care and a large number of temporary props put in place.

The villagers were becoming more and more incensed at the delay, and on the Thursday held a large public meeting which was addressed by Alexander McDonald, a leading trade unionist and champion of workers' rights. He urged the Blantyre miners to press for a full inquiry to establish what were seen as the management's failings in running the mine, and if necessary to prosecute the owners.

Temporary partitions

An inquiry had in fact already been announced. It proceeded rapidly, examining 48 witnesses including managers, foremen and miners, and was concluded by 23 November. Concern was expressed at the many temporary 'brattices' used in partitions between shafts and galleries, and at the frequent use of naked lights in what was known to be a gassy pit.

A small explosion had in fact occurred on 20 August 1877. One miner, Joseph McInulty, was killed, and his two brothers were injured. One of them, Andrew, then only 17, later became president of the Lanarkshire Miners Union. There was found to be negligence on the part both of management and of the miners themselves. Although supervision was inade-

quate, some practices such as shot-firing in the stoopings had at least the tacit approval of the men.

The inquiry failed to identify the precise cause of the explosion. Most likely it was a sudden escape of gas from a seam or pillar after a small roof fall, ignited by a flame, and exacerbated by the ever-present firedamp and the poor ventilation. It was also felt that the mine had been developed too quickly, without proper thought being given to the way shafts were driven.

The precise cause seemed irrelevant to 92 widows and over 250 fatherless children in High Blantyre. The total death toll was to reach 207, many of them young men in their teens. It remains Scotland's worst mining disaster.

Another explosion

The High Blantyre mine continued working after the disaster of October 1877. On 2 July 1879, less than two years after this terrible tragedy, another explosion shook the village. This time it was no 1 pit that had suffered, and a further 28 miners lost their lives. It appeared that the lessons of 1877 had not been fully learned, for several of them were found to have matches and pipes on them when the bodies were recovered.

1 General view of the **High Blantyre** district, looking south.
2 'Shankers' descending the 'kettle' to clear the 'shank'.
3 Some of the first volunteer explorers.
4 Volunteer 'shankers' waiting their turn to descend.

American mining disasters

1907–72

A series of tragedies

*Coal and silver mining
take a high toll.*

Deep mining is hazardous wherever it is carried out, and there have been a number of disasters affecting mines in the USA. There was a particularly bad year in 1907, with over 3 000 deaths in total. The worst accident was at Monongah, West Virginia. A loaded mine train got out of control, ran down a gradient and broke power lines, creating sparks which started a fire. There was a powerful explosion and 360 men died, either from the explosion, fire, suffocation or being crushed by falling debris.

Two years later it was the turn of Cherry, a small town in Illinois, to grieve. The accident here did not even start in the mine: it began with haybales catching fire near the mine entrance. The flames spread to the shaft timbers and were soon out of control. A few of the miners managed to escape but most were trapped below ground. Rescuers got the signal that a cage was coming up, but when it reached the surface all the men inside it were dead,

No records

Underground rescue is always more difficult when precise numbers are unknown: at Mannington, West Virginia, explosions at a coal mine on 20 November 1968 destroyed the office where shift records were kept, so an individual check had to be made at miners' homes. It was found that there were 99 men missing: 21 were rescued, but further explosions of tremendous force shot flames from the mine high into the air, ending rescue activity.

overcome by the choking fumes, which contained methane. The fire burned for over 24 hours before any further attempt to locate either bodies or survivors could be started, and the final toll was not established for another four days. The accident took the lives of 259 men. Some, it appeared, had been shot by their workmates, presumably to spare them further suffering from terrible injuries.

Ironic name

It is, of course, not just coal which comes from deep mines, and there was another tragic accident at the ironically-named Sunshine silver mine in Kellogg, Idaho, where the shafts are nearly 5 000 feet (1 500m) below ground. The men worked under very difficult conditions, with extremely high temperatures demanding a break every 30 minutes. On 2 May 1972 a fire started in a part of the mine no longer being worked, possibly through old timbers spontaneously igniting. Rescuers did everything possible, sealing off as many shafts as they could and trying to maintain a supply of air through the remaining shafts while they searched for survivors. It was known that about 100 men were unaccounted for.

Searches continued for a week, by which time 50 bodies had been recovered, and then a miracle occurred: two miners were found weak, but still alive, in a shaft 4 800 feet (1 465m) below the surface. They were the only survivors of a group of seven who had escaped the fire. As the days passed, five of the men succumbed to the heat, dehydration and exhaustion, but two lasted out, helped by the air continually being pumped through the galleries. The final death toll at Kellogg reached 91.

The Senghenydd pit fire

14 October 1913

Britain's worst mining disaster

Over 400 South Wales miners killed as a mine becomes a furnace with no escape.

For much of the 19th and 20th centuries, South Wales was renowned as a coal mining area. There were hundreds of pits in the Taff, Rhondda, Merthyr and Aberdare valleys, and many thousands of men relied on the mines for work. It was common for boys to leave school with no thought other than to follow their fathers down the mine. Communities were close-knit, and were, far too often, bound even closer together by tragedy.

The South Wales mines were known for two things: the high quality of the coal produced, and their gassy seams. Explosion followed by the spread of the dread firedamp was a constant fear. The first serious accident happened at Risca on 14 January 1846, when 35 miners were killed. As mines grew larger, and shafts were dug ever deeper and longer, so the number and scale of accidents rose also.

High toll

Between November 1867, when an explosion at Ferndale, Pontypridd, killed 178 men, and July 1905, when 119 died at Wattstown, eight serious accidents in South Wales mines took a toll of 1 364 miners; more died in smaller incidents. The death rate per 1 000 miners was higher than for any other British coalfield. The greatest disaster during this period was at Abercarn in September 1878, when 268 succumbed. Senghenydd was to eclipse them all.

The Universal Colliery at Senghenydd, at the head of a small valley some miles north-west of the town of Caerphilly, was owned and operated by Lewis Merthyr Consolidated Collieries. It started producing good coal in 1896. The village of Senghenydd depended on the mine, but disaster came early to the pit. In May 1901 a large explosion went through the whole series of workings. Of 82 men underground at the time, only one survived.

The mine remained liable to sudden escapes of gas; measurements taken in September 1913 showed an alarmingly high amount of firedamp in the atmosphere. Yet work continued, with the mine producing up to 1 800 tons of coal each working day from its numerous galleries, many of which bore names of Boer War battles — Mafeking, Ladysmith and so on. A large steam fan circulated air at 2 000 000 cubic feet per minute. Critically, this ventilation flow could not be instantly reversed, as happened in other pits. The disaster inquiry focussed on this point as being a major contributory factor to the very high toll.

The explosion

The mine was examined for gas as usual in the very early morning on Tuesday 14 October 1913, before the first day shift went down at 6am. Then, at 8:10am, the village was shaken by the unmistakable sound of an explosion from the colliery. The mine manager, Edward Shaw, ran across the yard to the top of the Lancaster shaft, to find it blocked by a mass of wreckage, with the banksman dead beside it. With over 900 men underground, rescue had to start immediately, but there is evidence that precious time was lost: the fire brigade at Porth, not far away, were not called until 10am, for instance.

Senghenydd had its own trained rescue team — but no proper breathing apparatus, so they had to wait for the firemen. Nonetheless, Shaw and an overman, Thomas, went down the other shaft, the York, to start their investigation. When they finally reached the Main West Level, a roadway two miles long, they were horrified at what they saw. 'It was like looking into a furnace' said Thomas later. There was nothing they could do until the rescue services arrived.

Wall of fire

With the best available teams assembled at the mine, further attempts were made to reach the trapped men. But a 'wall of fire', to quote one report, stopped them. Relatives and friends gathered at the pit, standing quietly and waiting for the news they feared most. A reporter for *The Times* commented on their dignified demeanour. By the evening only 12 bodies had been recovered, and over 400 men were still unaccounted for.

Early next day there was a small breakthrough. Some 16 hours after the explosion, a group of men, still alive, was found in the Bottanic District of the mine. One by one they came up, 18 in all, including a boy who revived after two hours' artificial respiration. The fact that they survived confirmed the view of the inquiry that reversible ventilation might have saved many more.

Money from the king

It was many days before all the bodies were recovered. The final toll was 439 miners and one fireman dead, Britain's worst mining disaster. One Senghenydd woman lost her husband, four sons and three brothers; another gave birth to her 12th child while her husband and a son were still lying underground, dead. A relief fund was opened. King George V gave £500 and money poured in from a shocked nation to support the widows and children of Senghenydd.

The inquiry which followed was long, controversial and set important precedents. It was a judicial inquiry, ordered by the Home Secretary, Reginald McKenna, who had himself visited Senghenydd — only the second Home Secretary ever to go to the scene of a pit accident. The inquiry had two expert 'assessors'. Robert Smillie, president of the Miners Federation of Great Britain, represented the miners, and Evan Williams, chairman of the South Wales Coalowners Association, the owners.

There was much wrangling over the type of lamps used at the mine, the failure to keep seam walls and ceilings free of dust, and over the possibility that one of the battery-operated electric signalling sets not long introduced into the mine could have produced a spark to set off the explosion. Bare galvanised steel wires from these sets ran along the sides of the roadways. To produce a signal, the wires were bridged with a knife or file. When the implement was removed, sparks were often seen. But the tests carried out were inconclusive and the point remained unproven.

The inquiry produced sufficient evidence for the Home Office to start legal proceedings against the mine owner and manager. In the event, only the manager was convicted, and on five counts was fined the sum of £24, which the outraged people of Senghenydd quickly worked out at roughly one shilling (5p) per dead man. On appeal, the case went back to court, creating an important precedent, but before the matter was concluded, the 440 deaths at Senghenydd were overshadowed as the carnage on the Western Front ran into untold thousands.

The Honkeiko disaster

The world's worst-ever pit disaster is recorded as having happened in the Honkeiko region of China in April 1942, when up to 800 miners died, entombed after an explosion had caused a major rockfall. The disaster happened in wartime in a country where there was in any case very little reporting of such events, and few details have ever emerged. More miners than this died as the result of the Tang-shan earthquake of 1976, but that was not specifically a pit disaster.

The Halifax Harbour explosion

7 December 1917

The Nova Scotia town is devastated

A ship loaded with explosives blows up, causing enormous damage and killing thousands.

The 3 000-ton French freighter *Mont Blanc* loaded up in New York in early December 1917 with vital materials for the battles being fought in Europe: TNT, picric acid, benzene and gun cotton. The *Mont Blanc* sailed north to Halifax, Nova Scotia, where the British cruiser HMS *High Flyer* was waiting to escort her and other merchant ships across the Atlantic. The *Mont Blanc* reached Halifax at about 9am on 6 December. The harbour is an excellent natural deepwater anchorage extending for several miles, generally about one mile (1.5km) across but narrowing at one point to less than half a mile (800m).

As the *Mont Blanc,* with a pilot on board, neared this point, her crew saw with alarm that another vessel was closing on them. It was a Belgian freighter, the *Imo.* The *Imo* should have passed to starboard of the *Mont Blanc,* but signalled that she was coming to port. The captain of the *Mont Blanc* put his rudder hard to port, but it was too late to stop a collision, and the *Imo* rammed the French ship near the hold where the acid was stored. The *Imo* managed to reverse off, then lay helplessly wallowing in the narrow channel.

Floating bomb

On board the *Mont Blanc,* fire broke out and the crew abandoned ship, reaching the shore safely. The blazing ship could be seen drifting slowly towards Halifax and neighbouring Richmond and the townspeople, realising only too well what cargo was aboard, began an exodus, uphill, away from the harbour and what they rightly perceived as a floating bomb of unimaginable proportions.

Another munitions ship, the British *Pictou,* was moored at Pier 8, and her crew also abandoned her. Bravely, men from the *High Flyer* set off in a launch for the *Mont Blanc* hoping to scuttle her before disaster struck. But they were too late. About 15 minutes after the collision, the explosives on the *Mont Blanc* went up in a terrific explosion. People who had not seen the ship thought that the town was under German air attack. The effect was just as devastating. Half of Halifax was flattened by the explosion, its blast effect, and by fire. The impact was heightened by the topography, the deep channel concentrating the force of explosion instead of spreading it. Many people were killed as the railway station, an imposing brick and stone building in downtown Halifax, collapsed on top of them. Hundreds of schoolchildren, just assembled for morning classes, died in their classrooms. Of 550 children in the affected area, only seven are said to have survived. Nearly all the buildings in the harbour area, with many hundreds of workers, were completely destroyed. In Richmond, where many houses were of wood, fire and blast wrecked whole streets.

Tented village

Those who survived gathered in a state of shock on higher ground and on the town's large common. Fire spread rapidly through Halifax, Richmond and Dartmouth, the communities either side of the river, and by the day's end 25 000 were homeless. The weather worsened and a snowstorm started, adding to their misery. Fortunately, rescue workers were soon on the scene. Troops arrived too, and a tented village rapidly arose on the common, providing at least some shelter for the injured and homeless; and at least the snow had the effect of dampening the fires.

The *Pictou*, meanwhile, was still anchored at Pier 8 and there was a very real danger of another large explosion. That danger was averted by the very brave action of a marine superintendent, J W Harrison, who got aboard the ship, opened all the sea valves, and scuttled her.

News of the tragedy spread rapidly. A special train left Moncton carrying doctors, nurses and medical supplies. Other trains took people from Halifax to temporary accommodation elsewhere. The girls at St Vincent's Academy, which was fortunately outwith the affected area, tore up sheets and spare uniforms to provide makeshift bandages after an appeal for help.

The total number of civilian casualties in Halifax and Richmond has never been precisely established. Most estimates put the figure at between 2 000 and 3 000. The whole town centre area — 2.5 square miles

— was flattened. Thousands of homes were destroyed in a tragedy which shocked the whole of Canada and brought home to that nation, perhaps for the first time, the horrors of war.

Military casualties in the explosion were light — some 12 soldiers in the harbour area died. It was the innocent civilian population which suffered. As well as all those killed, over 8 000 were injured and then there were the homeless and those with ruined businesses. And all because of a confusion over ships' signalling.

A radio message

Seeing the stricken *Mont Blanc* heading towards him, the telegraph operator in Richmond, Vincent Coleman, sent a hurried message over the wire: 'A munition ship is on fire and heading for Pier 8. Goodbye.' He then left to return home, having been married only a few weeks beforehand. Tragically, he was among those who died. His message was picked up in a number of places and helped to get rescue services to Halifax shortly after the explosion.

The Texas City disaster

16 April 1947

A deadly cargo explodes

A freighter loaded with chemicals blows up, setting fire to oil tankers and devastating a city.

A chain reaction of dreadful proportions was set off when fire broke out on board the freighter *Grand Camp* in the harbour of Texas City, on the Gulf of Mexico, on an April day in 1947. The freighter was loaded largely with highly combustible ammonium nitrate, and once this deadly cargo was set alight the consequences could only be disastrous.

There was little time to warn other vessels, or indeed the people of the town. The fire swiftly took hold and as the chemicals ignited and vapourized, a tremendous explosion took place. Burning debris was flung high into the air, raining down on other ships in the harbour and on nearby buildings. What was sitting there as if waiting for the fire was a mixture which could hardly have been more potentially catastrophic if it had been deliberately designed.

Burning oil tankers

The harbour contained about 50 oil tankers, in varying stages of loading. One after another they caught fire and began to burn, setting off further explosions and filling the air with dense black smoke to add to the choking, toxic fumes from the *Grand Camp*. Before long the fire reached a chemical plant nearby. It seemed there was to be no end to the holocaust. It was quite impossible for the fire services to contain a blaze of this magnitude, with more fires starting all the time. Fires continued burning for days afterwards, and in the end some 90% of all the buildings in Texas City were either damaged or destroyed.

As can be imagined, there was considerable loss of life. Many people in the dock area and on board ships were killed instantly by the terrific blast from the *Grand Camp*. Others died in the city as buildings burned and collapsed around them, or from the effects of the smoke and fumes. It is recorded that two people died when their light aircraft was blown apart by the blast as it flew over the city. Windows were smashed at a distance of 12 miles (20km) from the explosion.

An unbelievable tragedy

Two days after the explosion, the American Red Cross estimated that perhaps 800 people had died. The number may well have been higher. Even as that figure was being set, further explosions and fires were happening. Another freighter, the *High Flyer*, blew up the day after the *Grand Camp*, causing further death and damage.

It was an unbelievable tragedy for a major port and industrial city to suffer, and it took many years for Texas City to recover and rebuild itself and its prosperity. Damage costing millions of dollars was caused, and the area was declared a disaster zone.

A bad month

Texas City was the third disaster to hit the USA in spring 1947. Less than a month beforehand, a pit explosion in Illinois had killed a number of miners, and in early April a severe tornado swept through parts of Texas and Oklahoma, claiming over 100 lives.

The Aberfan colliery tip

21 October 1966

Children buried by colliery waste

A tragedy that shocked a nation when an unstable tip engulfed a village school.

Like many other mining villages, the people of Aberfan in the Merthyr Valley, South Wales, became used to living in the shadow of a large and ever-growing tip of waste material. By 1966 the Aberfan tip, started in the 1930s, was 800 feet (250m) high. Material had moved from it before, in 1959 and 1964. On the latter occasion, Mrs Gwyneth Williams, the local councillor, made the prophetic statement that: 'We have a lot of trouble from slurry causing flooding. If the tip moves, it could threaten the school.'

Beneath the tip, rainwater continued to build up, adding to its mass and continually weakening it. There was also, unknown to most people, a spring running under the tip. It was measured after the disaster and found to be discharging water at the rate of 100 000 gallons (450 000 litres) an hour. Little wonder that the tip moved.

On the morning of 21 October 1966 the tip finally gave way under its own weight and that of the water inside it. It rumbled down the hill slope for half a mile (800m) and, as Councillor Mrs Williams had predicted, engulfed the school, and a number of houses besides. It was clear that a disaster of awful proportions had occurred. The school was full of children at morning assembly, the tragedy made worse by the fact that at noon on that day they were due to break up for a week's half-term holiday.

A frantic rescue effort immediately started, with men and women using every available tool and device to shift the filthy mass of slurry, dust and mud to try to find any living souls underneath. The news soon reached the miners themselves, many of whom left their shifts underground and came up to join in the digging. From nearby towns, wooden pit props, sandbags, scaffolding and other materials were brought in. As the day progressed, traffic problems became severe, with ambulances unable to reach the village along the narrow valley roads, and the army were brought in to help control the situation.

Few found alive

In the area around the school, bulldozers worked where they could, but most of the work had to be done by hand and long lines of people snaked up and across the slope, passing empty sandbags to be filled and full ones to be taken away. The work continued all through the night, but despite all this effort, very few children were found alive. The final toll was 144 people dead under the slurry, 116 of them children.

The disaster shook the whole nation. There was a real feeling of national grief at the death of so many children, and the mass funeral of 81 of the victims was attended by 10 000 mourners. Shortly after this, an inquiry headed by Lord Justice Edmund Davies, who was born at Mountain Ash, only a few miles from Aberfan, began work. It uncovered a sorry state of affairs. The safety aspect of colliery waste tips had been scandalously ignored. There was no record of any official visit to the Aberfan tip since 1962, and no explanation for this lapse either. There was no proper policy for the management of tips, and clear danger signs and warnings were repeatedly ignored.

Bungling ineptitude

The inquiry report was published in August 1967. It pulled no punches, laying the blame firmly at the door of the National Coal Board and calling Aberfan 'a terrifying tale of bungling ineptitude by many men charged with tasks for which they were totally unfitted, a failure to heed clear warnings, and a total lack of direction from above'.

All this was of little comfort to the bereaved families of Aberfan. But, as with many communities struck by disaster, they closed ranks and helped each other. Very few people moved away; they took the braver course of staying to rebuild their lives. A disaster fund was set up, and reached over £1.6 million before it was closed in 1967. Its proceeds were used not only to give compensation to the people of Aberfan but also to build them a splendid new community centre, opened by the Queen in 1973 and in her words: 'A symbol of the determination that out of disaster should come a richer and fuller life'.

A modern problem

At the time of the Aberfan disaster, there were about 500 colliery tips in Wales and many others in Yorkshire, Scotland and elsewhere. Checks showed that dozens of these tips were in an equally unstable condition, and much work has been done since then on stabilising them and on finding alternative uses for the waste. The tips only grew with the onset of mechanical mining in the early 20th century. This meant that less pure seams of coal could be mined, leading to a greater accumulation of waste per ton of coal. With the considerable reduction in deep mining in Britain, these tips are now considered to be under proper control.

*A classroom in **Aberfan** village school engulfed by coal waste.*

Piper Alpha

6 July 1988

North Sea oil's worst tragedy

*A platform is destroyed by
explosion and fire.*

The development of the North Sea oil-fields, between Britain and Norway, has been one of the great technological success stories of the later 20th century. Using new techniques developed for this inhospitable location, companies and governments have worked together to exploit the vast resources of oil and gas locked below the seabed. The different fields are given names and as they are opened up are leased to operating companies.

The Piper field, operated by Occidental Petroleum, came onstream in 1976. Piper Alpha, about 120 miles (200km) northeast of Aberdeen, was the largest platform in the field. Weighing 34 000 tons, it acted as a control centre for the field and had a crew of about 200, working shifts. The rig was fully equipped with accommodation module and helicopter deck. It produced up to 160 000 barrels of oil a day.

Flared off

All North Sea oil has a high gas content. At first, as fields were developed, this gas was simply 'flared off' — burnt at the platform — but it became regarded as a valuable by-product, and installation of gas recovery equipment was compulsory for the later fields. Piper Alpha was therefore handling not just crude oil but also methane and 'liquid gases' such as propane and butane. Gas was also used as fuel on the platform. It may have been this 'cocktail' of oils and gases that triggered off the explosion.

Whatever happened started very suddenly: there was no time for the rig to send an SOS signal. The first news of the disaster came from the support vessel *Lowland Cavalier,* which flashed a Mayday call to the coastguards at 9:58pm on 6 July 1988 saying there had been an explosion on Piper Alpha and the platform was on fire. At the same time, another support vessel, the *Tharos,* sent a message to Occidental's headquarters in Aberdeen. Helicopters were scrambled from RAF rescue bases as it became clear that a major incident had occurred.

On the platform, men were desperately seeking ways of escape as fire seared the rig. A helicopter pilot reported that he was flying at 200 feet (60m) and the flames were reaching above him. The *Tharos* edged as close as possible and began spraying Piper Alpha with water from her fire nozzles. She also launched dinghies to pick up survivors from the water.

One survivor, Roy Carey, said later 'I didn't have time to think it over. It was a case of fry and die or jump and try. There was clear water below me so I just went straight through the railings'. The heat on the platform was enough to melt helmets, and other survivors described how the soles of their boots melted as they ran across the rig to jump into the water.

At about 10:30pm there was another major explosion, and the platform superstructure keeled over towards the sea as rescuers watched helplessly. Iain Letham, who was in a dinghy launched from the support vessel *Sandhaven,* said: 'Flames were going everywhere. All my gear melted, and I thought I was going to die'.

Medical help

By this time there were 15 helicopters in the area. Some were used to take nonessential personnel off the *Tharos* to make room for survivors. The *Tharos* had medical facilities and injured men, many of them badly burned, received initial treatment there. Nine specialist doctors were flown out to the ship from Aberdeen to help.

The airlift of survivors began in the small hours, the first helicopters arriving in Aberdeen at about 3am. The night is very short at these latitudes in July and by 3:30am it was light, assisting rescue efforts. The fire was dying down but the blackened skeleton of the platform held out little hope of yielding further survivors, and rescue vessels began to pick bodies from the sea. Many were never recovered: the wreck of Piper Alpha was deemed to be a safety hazard and was sunk some months later.

The precise cause of the explosion is difficult to establish. After the disaster there was considerable criticism of safety standards in the North Sea, and regulations were tightened up, but when such volatile materials are being handled there is always an attendant risk. There may have

been a gas leak which was ignited by a chance spark. That could well be sufficient to set off a fire large enough to cause the fatal explosion.

The Piper field has resumed production, and an impressive memorial to the 173 men who died on the Alpha platform has been erected in Aberdeen, the Scottish centre for the oilfields. It is a constant reminder of the hazards under which men work so that our essential supplies of oil and gas can be brought ashore.

Norwegian disaster

The full toll from accidents in the North Sea is over 500. The worst incident before Piper Alpha was on the Norwegian accommodation rig the *Alexander Keilland,* in the Ekofisk field. In March 1980, during the spring equinoctial gales, the rig broke up and capsized, killing 123 men. Metal fatigue in one of the rig's support legs was thought to be the cause of the disaster.

*The remains of **Piper Alpha** burn while a fire fighting platform lies a short distance away.*

Incirharmani mine

Turkey, 4 March 1992

Turkey's worst pit disaster

Methane gas explosion starts a disastrous fire.

There is extensive coal mining in the northern part of Turkey, near the Black Sea. The Incirharmani mine is below Kozlu, a town of 60 000 people, of whom about 5 000 worked at the mine. The explosion occurred at 8:10pm on Wednesday 4 March, at a time when there were about 700 miners underground. There appears to have been a very rapid build-up of methane gas, and there was no time to warn miners before the explosion sent shockwaves and fire through the underground galleries.

One survivor, Cevat Engin, said 'Everything happened suddenly. I saw rocks and bits of iron flying through the air' and another, Salih Yanik, described 'a noise like a rushing wind . . . the passages were full of bodies as we ran for the upper levels'. The explosion happened 1 800 feet (550m) underground. Rescue teams were sent down as soon as possible, and over the next 12 hours, 400 men were brought out alive, though many were injured.

Government concern

The injured were taken to hospital in Zonguldak, another Black Sea town, where they were visited by the Turkish Prime Minister, Suleyman Demirel, his deputy, Erdal Inonu, and other high-level officials. The government team also visited the stricken mine and talked to relatives and friends of those killed.

According to the director of Turkey's state-run Coalmining Agency, Ozer Olcer,

the build-up of gas took only 30 seconds. He said that the explosions happened when the volume of gas was just below the level which would have triggered alarm systems. The mine was regarded as one of the better-equipped in Turkey.

As with other mining disasters, most of the deaths resulted from fire or asphyxiation rather than the explosion itself. Many of the corpses were so blackened and burnt as to be unrecognizable. At first it was thought that only about 100 men had died. By the day after the explosion the figure had risen to 122, with a further 148 men still missing.

At this stage a decision was taken to seal the mine to cut off the air supply, as fires were still burning fiercely underground and there were fears of fresh explosions sending toxic clouds up to the surface. Once the mine was sealed and the fire was out, the difficult operation to recover the bodies of the missing miners could restart.

Rescue teams coming up to the surface reported new fires breaking out and said there was no chance at all of finding further survivors. The mine was described as 'a poisonous inferno', with carbon monoxide gas at dangerous levels. Grieving relatives waited beneath the large sign at the entrance to the mine, with its notice reading: 'Be safe! They are waiting for you at home'. For 270 men, the sign was tragically untrue.

> **Bad reputation**
> The Turkish coal industry does not seem to have a good reputation for safety, and this was the sixth explosion at the same pit since 1945. In the other five, 107 men were killed. In the years from 1980 to 1991, 405 miners were killed in Turkey.

Explosions in Guadalajara

22 April 1992

Leaking gas infiltrates the city's sewers

Many buildings destroyed in Mexico's second city

A series of powerful explosions rocked Guadalajara, the second largest city in Mexico, on 22 April 1992. There were at least 15 major blasts plus further smaller explosions, and they caused enormous amounts of damage, with whole streets being ripped up and buildings collapsing.

Eye-witnesses told of cars and even buses being flung into the air with the force of the explosions. Twenty street blocks were badly affected in the Reforma district, which had a population of about 150 000. The total population of Guadalajara, which is 270 miles (450km) north-west of Mexico City, is about three million.

When rescue services rushed to the area, they found chaotic scenes. A spokesman for the Jalisco State government said that it was 'like a major earthquake. Streets have been torn open, with holes 15 metres deep. There are cars on top of houses'. With the death toll still uncertain, the state's Red Cross director, Fernando Pérez Jimènez, estimated that over 600 people had been injured, many of them seriously.

Some buildings had been sliced in two, with furniture and fittings still upright and undisturbed inside one half, while the other half of the building lay in rubble below. Dazed survivors wandered the streets looking for missing relatives, and when the state governor, Guillermo Cosio Vidaurri, toured the area, they accused him of ignoring warnings given the day before.

Smell of chemicals

As an inquiry into the cause of the disaster began, it emerged that local people had alerted the authorities to a strong smell of chemicals or gas 24 hours earlier, but little had been done. A fire service spokesman said that manhole covers in the area had been opened to try to disperse the gases. A policemen, Martin Bonales, said his wife had reported a smell of petroleum to the authorities and was told that everything was under control.

Suspicion fell on the state oil company, Pemex, who were accused of allowing petroleum to spill into sewers. The company at first denied the charge, saying that the explosions were caused by a leak of hexane caused by a private company manufacturing cooking oil. Hexane, a volatile solvent, is used in the process of extracting oil from seeds.

As further facts emerged, Pemex again became the prime suspect. Mexico's Attorney-General, Ignacio Morales Lechuga, said that the evidence so far collected pointed to the disaster being caused by a leak of petrol from a corroded Pemex pipeline. The petrol combined with other volatile gases and liquids in the confines of the sewers, leading to the explosions.

Mayor resigns

The mayor of Guadalajara, Enrique Dau, resigned, although denying he was in any way to blame. The city's fire and sewerage chiefs also resigned. Mr Lechuga said that nine public utility officials and two private citizens would be charged with various offences including possibly negligent homicide.

The final death toll rose to 230, with over 1 000 people suffering injuries. Services in the city were badly disrupted, with electricity and water supply lines cut in the affected areas. The Mexican government sent army personnel to Guadalajara to ensure that order was kept and to stop looting.

The government also pledged state aid for the victims of the disaster. The ruling Institutional Revolutionary Party were accused of an inadequate response after the Mexico City earthquake in 1985, and were clearly determined to show a quick and positive response following this tragedy.

There were claims that the Reforma area should have been evacuated after the leaks were reported the night before the disaster. On the day following the explosions, many people were in fact evacuated from their homes while another gasoline leak discovered in a Pemex pipeline was sealed.

A major rebuilding programme is required to restore housing, shops and offices in the area affected by the explosions, and it is bound to be many months, if not years, before the scars caused by the disaster are healed.

Bus in a hole

A number of people had a fortunate escape when a bus in which they were travelling sank into a hole which opened up in a street in Reforma. Although the bus was damaged, its structure stayed largely intact, and rescue services were able to free the trapped passengers, most of whom had only minor injuries — and an extraordinary story to tell.

*Explosion damage in **Guadalajara**.*

Pandemics

The rapid spread of disease has happened many times. Most often, particularly since medicine became a more exact science, it has proved possible to confine epidemics to one area or country, though the effects can still be serious. There have been epidemics of this kind in Britain this century involving typhoid, several types of influenza, whooping cough and other diseases, and in other parts of the world they are also quite common.

The three cases reported here are different. They fall more into the category of pandemics, sweeping across large areas of the world and attacking indiscriminately, felling thousands of previously otherwise healthy people. Whereas localized epidemics may perhaps concentrate their attack on children or the elderly, these pandemics strike across ages and classes.

They span over 500 years. The first is the infamous Black Death, the bubonic plague of the Middle Ages which reduced the population of Europe perhaps by a half and also killed many millions in Asia. Medicine was in its infancy then and physicians were powerless. They turned to the priests for help, but the power of prayer was also insufficient to stop the disease, spread by rats and fleas.

The 'Spanish flu' pandemic followed directly on from the Great War of 1914–18, and indeed overlapped it, affecting thousands of troops. It too swept across continents, aided by modern, rapid means of transport such as trains and steamships. For two years it ran riot, and by the time it subsided in 1920 it had taken more victims than all the guns of the previous four years.

The third pandemic, AIDS, is with us today. Its final effects are unknown but the prognosis is not good, with an estimate of at least 40 million people infected by the year 2000. The origin has still not been properly identified, nor (in early 1992) has any effective cure. Like famine, epidemics may have been thought a thing of the past, but however hard we try, we cannot eradicate disease, and new strains continue to emerge almost as fast as cures for old ones are found.

The Black Death

1338–50

The world's worst pandemic so far

Kings and commoners alike fall victim as the plague sweeps across continents and kills untold millions.

The Black Death spread throughout Asia and Europe: plague is no respecter of boundaries. It lingers in the folk memory of many nations; hardly surprising, for this was by far the worst pandemic the world has known so far. The total number of deaths may have been as high as 75 million, and in some countries, 90% of the population was wiped out in the space of two or three years.

The first record we have of the plague is from headstones in the Central Asian state of Kirghis dated 1338, though the disease may have started to spread before this. It affected many Asian countries before reaching the Near East and then Europe in 1347. It spread rapidly from Sicily through Italy to Germany, France, Scandinavia and Britain, where it arrived in 1349.

Primitive medicine

Doctors were powerless. Medicine was in any case at a very primitive stage, and even today it has proved difficult to contain rapid epidemics in African and Asian countries. The papal physician, Guy de Chauliac, observed two forms of the plague: one in which the victim fell sick with a fever, coughed blood and died in two or three days, and another with tumors or 'buboes' and black spots in which death took four or five days.

His observation was accurate, though there are in fact three forms of the plague. The bubonic form, with tumors, is contracted from fleas, often carried by rats. The feverish form, septicemic plague, kills by poisoning the blood. The third form is pneumonic, in which bacteria are passed on by sneezing or coughing. All were rife in the mid-14th century.

Reports came from all over Europe of populations decimated by the Black Death. Half the population of Florence perished. Boccaccio recorded that 'Between March and the ensuing July, upwards of a hundred thousand people lost their lives. Grand houses once full of lords and ladies and their retainers were left desolate, even to the meanest servant.' In Siena, work on the cathedral had to stop, so many workmen had died. Over 50 000 dead were reported from Marseilles, and in Holland a contemporary writer says the death toll was 'impossible to believe', so great was it.

Mass burials

In Britain, as in other countries, whole villages were simply wiped out. The rebuilding of Winchester Cathedral was halted, and instead of the planned, elaborate west front a temporary façade was put up. It is still there, and is admired today as fine 14th century architecture! Everywhere people were dying at a rate that made it impossible for proper burials to be carried out. Huge pits were dug to take the bodies, or they were thrown into rivers. In France, the Rhône was hastily consecrated so that bodies could be tipped into it.

One of the most gruesome stories comes from the Crimea, where a Tartar army was besieging the then Genoese port of Caffa (now called Feodosiya). The Tartars actually used catapults to hurl plague victims' corpses over the walls so that those inside would be infected. The Tartars themselves caught the disease, and their galleys brought it back to the Mediterranean. On the other hand, so many English and French soldiers died that the Hundred Years War between the two countries was temporarily halted.

Jews massacred

At any such time, scapegoats are sought, and in many parts of Europe the unfortunate Jews, as before and since, were held to be responsible for the dreadful toll of death, and were massacred. This happened in France, Switzerland, Germany, Flanders and Spain. In other places, groups of penitents called Flagellants went round whipping themselves as a form of penance for the sins that they believed had brought the pestilence upon them.

No-one was immune. King Alfonso of Castile in Spain died of the plague, as did the son of the Byzantine Emperor. The Archbishop of Canterbury succumbed; his successor was no luckier, lasting only a short while before catching the plague himself. Priests were always vulnerable, as it was their duty to tend to the sick and dying. Despite wearing masks, they often caught plague from their congregations.

The plague abated after 1350. It is estimated that one third of the population of Europe died within 15 years. In Britain, as many as 2 500 000 people may have died; London is said to have lost half its then population of 70 000. The toll in Asia was probably even higher. Such a pandemic is hard to envisage today: AIDS (see p144) is our nearest modern equivalent.

Further plagues

Though the Black Death diminished greatly after 1350 in Europe, that was not the end of plagues, and there were several serious outbreaks in the centuries that followed. There was a widespread plague in Britain in 1625, written about by the contemporary chronicler John Taylor under the title *The Fearfull Summer*. The book speaks of 'the grievous and afflicted state of the Towne of Newcastle upon Tine' and of 'London's Calamitie'. Further plagues struck here in 1665–66, described, though in rather overblown terms, by Daniel Defoe in his *Journal of the Plague Year*.

Spanish Influenza epidemic

1918–20

A worldwide spread of deadly virus

*In a few short years, disease takes
more victims than the
guns of war.*

In early 1918, there were reports of wide-spread outbreaks of influenza from different parts of the world, including China, the USA and Spain. Although thousands of people were infected, there were as yet few deaths from this new strain of the disease, which became known as 'Spanish 'flu' from one of its apparent points of origin.

World War I still had nine months to run, and its carnage had been terrible. In the words of the war poet Wilfred Owen (himself a victim of the slaughter), it had taken 'half the seed of Europe, one by one'. No-one could have foreseen that the influenza epidemic that was to sweep the world in the next two years would lead to the death of even more people.

The real assault started in September 1918, and modern transport such as trains and steamships helped to spread it far more rapidly than would previously have been the case. A train could traverse most European countries in under a day, or the USA and Canada in a few days; a ship could cross the Atlantic in under a week.

Flanders gripe

There were reports of large-scale deaths from South Africa, Russia, North and South America, Europe, Asia . . . it seemed the whole globe was under attack from the virus. Soldiers in the trenches were far from immune. US troops in France suffered thousands of cases of influenza: fortunately for them and the British, the German troops were also badly hit. The British soldiers called the disease 'Flanders gripe'. In England, over 1 000 German prisoners of war in a single camp died; in the confined space of the camp the virus, once it had taken hold, was impossible to check.

The disease attacked indiscriminately and violently, with many reported cases of people dropping dead in the street. There were reports of cars and others vehicles colliding as the drivers fell ill, and off the Irish coast two ships collided because no-one on board was well enough to steer correctly.

Many of those affected developed pneumonia, further weakening them, and a common symptom was for the victim to turn blue in the face as the virus attacked the lungs and starved the body of oxygen. In such cases, death often followed within two or three days. In poor countries and among superstitious or religious people, windows were kept firmly shut to try to exclude the disease; in fact the lack of fresh air was merely helping the virus in its deadly work.

No effective vaccine

There was little doctors could do, in the absence of an effective vaccine. Some did try vaccination, but it was more of a placebo than a true defence. People wore masks in many countries to try to stop inhaling the virus. In the USA notices were posted reading 'It is unlawful to cough or sneeze in the street. Offenders will be fined $500.'

Desperate measures were tried, many based on 'old wives tales' without any medical base. Some people smeared themselves with bacon fat, others sat for hours inhaling hot eucalyptus oil. Bathing in water as hot as the body could stand was recommended: so was bathing in ice. One remedy tried in the USA was wearing plasters soaked in vinegar. Few of these 'home cures' had any effect other than to make the victims acutely uncomfortable.

Business was badly affected. Banks and offices closed for lack of staff, trains and ships lay idle, and in New Zealand the parliament was suspended as nearly all its members were affected by the disease. The epidemic had reached that country on a ship from Europe, the *Niagara*. No quarantine was imposed on its passengers, and more than 50 000 New Zealanders died as the disease swept the country.

Harvests neglected

The third wave of the virus hit in early 1919. By now the war was over, but the returning troops found themselves facing a threat to life every bit as dangerous as the guns and shells they had so recently left. In Barcelona, the daily death toll reached 1 200. In Bombay it was 700, and similar figures were reported from Canada and South Africa. Harvesting was neglected in many countries, seriously affecting food supplies. Children were especially vulnerable, and infant mortality rates soared.

By 1920 it seemed that the peak had passed. The virus had done its worst. Estimates of deaths worldwide vary, but 20 million is commonly accepted as a probable figure, of which 16 million were in Asia. Oddly, the disease struck hardest at younger people: over 80% of those who died were under 40. In a few short years, war and disease had reduced the world's population by over 30 million.

More epidemics

Influenza epidemics still rear up from time to time. There was one in 1976, but by then an effective vaccine had been developed, and the outbreak was largely confined to the USA. In the same year, Legionnaire's Disease, a new type of pneumonia, was first identified, taking its name from ex-servicemen, 20 of whom died in one outbreak. An antibiotic has been located which is effective in countering the disease. Other recent diseases have included Lassa Fever (named after a small town in Nigeria) and Green Monkey Disease, brought to Europe by animals being used in laboratory experiments.

'Flu mask in use, February 1919.

AIDS

1950s–

A world problem

The HIV virus creates possibly the greatest-ever public health disaster.

There can be no doubt that AIDS (acquired immune deficiency syndrome) is a global catastrophe of immense proportions. The infecting agent is HIV (the human immuno-deficiency virus) and those infected are said to be 'HIV positive'. The infection spreads through contact with infected blood or body fluids.

Its origins are still a matter of considerable debate. There appears to be general agreement that the virus originated in Africa some time in the 1950s, possibly in monkeys in the central part of the continent, and was transmitted to man through bites from the animals, which were used in cancer research experiments in laboratories in a number of countries. There have been other, more fanciful, theories including one that the virus was deliberately created by germ warfare scientists, then tested on prisoners who were later released into the community, spreading the disease — a real-life science fiction story.

Rapid spread

Whatever the truth, AIDS has spread at an exponential rate. It first began to be recognized as a major problem around 1980. Medical centres in the USA reported a new disease among homosexual groups, and similar reports began to appear in medical journals from other countries, including Britain. It soon became clear that the disease could be spread by heterosexual contact as well. Another group greatly at risk were drug-users, if they shared needles.

In 1982 there were about 1 000 reported cases in the USA and just three in Britain. By 1985 the figures had jumped to 10 000 and 200 respectively. In 1991, over 120 countries had reported cases of people dying from AIDS. The number of deaths in the USA was expected to reach over 50 000, and the cost of treating HIV-positive patients there was put at $66 billion: more than half of the entire health budget for the state of California was taken up in AIDS-related work.

Future forecasts

Forecasts for the future spread of the disease are almost impossible to take in. The World Health Organization has estimated that by the end of the century there could be at least 40 million cases of AIDS worldwide. Africa, where the disease may have originated, has suffered very badly, as have many Asian countries. In larger cities in these continents, as many as a third of the population are believed to be infected.

Vast resources are being applied to try to find curative and, if possible, preventative measures, but (up to early 1992) without success. The effort is international, with cooperative research proceeding at an intense level. Nothing so far seems to have even slowed down the spread of AIDS, and it appears we may be facing the most serious pandemic of the 20th century.

> **Stars die**
> A number of popular entertainers have died from AIDS. One of the best-known of these stars was Freddie Mercury, lead singer with the rock group Queen, who died of AIDS in 1991. Large-scale charity concerts were organized by the remaining members of the group, all the proceeds going to benefit AIDS research and hospices for sufferers.

Rail and road disasters

Rail travel developed very rapidly throughout the second half of the 19th century and into the 20th. One of the very first trials was attended by tragedy when an English MP was killed by falling under a train, but in general trains proved to be a safe, if initially rather dirty, means of travel. There is great romance in long rail journeys such as those across North America, Australia or the vast expanses of Russia, but sometimes things do go wrong. There have been a very large number of rail crashes involving loss of life. A small selection is included here: every loss of life is a personal tragedy for the people involved, but relatively few rail crashes come into the 'catastrophic' category.

The collapse of the Tay Bridge in 1879 shook the railway world. This was the longest bridge ever built. Its designer had been knighted by Queen Victoria, and it was acclaimed as a masterpiece. For it to give way so soon after its opening was almost unbelievable. The terrible tragedy in Russia in June 1989, when many children died as gas exploded by a railway line, is one of the two worst in recent years. The other, in Bihar, India, holds the unenviable record of the greatest loss of life in a single rail accident.

Two other crashes are included: one from Scotland — Britain's worst, at Quintinshill — and one from New Zealand. They are representative of many others. As with air travel, it should be stressed that rail travel is still, statistically, very safe, and there is certainly more chance of escaping from a train than from an aircraft in difficulties. The inexplicable tragedy at Moorgate on the London Underground is also described. City subway systems are in use in many of the world's great world metropolitan centres, and in general operate with efficiency and safety. On this one occasion, either human error or a sudden seizure led to disaster.

Like the train, the motor car has been of great benefit, and has totally revolutionised personal travel. It has also been an instrument of slaughter throughout the 20th century. The numbers killed in motor accidents must by now run into millions, but the vast majority of these accidents involve only a few people — often only one. The tragedy described here was different.

Salang was motor madness on a vast scale, with two convoys trapped inside a tunnel between Pakistan and Afghanistan, fire raging, and no ventilation. The numbers killed ran into hundreds, possibly even higher; the full facts have never emerged. It is a reminder that when things go wrong on the roads, they can go very wrong indeed.

The Tay Bridge disaster

28 December 1879

A world-famous bridge collapses

The world's longest railway bridge fails in severe winds with a train halfway across.

The latter part of the 19th century saw a great expansion of the railway network in Britain. As lines pushed further north across Scotland, two formidable natural barriers stood in the way of a fast service between Edinburgh, Dundee and Aberdeen: the broad estuaries of the Forth and the Tay.

The challenge to the great engineers of the day was irresistible. Proposals for bridging both rivers were brought forward, and it was the Tay crossing which got under way first, in 1871. The bridge, designed by Thomas Bouch, was nearly two miles (3km) long including the shore sections, and at the time was the longest bridge in the world. It stood upon 85 stone and iron piers and was on average 88 feet (26m) above the waters of the river.

The bridge was seven years in construction, and in that time 20 workmen lost their lives through falls or other accidents. It was officially opened on 1 June 1878 and cut the rail journey from Edinburgh to Dundee, which formerly had to be routed via Perth, by some 30 miles (50km). The bridge inspired tremendous feelings of pride: it was described as 'the very perfection of strength and beauty' and a rash of merchandise such as Tay Bridge Toffee appeared to mark its opening. Despite this, its builders had over-committed themselves financially and needed to recoup the money they had spent. They were never to do so.

Royal approval

The bridge came through its first winter safely, and in summer 1879 received the royal seal of approval when Queen Victoria crossed it on her way south from Balmoral. She was evidently impressed, for on 26 June 1879 its designer became Sir Thomas Bouch in a ceremony at Windsor Castle.

The latter part of December 1879 saw a number of severe gales striking northern Britain, and on Sunday 28 December the wind reached storm force. Many ships were wrecked and there was considerable damage in towns and villages in Scotland. The gale reached its height in Dundee in the early evening. Tay Bridge Station had a large part of its roof blown off, and some loaded coal wagons were blown along the track for 400 yards. The 5:50pm Newport to Dundee train crossed the bridge safely, though not without difficulty, the driver and passengers reporting that carriages were violently rocked by the wind.

The next train due across had come from Burntisland in Fife; it consisted of an engine, six coaches and a brake-van and when it left St Fort Station on the Fife side of the bridge just after 7pm it was carrying 71 passengers and a crew of four. The train set out on its slow passage across the Tay at 7:14pm. It was expected in Dundee no more than ten minutes later. When it was clearly overdue the Dundee stationmaster, James Smith, left for the bridge to find out what had happened. He met two men, James Lawson and David Smart, who had seen the train set off over the bridge and then what looked like a shower of sparks fall into the river.

Awful tragedy

James Smith then located his superintendent, James Roberts, and they crawled out onto the bridge from the Dundee end. Half a mile out, they saw with horror that there was nothing in front of them: the centre section of the bridge had gone, and of the Burntisland train there was no sign. The inescapable conclusion was that an awful tragedy had occurred. The weather made it very difficult to confirm what had happened, but at 9pm the postmaster in Dundee received news from Broughty Ferry, some miles to the east, that mailbags known to have been on the train had been washed ashore.

Next day, when the wind had abated and ships were able to get close to the scene, they saw that 13 spans had crashed into the river. There were no survivors from the ill-fated train. This accident had a tremendous impact, the bridge having opened only 18 months previously and having been hailed as a magnificent piece of engineering; the tragedy is still remembered today.

The Tay Rail Bridge was rebuilt to a stronger design; reopened in 1887, it still carries trains today. Thomas Bouch was ruined. He was to have designed a bridge over the Forth but that job was given to others and his name is remembered today for all the wrong reasons; yet he was without doubt a fine engineer. He was unlucky that his bridge was struck by a wind of exceptional ferocity, though doubts were also expressed about the quality of the stone and iron used for the support piers. Bouch was severely depressed by the tragedy and died within a year.

Was it a hurricane?

There was much debate over the actual strength of the gust that caused the central part of the bridge to collapse. A retired admiral in Fife reported that at 7:20pm a walnut tree in his garden was snapped in two by the wind, which he asserted from his long experience was hurricane force. At the same time, a church service in Dundee was halted because the minister feared the roof was about to collapse. Another eyewitness reported what looked like waterspouts roaring along the river and under the bridge. The official speed for a hurricane is 73mph (115kph) and it is more than likely that speed was exceeded on 28 December 1879.

*The collapsed **Tay Bridge**.*

The Quintinshill rail crash

22 May 1915

Britain's worst rail disaster

Four trains in multiple crash: a wartime tragedy kills many soldiers through signalmen's errors.

Britain's worst rail disaster happened in the confused circumstances of wartime travel. On 22 May 1915 a special troop train carrying 500 men of the 7th Royal Scots Regiment from their depot at Leith, in Edinburgh, was heading south on the first stages of a journey which would have taken the regiment to battle in the Dardanelles.

The disaster happened at Quintinshill Junction near Gretna, on the Scotland–England border, and involved five trains. Two overnight expresses from London, running late, were approaching Carlisle at 6am, the time when the Quintinshill signalman, George Meakin, should have been ending his night shift. His replacement, James Tinsley, was (illegally) hitching a ride on the local train from Carlisle, and would arrive at about 6:35, so Meakin stayed on. This arrangement had been going on for some time. It was against regulations but it suited both men. To cover, Meakin wrote train movements on a slip of paper until Tinsley could copy them into the official log on his arrival.

Carriages telescoped

Because the expresses were late, the local reached Quintinshill before them. Meakin had already placed a goods train from Carlisle into the loop of track beside the main

'down' line and an empty coal train into the 'up' loop. Only the two main lines of track were now free, and inexplicably, Meakin put the local passenger train, which had brought Tinsley, on the 'up' main line. Tinsley started on his paperwork while crew from the goods trains joined Meakin in the box for a chat. Following regulations, the fireman from the local came to the box to check on the situation. There were now too many trains for the section to handle, though neither Meakin nor Tinsley seemed to be aware of the fact.

At 6:38am Tinsley, now in change in the box, cleared the first express through his section, and at 6:42 he similarly cleared the troop train, apparently forgetting about the local standing on the track. It can only be assumed that he was preoccupied in his paperwork. Travelling fast, the troop train smashed into the local. The wooden carriages stood no chance; they were crushed and the train was telescoped into a third of its original length. Several of the carriages were turned sideways across the line.

Meakin, who had left the box, rushed back up the stairs and put the down signals to 'stop' in a vain attempt to halt the first express. With three others, he ran down the line, all of them waving frantically. But it was too late, and a minute after the first collision, the 600-ton express from the south, double-headed with two locomotives, careered into the wreckage, which by this time had spread to include the goods train on the down loop.

Extensive wreckage

A fierce fire had started in the tangled wreckage, fuelled by pieces of coal from the trains' tenders and by the gas which lit train interior lights at the time. Bullets in solders' belts and ammunition cases exploded as the fire spread. Many men injured in the troop train and unable to escape were burned to death. The fire service from Carlisle arrived at 10am but the fire was burning fiercely and there was little water available locally. The fire continued burning all day and through the next night.

It took a long time to clear and search all the extensive wreckage, which involved all the carriages of the troop train, the first three coaches of the express, and 12 wagons of the two goods trains.

The survivors were eventually assembled in a field near the railway line; of a battalion of 500 men, only 52 were present and able to give their names. The Battalion Roll was lost in the flames, but the final toll was put at 165 dead and a further 50 missing, presumed dead. The Royal Scots had lost 215 men.

Military honours

Driver Scott and his fireman, a man named Hannah, were also killed, and there were 10 civilian fatalities, bringing the total of lives lost to 227. The soldiers whose bodies were recovered were given ceremonial burial with full military honours at their base in Edinburgh. There is a memorial to them in the city's Rosebank Cemetery. Scott and Hannah's widows received a lump sum in compensation plus an annual pension for their children.

The inquiry into the crash, under the Chief Inspecting Officer, Lt-Col Druitt, found nothing to criticize in the state of the rolling stock or the equipment at Quintinshill. This might be thought strange in view of the fact that the troop train was made up of very old stock, such as wooden carriages without bogies, and yet was hauled by a powerful engine and scheduled to run as fast as a passenger express. However, it was wartime, and every available unit had to be pressed into service, and this was no doubt taken into account.

The late running of the two expresses from London was certainly a contributory factor; if they had been on time the goods and local trains would not have had to be 'held' at the junction. The outmoded gas lighting on the troop train was also mentioned as causing the fire to start and spread more rapidly than might otherwise have been the case.

It was found that Meakin and Tinsley had failed in their duty, and were therefore primarily responsible for the accident happening. 'Collars' should have been dropped over signal controls whenever a through line was blocked, to prevent the signalman throwing the lever and clearing another train through. This was not done, nor had the two men realized, it seems, that there were more trains than their section could handle. They should not have accepted the troop train when the line ahead of it was blocked.

The two unhappy men were tried in Edinburgh in September 1915 and convicted. Tinsley was sentenced to three years in prison and Meakin to 18 months. However, both suffered severe nervous breakdowns and they were released in a year. They had to live with the responsibility of causing what is still Britain's worst railway accident, and that involving the most trains.

Other wartime disasters

There have been other terrible rail disasters in wartime. In 1917, an overloaded train carrying French troops home from Italy ran out of control on a downslope. Friction from the brakes started a fire and the train was derailed at high speed, killing at least 450 soldiers and possibly as many as 700. In 1944, an Italian goods train crowded with people illegally hitching a ride came to a halt while climbing an incline in the Basilicata hills. The train was in a tunnel, and 509 people died from carbon monoxide poisoning: a tragedy without a crash.

See illustration on following page.

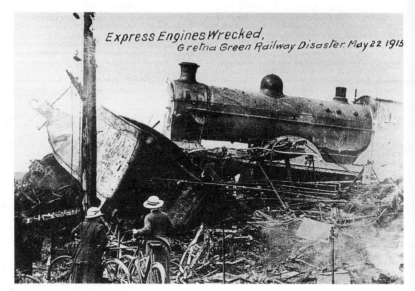

*Scene after the **Quintinshill** rail crash.*

The Tangiwai Bridge collapse
24 December 1953

A Christmas tragedy in New Zealand

*A flash flood destroys a bridge
as an express train is
halfway across.*

The main railway line travelling up New Zealand's North Island to Auckland crosses the Whangaehu River at a point called Tangiwai, a name which in Maori means 'wailing waters'. This name became tragically appropriate on Christmas Eve 1953. On that day the river seemed abnormally high and turbulent. There had been heavy rain, but not enough to account for the flood. The Tangiwai postmaster, Cyril Ellis, went down to look at the river, and as he did so remembered that an express train was due. The flood was subjecting the bridge — a strong structure standing on concrete piers — to a terrible battering. Ellis ran down the track to try to warn the driver to stop the train, but he was too late.

The combined force of the water and the weight of the train was too much for the bridge, and when the express was halfway across, the bridge gave way. The engine, its tender, and five carriages plunged into the icy waters below. The sixth carriage teetered on the brink for some minutes before it too fell into the river.

Oily water

The river was full of mud and silt and the carriages had rolled and tumbled some way. There was also a good deal of oil in the water, from the locomotive and tender. Cyril Ellis himself saved a number of people, and there were many other acts of great bravery. Four of those involved were decorated for their bravery, Cyril Ellis and

a man named John Holman receiving the George Medal. The train driver was also praised for applying his brakes as the train reached the bridge. If he had not done so, more carriages would undoubtedly have fallen.

One survivor described his experiences thus: 'We must have rolled over half a dozen times. Mud and water poured in. The car was washed about 200 yards (180m) downstream, then stuck on a sandbank on its side. That's what saved us.'

The cause of the flood was later found to be an eruption from the 9 000-foot (2 750m) Mt Ruapehu, one of a number of active volcanoes in New Zealand. The eruption spewed out lava and mud and took a considerable amount of water from a lake high on the mountain down into the headwaters of the Whangaehu. All this natural debris came rushing downstream, gathering force as it went, and it is little wonder that the bridge failed to survive.

Although rescuers were quickly on the scene, it was difficult to save many people from the train because of the mud and slime which covered the carriages. The eventual death toll was put at 131, with a further 20 people never accounted for. Many bodies were recovered completely stripped of clothing, showing the terrible force of the water.

Royal sympathy
The disaster happened the year after Queen Elizabeth II came to the throne, and at the time she and her husband, the Duke of Edinburgh, were visiting New Zealand as part of a Commonwealth tour. The Queen made her traditional Christmas Day broadcast from Auckland, and in it expressed her deep sorrow at the loss of life. The Duke attended a service held in Wellington for those who died in the crash.

The Moorgate underground crash
28 February 1975

An inexplicable incident

A train overruns the buffers, leaving the worst-ever casualty list on the London Underground.

The extensive underground railway network serving London encompasses over 250 miles of track and carries millions of people every week. Accidents are few and far between: the system has an excellent safety record, which makes disasters such as that at Moorgate all the more horrifying.

The Drayton Park to Moorgate branch of the Northern Line is one of the system's shorter spurs, with just five stations. The run only takes about ten minutes to complete. Moorgate, its City terminus, is one of the busiest stations on the underground, with ten platforms at three different levels. The Drayton Park trains come in to Platform 9, which ends with a short tunnel 20 yards long containing a 'sand drag' aimed at stopping any train which overshot the buffers.

Driver Leslie Newson, a quiet man in his fifties, had been on the Drayton Park run for about two months. On Friday 28 February 1975 he started work at 6am, taking the first train of the day into Moorgate. After several more runs in each direction, he set his train, no 272, off again from Drayton Park at 8:38am.

Through the buffers

The train picked up passengers at Highbury, Essex Road and Old Street, and approached Moorgate at 8:46am. Staff at Moorgate saw the train approach, but instead of slowing down it seemed to accelerate. At 40mph (64kph), the train shattered the buffers, hit the sand drag and ploughed into the wall at the end of the tunnel. The leading coach jack-knifed into a V-shape, its front end buried in the tunnel roof. The second coach ploughed under the first and the third rode up over the roof of the second. A huge cloud of black dust blew back into the station, then there was silence.

Rescue services were on the scene within minutes. It was a dreadful place in which to work. Sixty feet underground in the desperately confined space of the tunnel, and in steadily rising temperatures, specialist teams had to cut each piece of metal away by hand to try to release trapped passengers. The skill, patience and dedication shown by firemen, doctors, police and others that day was quite exceptional.

The last two survivors were not freed from the tangled mess of the first coach until 14 hours after the crash. Getting bodies out from the wreckage was even harder, and the body of Driver Newson was not released until the Tuesday afternoon, more than four days after the accident happened.

But why did it happen? Nobody knows. There was no fault on the train and no reason for it to fail to stop. An autopsy revealed alcohol in Leslie Newson's blood, but this seems to have built up by natural fermentation in the long period before he was released. He was a man of moderate habits and never drank before working. He was not slumped over the controls but still sitting upright at the moment of impact. We can only assume that he suffered some form of brain seizure. The crash killed 42 people and seriously injured another 82: the London Underground's worst single accident.

The Bihar rail disaster

6 June 1981

The worst-ever rail accident?

Many hundreds killed as a train plunges into a river in India.

The rail disaster in the state of Bihar, India, on 6 June 1981 is listed in reference books as the world's worst, but it is one of those cases where precise figures seem not to be available. The number who lost their lives is thought to be around 800. The train, travelling from Samashpur to Banmukhi, consisted of seven coaches plus the engine. The line crossed the Bagmati River on a high viaduct partway along the route. On the day there were very strong winds blowing, and some accounts speak of a 'cyclone' which might indicate that the bridge was hit by an exceptional gust as the train was crossing it.

In some respects there are similarities with the Tangiwai disaster (see p151). In both cases the train was at its most vulnerable, crossing an exposed section of track above a fast-flowing river. In both cases a bridge gave way, and in both cases rescue was hampered by the weather and the difficulty of reaching the wrecked carriages.

Blown off the track?

What actually happened as the train crossed the Bagmati River is difficult to ascertain. One account says that the train driver put his brakes on hard to avoid water buffalo that were on the line, and this contributed to the crash. Other accounts say that the train was actually blown off the track, but this seems hard to believe. After the accident, a spokesman for Indian Railways denied that the bridge was damaged before the train left it.

In any event, when rescue services finally arrived on the scene they found only the engine and two coaches still on the track. The remaining seven coaches had plunged into 60 feet (18m) of water, and there were few survivors. A team of naval divers was brought in, and worked round the clock, but the recovery of bodies was very slow, only 50 being brought out in the first 24 hours. Many bodies were undoubtedly washed away by the river.

The incident was treated as a national disaster in India, and a relief fund for the survivors and relatives of those who died was opened by the Bihar state governor, S R Kidwai. The then Prime Minister, Mrs Indira Gandhi expressed deep grief at the tragedy and ordered that everything should be done to help those affected.

There were no official figures for the number of people on the train (a common problem with railway accidents worldwide). At first the figure was put at somewhere between 200 and 500, but it was later revised upwards, and the estimate of 800 deaths seems likely to be close to the true number.

Tragedy in Tokyo

There was a serious rail accident in Tokyo in May 1962. A packed commuter train collided with a goods train, then a second commuter train hit the wreckage of the first two. Five carriages rolled down an embankment. There were 163 people killed in this accident and over 300 injured. In October 1972, a train in Mexico jumped the rails when travelling downhill and caught fire, killing 208 of the passengers.

The Salang Tunnel
3 November 1982

A horrific road disaster

Hundreds of vehicles trapped by fire in an unventilated tunnel.

Each road accident is a personal tragedy for the people involved, their families, friends and dependents; but the toll of lives lost rarely reaches double figures in any one accident. The disaster in Salang Tunnel may have killed over a thousand. As with other disasters on Soviet territory, conflicting reports of casualties have appeared at different times, and as this awful tragedy involved military personnel, there was little likelihood of it ever being fully reported. News and reports have, however, filtered out from time to time, and it seems very probable that we are dealing here with the world's worst single road accident.

The Salang Tunnel is 1.7 miles (2.6km) long and is on the main road through the Hindu Kush linking what was the Soviet Union with Afghanistan, which at the time of the disaster was under Soviet military rule. The tunnel was built as part of an 'aid' package in the late 1950s. At the time of the disaster it was apparently unventilated.

Two convoys

Normal practice was for traffic to run through in alternate directions, effectively operating a one-way system, but it seems that, on 3 November 1982, for some reason there were two convoys inside the tunnel, one heading north and one south. A collision occurred, and (according to one report) a tanker full of fuel caught fire. Both convoys contained military vehicles. Both convoys naturally stopped: it was very cold inside the tunnel, and many drivers left their engines running. Fumes rapidly built up inside the unventilated shaft, and most of those who died suffocated.

One report says that there was panic in the tunnel, some troops believing that an ambush was taking place. Both entrances were blocked (perhaps to prevent the 'ambushers' from escaping) thus literally sealing the fate of those inside the tunnel. But how many people lost their lives that day? The first official news came from the Afghan news agency Bakhtar on 18 November. It talked merely of 'loss of life'. For a Soviet report we have to wait until January 1984, when the Red Army newspaper, in an article about the Salang Tunnel, mentioned a 'sad event' when a truck stalled and fumes from idling engines led to 'several people dying from suffocation'.

At the time of the disaster, several unconfirmed reports from Kabul, and one from Pakistan, put the number killed at over a thousand — one report speaks of 700 Soviet soldiers and 400 Afghan civilians, another says the death toll could have reached 2 000. It seems certain that the numbers lost that awful day below the mountains of the Hindu Kush are to be measured in hundreds; a thousand or more is quite possible.

The conspiracy theory
Afghan resistance groups claimed responsibility for the Salang Tunnel disaster. One said that the lead vehicle in the southbound convoy was rammed by an Afghan hero, dressed in Soviet uniform, driving a petrol tanker. The report went on to claim that the Soviet convoy was carrying 'poison gas' for the base in Kabul. It says over 1 000 Soviet and 'pro-Soviet' soldiers and civilians died but denies reports of Afghan deaths. This report, whilst colourful, seems at the very least to be an embellishment of the facts.

The Trans-Siberian disaster

4 June 1989

Fire kills hundreds, including many children

Two Russian trains are caught in a wall of fire.

The disaster on the trans-Siberian line near the town of Ufa in central Russia was a freak. It originated not on the railway at all, but from a pipeline carrying gas from Siberia to Ufa, a major industrial town. A leak developed in the pipe — possibly some days before the disaster — and pockets of gas accumulated alongside the line, which is in a cutting at that point. The gas reached its critical temperature and ignited just as two crowded trains were passing the spot. It is believed that the air displacement effect of the two trains passing contributed to the explosion.

Between them, the trains were carrying at least 1 200 passengers, including many children travelling south to holidays in the Black Sea area and others returning north. As the two trains reached the cutting, there was a massive explosion and a fireball set them alight. Many of the carriages were wooden, and were burned out within minutes, giving those inside no chance of survival. Trees were felled up to two miles (3km) away and the explosion was clearly heard in Ufa, seven miles (11km) away, where the blast shattered some windows.

Flown to Moscow

There were about 40 carriages making up the two trains: most were reduced to twisted lumps of wood and metal, and rescuers faced great difficulty in locating the dead and those who survived. Many had been blown by the blast into surrounding woodland. Badly burned passengers were taken to Ufa and to Chelyabinsk, another nearby town. The worst cases were then flown to Moscow for specialist treatment at burns units.

High toll

As with other Soviet disasters, casualty figures varied widely. The official news agency Tass gave a figure of 192 dead the day after the crash, but this was clearly a considerable underestimate. General Moiseyev, the Chief of Staff, said that 'at least 400' were dead or missing, and the editor of the area's local newspaper, Gennady Kmitrin, put the death toll at more than 500. He also said that the figure of 1 200 given for the number of passengers on the two trains did not include young children who did not require tickets. Apart from those who died in the crash itself, others succumbed to their burns afterwards.

It is likely that the death toll from this disaster has been exceeded only by the 1981 crash in Bihar. It was an extraordinary piece of bad luck; the original problem, the leak in the gas pipeline, should have been located and dealt with before the gas built up to a dangerous level.

A bad record

There have been several other serious incidents on Soviet trains in recent years. In August 1987, 106 people were killed in a collision between two trains in the town of Kamensk-Shakhtinsky, 560 miles (900km) south-east of Moscow. In June 1988, 80 were killed and 700 injured at Arzamas when three wagons carrying explosives blew up. Less than a week after the Siberian disaster, 31 people were killed when a train hit a bus on a level crossing.

Disasters at sea

Men have been going down to the sea in ships since the beginning of recorded history, and throughout that time ships have foundered and been lost. As with the air and the land, the sea needs respect from travellers; it can be fickle, changing from calm to violent in a very short space of time, especially in the tropical latitudes.

Although many lives were lost in ships up to and including the 19th century, all the incidents included here are from the 20th century. The past 100 years have seen the rise to dominance of the great ocean liners, carrying hundreds of passengers in unparalleled comfort and style, and then their almost total eclipse by jet aircraft, a circumstance which the sea-lines such as P&O and Cunard would never have forecast in the years before World War II.

There are famous disasters described here, and some less well known. The worst of all in terms of lives lost, the *Dona Paz* ferry in the Philippines, happened very recently (in December 1987) yet is hardly remembered outside maritime circles, in contrast to the sinking of the *Titanic*, which occurred 75 years earlier. The loss of *Titanic* has become one of those events which seem pivotal in modern history. There are a number of ferry disasters here, including the *Herald of Free Enterprise*, whose tragic end at Zeebrugge was captured on television and caused national sorrow in Britain.

There are extraordinary stories such as the fire on the *Morro Castle*, a confusion of error upon error brought on by the sudden death of the captain; and the *Admiral Nakhimov*, a Russian cruise liner on at least her third life when she finally went down in the Black Sea.

It seemed for a time that large-scale maritime disasters involving people had gone with the demise of the great liners, to be replaced by disasters of the kind described in the 'environment' section of this book, but after a gap of 20 years from 1966 to 1986, four modern disasters appear here, the most recent being the sinking of a Red Sea ferry with great loss of life in December 1991.

Despite the best efforts of ship designers, sophisticated navigational aids and efficient rescue services, the sea continues to take its toll, and no doubt will continue to do so as long as we voyage on its broad waters.

Camorta
April 1902

Victim of a cyclone

No survivors from the sinking in the Gulf of Martaban.

At the beginning of the 20th century, ships were increasing in size and speed. There were regular passenger and freight runs on all the main shipping routes, and it was inevitable that as the number of ships, and the number of passengers carried, increased, so would the scale of tragedies.

The *Camorta* was typical of her day. She was built in 1880 by A & J Inglis of Glasgow, one of many yards on the Clyde, for the British India Line. Displacing 2 119 tons gross, she had a cruising speed of 11 knots, and was used for voyages both between Britain and India and in Far Eastern waters.

In April 1902 the *Camorta* left Madras bound for Rangoon, carrying about 650 passengers and a crew of 89. Whilst on passage through the Gulf of Martaban, one of the regular cyclones affecting the area blew up and the ship was lost. There were no survivors. In terms of lives lost, this little-known disaster ranks seventh behind the *Titanic, Empress of Ireland, Lusitania, General Slocum* and the two ferry disasters in the Philippines and Japan.

General Slocum
15 June 1904

A summer picnic ends in tragedy

A chartered ferry catches fire and sinks with great loss of life.

There was a happy mood as the large party from St Mark's School, New York, assembled on 15 June 1904. It was the summer picnic for children, parents, friends and teachers, and the weather was bright and sunny. A big ferry, the *General Slocum,* typical of the American riverboats of the period, had been chartered to take them to Throg's Neck, a popular spot for outings.

As the big boat went slowly down the East River, everyone was in high spirits, but below decks, unbeknown to the passengers, a fire had started. Accounts differ as to its source: some say it was from the stove in the galley, others that it started in a paint locker. Within minutes the boat was ablaze.

For an hour she continued slowly along the river as the crew fought vainly to control the flames. There was no escape for those on board, faced with flames at one hand and the deep river on the other. The *General Slocum* sank with the loss of 1021 lives. This terrible tragedy is still remembered in the USA, and indeed is marked by a plaque in New York Harbour, but is less well known elsewhere. Among the survivors was the master, Captain Van Schaick, who was later convicted of manslaughter and sent to prison.

Titanic
14 April 1912

The sinking of the 'unsinkable' liner

The maritime world is shocked as a maiden voyage ends in disaster.

In the early years of the 20th century, the battle between rival sealines for the lucrative North Atlantic market was intense. Following the launch of Cunard Line's *Mauritania* and *Lusitania*, the White Star Line, under its managing director J Bruce Ismay, resolved to build three luxury liners that would surpass in comfort and size anything else afloat.

The first of these liners, the *Olympic*, was launched in 1909. With electrically operated watertight doors, she was said to be the safest liner afloat. She performed faultlessly on her maiden voyage, and afterwards, and gave distinguished service in World War I as a troop carrier. The third of the trio, the *Britannic*, served as a hospital ship until sunk by a mine in November 1916. These two fine vessels are hardly remembered today; their sister ship, *Titanic*, is famous, though she failed to complete a single crossing of the Atlantic.

All three ships were designed to take about 2 500 passengers with a crew of nearly 1 000. *Titanic* was 882 feet (268m) in length with a beam of 92 feet (28m) and a gross tonnage of 46 000. She was launched in 1911 and her maiden voyage was set for 10 April 1912, leaving Southampton for New York via Cherbourg (France) and Cork in Ireland. Disappointingly for her owners, but fortunately in view of what happened, the ship was only half full of passengers – possibly because the *Olympic*, which already had a reputation for speed and comfort, had sailed just a week beforehand.

Respected captain

In command of Titanic was Captain Edward J Smith, known to his men as 'EJ.' He was 59 and planned to retire after launching *Titanic*. He had been a captain for 25 years and was a man of immense experience, much admired and respected by his crew. He had commanded no fewer than 17 ships for the White Star Line. His officers were similarly experienced. With such a vessel and such a crew, surely nothing could go wrong?

The voyage nearly began in disaster. *Titanic* displaced so much water leaving dock that the surge actually pulled a smaller liner, the *New York*, from her moorings and only quick work by tugs averted a collision. After calling at Cherbourg and Cork, *Titanic* steamed west carrying 1 316 passengers and 891 crew.

There were reports of icebergs from the start, but they were north of *Titanic's* track and the weather was good. Ismay, by all accounts a vain man, urged the captain to make all possible speed, and in her first full day at sea, *Titanic* made an impressive 546 miles (873km). Reports of ice continued to come in on the radio, now much nearer to the ship's intended track, but no slowing down was ordered. It was in fact common practice to continue steaming in clear weather despite the threat of icebergs: with ships making mostly around 10 knots this was an acceptable risk, but *Titanic* was travelling at 22 knots, and was a much larger vessel and thus slower to manoeuvre.

Raising the alarm

On the evening of 13 April, lookouts were posted as usual to watch for icebergs. The captain retired to his cabin, saying 'If it becomes at all doubtful let me know; I'll be just inside.' At just before midnight, able seaman Frederick Fleet saw something ahead. Realising it was a large berg, he telephoned down to raise the alarm. The ship was put hard to port and the engines to full astern; but the *Titanic* was too near the berg to escape, and her bow struck the mass of ice underwater. Most people on board felt only a jolt, and the extent of the damage was not realised. The emergency doors were immediately closed, but the water had penetrated too far into the vessel for them to be effective.

Captain Smith resumed command, and with Thomas Andrews, who had supervized the ship's construction, went below to assess the damage. The news was bad. Andrews gave the *Titanic* two hours before she would sink. An SOS was radioed — the first time this new distress code had been used — and a number of vessels turned towards the stricken liner, including the Cunarder *Carpathia*, only about 50 miles (80km) away. On board *Titanic*, the order to 'abandon ship' was given.

The ship was carrying 20 lifeboats with a total capacity of 1 178 people: this was in accordance with the regulations of the day, which prescribed the number of lifeboats on the basis of tonnage, not people. The *Titanic's* sister ships were similarly equipped. Inevitably, many people failed to make the boats in the panic that followed. Bruce Ismay did escape — and was pilloried by the press for doing so, the feeling being that he should have gone down with his ship.

The *Titanic* sank at about 2am on 14 April. The *Carpathia* arrived less than two hours later, and picked up survivors from the lifeboats. In all, 815 passengers and 688 crew perished in the cold sea, an unprecedented toll for a passenger ship. There were many famous and wealthy people on board. Those who died included the American millionaire J J Astor.

Seeking scapegoats

In the aftermath of the disaster, scapegoats were sought. Blame was laid on Captain Smith (who went down with his ship) for continuing at full speed into the iceberg zone; on Bruce Ismay for encouraging his captain to take what was seen as an unwarranted risk; and on the unfortunate Captain Stanley Lord, master of the *Californian,* which was (according to some reports) only a few miles from the *Titanic,* saw distress rockets, yet did not go to investigate. His name was cleared in May 1992 by a fresh inquiry.

Many people asked how such a disaster could befall an 'unsinkable' ship. That actual claim was certainly never made by the owners, but seems to have stemmed from a feature in the respected journal *Shipbuilder* which said that: 'The captain can, by simply moving an electric switch, instantly close the watertight doors and make the vessel practically unsinkable'. Thus a legend started.

The Board of Inquiry concluded that Captain Smith 'made a very grievous mistake, but one in which, in face of the practice and past experience, negligence cannot be said to have had any part; and in the absence of negligence it is impossible to fix Captain Smith with blame'. Sailing practices were altered afterwards to try to ensure that the tragedy of the *Titanic* would never be repeated.

Raising the *Titanic*

It was many years before the wreck of the *Titanic* was located. It was finally found in September 1985 by a joint American/French team using a special submersible called the Argo. Dramatic film was obtained showing that the ship was split in two; many of the superb fittings could be seen, still intact. There has been talk several times of raising the old liner, but such a task would be exceptionally difficult, and in deference to those who died, the researchers have not disclosed the precise location. *Titanic* seems likely to stay for ever in her deep, cold grave.

The **Titanic** 15 minutes before she disappeared.

No	Words.	Origin. Station.	Time handed in	Via.	Remarks.
69	#	Titanic	11.55 M. april 14th - 15		Distress Call Sigs Loud

Cqd - SOS   from old m. G. Y
  We have struck iceberg sinking
fast come to our assistance.
Position Lat 41·46 n. Lon. 50 14 w.
          mgy

                      S. L. Cannon.
                      JBWard.

Message received about five minutes after the **Titanic** had struck the iceberg.

Empress of Ireland
29 May 1914

A tragic collision

A great liner is lost in fog off the coast of Canada.

The *Empress of Ireland* was built on the Clyde, like so many other great liners. She came from the Fairfield yard and was launched in 1905 with a gross tonnage of 14 191. Designed to cruise at 18 knots, she went into service with the *Empress of Britain* on the Liverpool to Quebec run, operated by the Canadian Pacific Line, and could carry over 1 400 passengers in considerable comfort.

In 1914, the maritime world was still trying to overcome the shock of the loss of the *Titanic*. Another Fairfield-built ship, the *Volturno*, had been lost in the Atlantic after a fire in October 1913; 136 people perished. Worse, however, was to follow.

The *Empress of Ireland* left Quebec on a regular service run on 28 May 1914 carrying 1 057 passengers and a crew of 420, with Captain Kendall in command. Early the next morning, the pilot left the liner as she passed Father Point, ready to steam out into the Atlantic. Lights were sighted at a distance of about six miles. This was the Norwegian collier *Storstad*, with a cargo of 11 000 tons of coal.

Bank of fog

Visibility lessened dramatically as a bank of fog rolled over the two ships; on each, lookouts strained their eyes to locate the other vessel. Action when it came was too little and too late. Sighting the *Storstad* alarmingly near, Captain Kendall ordered first 'Full Speed Ahead', then 'Hard Astern'. On the Norwegian vessel, Captain Thomas Andersen sounded his whistle and also tried to change course.

The collier struck the *Empress of Ireland*, tearing a hole in her side. In a last effort, Captain Kendall ordered 'Full Ahead' to try to reach the shore and beach the liner, but water was pouring into her at a tremendous rate.

Sleeping passengers

Nearly all the passengers were in their cabins asleep. The great ship started to sink within 15 minutes of the collision, and very few had any chance of even reaching the deck, let alone finding a lifeboat. Within half an hour of the *Storstad* striking her that fatal blow, the *Empress of Ireland* had gone to the bottom.

Of the passenger complement of 1 057, only 217 survived, making this, at the time, the second worst maritime disaster involving a passenger ship. Of the crew, 172 perished, giving a total death toll of 1 012: a lower number overall than the *Titanic*, but with 25 more passenger deaths. The tragedy was widely reported at the time, but excited less attention than the *Titanic* because of the latter ship's 'unsinkable' reputation and the famous people she was carrying.

> **Passing safely**
> There have been many accidents in fog, and the area known as the Grand Banks off the eastern Canadian coast is notorious for its mists. In such circumstances, if ships appear to be in any danger of colliding, the normal procedure is for one or both to turn to starboard, thus (in theory) widening the distance between them, as, if they are using shipping lanes correctly, they should be passing port to port. Even with modern radar, this system is not foolproof, and collisions still occur.

The Lusitania torpedoed
7 May 1915

A victim of submarine action

A Cunard liner becomes a tragic statistic of war.

Built on the Clyde by John Brown & Co, the *Lusitania* was the first of Cunard's luxury liners. She made her maiden voyage in September 1907, and in 1909 won the 'Blue Riband' for the fastest transatlantic crossing with an average speed of nearly 26 knots. She had a passenger complement of 2 160, of whom 563 travelled First Class.

The British government had been aware for some time of the possibility of war breaking out, and all large passenger ships had to be capable of partial conversion to 'armed cruiser' status in the event of hostilities breaking out. Cunard did not wait for war to arrive: in May 1913 the *Lusitania* was secretly refitted to take eight six-inch guns — four either side — and two large ammunition stores, or 'magazines'.

Auxiliary cruiser

On the outbreak of war in August 1914, the job was completed, and on 17 September the liner was officially listed as an armed auxiliary cruiser, in which guise she continued carrying passengers across the Atlantic on a regular monthly schedule, despite a statement from the German High Command that all open seas were considered to be a war zone and that any ship flying the British flag was liable to be attacked.

On 1 May 1915, the *Lusitania* left New York carrying 1 257 passengers, a crew of 702, and 1 400 tons of what was described on the ship's manifest as 'general cargo'.

It actually included 1 250 cases of shells and nearly 5 000 boxes of cartridges, most of which were stowed close to no. 1 boiler room. The first half of the voyage was without incident, but on 6 May the liner received warning from the Admiralty of German submarine activity west of Ireland. Captain William Turner ordered the lifeboats to be swung out and readied, all watertight doors and bulkheads not essential to the running of the ship to be closed, portholes to be blacked out and double lookouts posted.

Struck by torpedo

The German submarine U-20 sighted the liner, sailing in a straight line rather than zig-zagging as might have been thought prudent, at about 1:30pm on Friday 7 May. After tailing the *Lusitania* for a while, the submarine fired a torpedo at 2:10pm. It struck the ship in the worst possible place — just below the bulkhead leading to no. 1 boiler room. The ship began to list, and there was a large explosion, caused by the ammunition stowed near the boiler room.

Because of the increasing list, the port side lifeboats could not be used, and there was great confusion as passengers tried to reach the boats on the starboard side. The ship went down within 20 minutes of being struck; 785 passengers and 413 crew lost their lives.

Another victim of war
In November 1915 the *Ancona*, operated by the Italian ISNV Line of Genoa, was fired on in the Atlantic by a submarine flying the Austrian flag. Of the 446 people on board, 194, including 11 Americans, perished; the French cruiser *Pluton*, which was nearby, picked up many survivors.

Principe de Asturias

3 March 1916

Lost in fog off Brazil

Pride of the Spanish fleet runs aground.

Built by Russell & Co in Port Glasgow, the *Principe de Asturias* displaced 8 371 tons gross and had a capacity of 2 000 passengers, of whom 1 750 travelled Third Class. She went into service in August 1914, making regular sailings between Spain and South America.

On her sixth voyage, she left Barcelona in late February 1916 bound for Buenos Aires. On 3 March she was off the coast of Brazil in a thick fog, and during the night she ran aground on rocks near Sebastiao Point. The ship's bottom was torn open, and the inrush of water caused several of her boilers to explode. A fire spread rapidly and within a few minutes the *Principe de Asturias* had broken in two and sunk.

Of her complement of 395 passengers and 173 crew, 415 were lost. It was said that the captain was keeping close to the Brazilian coast because many of his passengers were German and he feared interception by British warships which were in the area at the time.

Valbanera

2 September 1919

Overwhelmed in the Caribbean

Another Spanish ship founders.

Like the *Principe de Asturias*, the *Valbanera* — operated by Pinillos, Izquierdo & Co of Cadiz — made regular runs between the Old World and the New, often carrying emigrants. Built in 1906, she displaced just over 5 000 tons gross and could carry more than 1 000 passengers, typical of her day.

In September 1919 the *Valbanera* left Spain bound for New Orleans with about 400 passengers and 88 crew. As she entered the Caribbean, there were warnings of a severe hurricane. The ship neared Havana, Cuba, but the master, Captain Ramos Martin, felt it more prudent to try to ride out the storm, and took the ship out to sea again. The last contact with the ship was at 1:15pm on 12 September when both Havana and Key West in Florida picked up radio messages from her asking about the weather forecast.

She was not seen again until 19 September, when an American submarine chaser vessel located a wreck near the Rebecca Shoals light, 50 miles (80km) west of Key West. Could this be the missing Spanish vessel? Divers were sent down to examine the ship, and found it was indeed the *Valbanera*. All the lifeboats were intact and there was no evidence of any major damage to the ship. It was concluded that she must have been overturned by an enormous wave, very suddenly, and was thus unable to take any action to save herself or her passengers and crew. There were no survivors.

Afrique

13 January 1920

Sunk on a Biscay reef

Rescue ships can only watch as French vessel goes down.

The *Afrique,* built at Swan Hunter's Newcastle yard in 1907, was a one-funnel steamship displacing 5 400 tons gross. She was operated by the Compagnie des Chargeurs Réunis of Marseille, sailing regularly from her home port to the French colonies in West Africa.

On Saturday 12 January 1920, the *Afrique* was on passage from Bordeaux to Dakar, carrying 458 passengers and a crew of 127. While crossing the Bay of Biscay in poor weather conditions the ship developed engine trouble. Unable to maintain course, she found herself being driven towards the treacherously shallow waters around the Roche-Bonne Reef, some 50 miles (80km) from La Rochelle.

A distress call was sent out and three ships arrived to help, including the *Afrique's* sister ship, the *Ceylan.* Unfortunately, the stricken ship was steadily incurring more and more damage from the reef and at 3am on 13 January she sank, with the three other ships still watching helplessly. There were only 32 survivors, making this one of the worst disasters to befall a French-registered ship in peacetime.

Principessa Mafalda

25 October 1927

Italian liner sinks off Brazil

A chapter of accidents after a propeller shaft breaks.

The *Principessa Mafalda,* an Italian-built vessel of some 9 210 gross tonnage, was launched in 1909 and was part of the fleet of Navigazion Generale Italiana (NGI), a company created by the merger of the Florio and Rubattino Lines.

She was a comfortable, well-appointed ship with capacity for about 1 700 passengers and a crew of around 300. Her run to Rio de Janeiro in October 1927 seemed no different from many others she had completed. She left Cape Verde Island carrying 971 passengers and 288 crew.

Off the Brazilian coast on 25 October, near Abrolhos Island, the ship's port propeller shaft broke, causing damage and a sizable hole, through which water poured into the engine room, filling the boilers, which exploded — accidents which could never have been foreseen.

Captain Guli radioed for assistance as the ship settled in the water, listing to port. There seemed no immediate danger of her sinking. Fortunately, there were other ships in the area, and six arrived including another liner, the *Empire Star.* Boats were launched and a large number of passengers were rescued before the *Principessa Mafalda* finally sank, four hours after the explosion, taking 303 people with her.

Morro Castle

8 September 1934

The death of a master at sea

Suspicious circumstances surround fire and grounding of an American liner.

Although in terms of lives lost the *Morro Castle* disaster is not amongst the most terrible, it became a *cause célèbre* because of the combination of a number of unexplained incidents, including the death of the ship's captain, Robert Wilmott, possibly by poisoning.

The ship was built at Newport News and launched in 1930. Displacing 11 520 tons gross, she carried up to 530 passengers in considerable comfort and was operated by the New York and Cuba Mail Steamship Company (Ward Line) between New York and Cuba, which at the time was a popular holiday destination.

Ship's crews, particularly the lower-paid members, operated under poor conditions in those years, and the *Morro Castle* was no exception. There had been a number of incidents on the ship, including a fire in a hold carrying explosives, seemingly started deliberately. The seamen's union was under considerable Communist influence, as was the island of Cuba, and American ships were always liable to find trouble on that run.

Tailor's dummy

All this hardly made for a happy ship, a situation worsened by tension between Captain Wilmott and his senior officers. He did not get on with the chief officer, William Warms, a dour character, and Warms in turn had no time for the chief

engineer, Eban Abbott, whom he described as a 'stuffed tailor's dummy'. The chief radio operator, George Rogers, who emerged from the disaster as a hero, was in fact a psychopath with a criminal record and it was suspected that he might himself have started the fire that wrecked the vessel.

On the surface, all seemed well as the *Morro Castle* steamed towards New York on 7 September 1934. However, Captain Wilmott, a nervous man at the best of times, had become convinced that someone on the ship was out to harm him and instead of mixing with the passengers, stayed either on the bridge or in his cabin, even at mealtimes. On that evening, after eating some melon, Wilmott suffered violent stomach pains. The ship's doctor was summoned but by then the captain thought he might merely have severe indigestion — a complaint he had been troubled with before — and assured the doctor he would be all right.

At about 7:45pm Warms (who had been alerted by the doctor) went to see the captain. He found him dead. A brief message was sent to the ship's owners, and Warms took command. The weather was poor, with heavy rain and strong wind. The evening passed without further incident, but at about 2am on 8 September, a passenger found a fire in a writing room, and alerted a steward, who tried to put it out, but (crucially) failed to alert the bridge.

Hoses missing

As was common at the time, there was much wood panelling in the ship, and fire was liable to spread rapidly. By the time Warms on the bridge heard of the fire, nearly an hour later, it had strong hold. To make matters worse, a number of fire hoses were missing, and some of the hydrants were capped and unable to supply water. This had been done on Wilmott's orders — a lady passenger had sued the company when she was injured after slipping near a leaking hydrant. Further, no proper passenger drills had been held — again, seemingly because Captain Wilmott felt them an unwelcome interruption of routine. At the inquiry which followed the disaster, passengers confirmed that they had received no instructions as to what to do in an emergency.

The combination of events was to prove disastrous. Warms, unused to command, was unable to cope with a situation that was out of hand anyway. Chief Engineer Abbott cracked under the strain and was one of the first into the lifeboats. Warms was concentrating on steering the ship, which was approaching its pilot station, and no SOS was sent for some time. Rogers sent messages for as long as he possibly could, and undoubtedly saved many lives by doing so. Eventually the generator exploded, putting the radio out of action.

With the fire completely out of control, those left on board gathered either at the bow (mainly crew) or the stern (mainly passengers). There was no organisation of the evacuation, and of the first 98 people to escape by lifeboat, 92 were crew. Other vessels arrived, including a small fishing boat, the *Paramount*, which plucked 35 passengers from the water. The British liner *Monarch of Bermuda* saved 71 more, and the tanker *City of Savannah* a further 65. The *Morro Castle* ended up off Asbury Park, New Jersey, where she attracted large crowds. The fire and rescue had been widely reported in the newspapers and on film newsreels. In all, 137 people died.

Guilty of negligence

A full inquiry was held, and the facts began to emerge. Although there was some sympathy with William Warms's position, he was in command and was found guilty of negligence. He was sentenced to two years imprisonment: Abbott received a five-year sentence, and the vice-president of Ward Line, Henry Cabaud, was given a suspended sentence of one year and a fine of $5 000. The company was fined $10 000, the maximum penalty under the law of the time.

Compensation and correction

Survivors and relatives of those who died on the *Morro Castle* filed many suits for compensation, and in 1937 the company had to pay out over a million dollars. At the same time the indictments on both Warms and Abbott were set aside, the appeal court finding that they were not guilty of criminal conduct. Some good came out of this sordid affair: a Senate investigation led to much improved conditions for crew and to safer construction and fitting for passenger ships.

Toya Maru

26 September 1954

Over a thousand lives lost

A large ferry is among many ships sunk by a Japanese typhoon.

Japan's most northerly island, Hokkaido, was struck by a violent typhoon on 26 September 1974. Sea traffic was severely affected, and among a number of vessels which foundered was the 4 300-ton passenger and freight ferry *Toya Maru*. The ferry was outside Hakodate harbour at the height of the storm. A big box-like vessel designed to carry railway trains as well as large numbers of people, she was liable to roll even in light seas; in weather like this she lurched alarmingly.

Among her load that day were 45 railway carriages. As the wind rose and the ferry wallowed from side to side, these carriages strained at their shackles. Eventually the strain became too much; the carriages broke loose and crashed to one side of the ferry.

She was now extremely unbalanced. The captain and crew tried to beach her, but the high seas took her onto rocks, where she overturned. The *Toya Maru* was reported to be carrying about 1 250 passengers, of whom at least 1 000 are thought to have perished. As with other similar disasters, many bodies were never recovered.

Terrific lurch

Despite the nearness of the land, conditions were such that only a few fortunate people managed to escape the stricken ship. One survivor, Kaichiki Yamakazi, described what happened. 'I felt a terrific lurch. The floor listed about 45 degrees and water began pouring into the ship. In the dark, everyone was thrown together. Some were pushed over, some were stepped on. They were screaming and shouting in the dark. It was like a hell on earth'. The *Toya Maru* was not alone in the battering she got from the typhoon. Two other passengers vessels, the *Hidaka Maru* and the *Daisetsu Maru*, another ferry, the *Tokachi Maru*, and a freighter, the *Shinsei Maru*, put to sea from Hakodate to try to ride out the storm, fearing that if they remained in harbour they were be dragged from their anchorages and damaged. All four foundered, with the loss of over 200 crew members.

Hundreds of small craft were also lost during the storm, one of the worst to hit Japan for some years. Winds were measured at up to 110mph (180kph) as the storm passed across Hokkaido. Just when it seemed to be continuing over the Sea of Japan, the typhoon turned back along the reverse of its previous course and battered the island, and the seas around it, a second time.

> **Widespread damage**
> The typhoon caused widespread damage across the island of Hokkaido. Roads and railways were blocked or cut, and the town of Iwani, 90 miles (150km) north of Hakodate, was severely hit. Two-thirds of its houses — over 3 000 buildings — were destroyed in a few minutes, and at least 50 people died.

The Andrea Doria collision

25 July 1956

A successful rescue operation

A fine ship lost, but most of the passengers are saved.

The *Andrea Doria*, displacing 29 000 tons gross, was launched in 1953 from the yard of Ansaldo in Genoa. She could carry 1 250 passengers and was luxuriously fitted out with 31 public rooms, each in a different style, and three outdoor swimming pools. She went into service for Italian Line on the Genoa to New York run, with stops at Naples, Cannes and Gibraltar.

She completed 50 crossings with no problems, and set out on her 51st on 17 July 1956 with Captain Calamai in command, as he had been since the liner was launched. She was carrying an almost full load of 1 134 passengers plus 572 crew, 400 tons of freight and nine cars. The voyage was scheduled to last eight days and all went according to plan until the final stage.

Banks of fog

On 25 July, as the *Andrea Doria* sped west, she encountered banks of fog in the area of the Nantucket Lightship. With visibility reduced to half a mile or less, speed was cut to 21 knots and a close watch was kept on the radar screens for other vessels. At 10:45pm a blip was seen on the screens. It appeared that the other vessel would pass to starboard. Meanwhile, on the Swedish liner *Stockholm*, the blip representing the *Andrea Doria* was being monitored and the same conclusion arrived at — the vessels would pass each other safely. One or other must have been wrong.

As the two vessels closed, at a combined speed of some 40 knots, it became obvious to each that there was little if anything to spare. By the time visual contact was established, it was too late. The *Stockholm* was heading across the *Andrea Doria*'s course and struck her hard on the starboard side. The effect of the collision was serious enough, but was made worse by the fact that the *Stockholm*'s bow was toughened as an ice protection measure.

The rescue

The *Andrea Doria*'s side was ripped open. The *Stockholm* was able to reverse slowly and get herself free, but the Italian liner had already begun listing badly. Only the starboard side lifeboats could be used. Fortunately there were a number of other ships in the area, and no fewer than six responded to the *Andrea Doria*'s SOS signal, including the great French liner, the *Ile de France*.

These ships, together with the *Stockholm*, gathered in all but 47 of those aboard the *Andrea Doria*. Most of those who died did so because of the impact. By 5:30am on 26 July the ship was abandoned, and a few hours later she sank. She was only three years old.

> **Sad end for a great liner**
> The largest liner ever built, the 83 000-ton *Queen Elizabeth*, enjoyed a deserved reputation for comfort and speed. With the advent of jet air travel, she became uncommercial, and in 1968 she went to Florida as a conference centre. This did not work out, and in 1971 she made her final voyage to Hong Kong, where she was to be a floating college, renamed the *Seawise University*. On 9 January 1972 the ship caught fire, burned out and sank: a sad end to an illustrious career.

Dara

8 April 1961

The victim of terrorist action?

A laden pilgrim boat is blown up off Dubai.

The *Dara* was one of four ships built for British India Line's service between Bombay, Karachi and Basra. Named after a Persian prince, she came from Barclay Currie's yard on the Clyde and was able to carry nearly 1 000 passengers.

The ship frequently carried hundreds of pilgrims in this way, to Saudi Arabian ports from where they travelled overland to the holy city of Mecca. Perhaps fortunately, April, when she met her end, was not the pilgrim season, and although the ship was carrying 600 passengers, she was far from full. Her voyage started from Bombay on 23 March 1961. She reached Basra safely, with the usual intermediate stops, and started back, calling at Korramshahr, Kuwait and Bahrain before reaching Dubai on 7 April.

Gale-force winds

The weather was unseasonably bad, with high winds and rainstorms, almost un-heard-of in the Gulf in April. As the *Dara* was loading, a severe hailstorm started, accompanied by gale-force winds. Captain Elson felt the vessel would be safer at sea and he took her out. Most of the passengers had boarded, and there were also about 70 unwilling extras such as port officials on board.

The *Dara* steamed slowly northwards in a thunderstorm. The weather slowly improved, and at 4am on 8 April the captain decided it was safe to return to Dubai. Her position was fixed and a course set. At about 4:45am the vessel was shaken by a loud explosion, followed immediately by the outbreak of fire. The officers thought it had come from the engine room: the engines had stopped and the steering was out of action.

It quickly became apparent that there was no way of controlling the fire, and the order to abandon ship was given. With the radio also out of action, no SOS could be sent, but a converted landing-craft, the *Empire Guillemot*, was only a few miles away, saw the fire, and sent a distress signal on behalf of the *Dara*.

Panicking passengers

On the stricken ship, efforts were made to launch at least some of the lifeboats, hampered by panicking passengers. The starboard boats could not be used because of the fire, and the others were difficult to launch as their falls were power-operated. Some were however lowered into the water and passengers began to climb in. The *Empire Guillemot* was alongside, rescuing those it could, and was joined before long by several other vessels. In all, 584 people were saved by various means, but 238 still died at the time, and three later as a result of their injuries.

A rebel bomb

The cause of the explosion and fire was not established until divers examined the *Dara* six months after she sank. It was found that an explosive device had gone off in an alleyway just above the engine room. The charge was estimated at 20lb (8kg), which would have created a fireball of up to 12ft (3.5m) diameter. Little wonder the fire spread so rapidly. The explosion was thought to be the work of Omani rebels, but this was never fully established.

Heraklion

8 December 1966

An Aegean tragedy

A Greek ferry founders in stormy seas.

The ship which eventually went down in the stormy Aegean Sea was built as the *Leicestershire* by Fairfield's on the Clyde in 1949. Originally operated by Bibby Line on their UK to Burma run, largely as a freighter but with some space for passengers, she was chartered to British India for some years, sailing between London and ports in East Africa.

In 1964 the ship was sold to the Greek shipping line Typaldos and underwent a major refit for use as a car and passenger ferry, running between Piraeus, the port for Athens, and Heraklion in Crete, after which city she was renamed. In her new guise she could carry 300 passengers and a large number of cars, buses and trucks. The service operated all year round.

Stormy weather

The weather in early December 1966 was very stormy, and on Wednesday 7 December, as the *Heraklion* nosed out of harbour into the Aegean, she met a gale. Under such conditions it is questionable whether vehicle ferries should put to sea; if they do, the vehicles must be very strongly fastened or lashed down. This was, unfortunately, not the case with the Heraklion. A number of vehicles were either unfastened or insecurely tied and before long were starting to move around in the hold. Once large vehicles in particular begin to move it is difficult and highly risky to stop them.

The ship continued steaming south, but the situation on the vehicle deck was getting worse, with cars and lorries banging against the sides of the vessel and against each other. Finally, a large refrigerated lorry and trailer smashed into the bow door and forced it open. The crew were unable to close the door and the *Heraklion* began shipping water, driven by the gale. At 2am on 8 September an SOS was sent out, giving the ship's position as near the small islet of Falconcra in the Cyclades and saying she was in danger of sinking.

Few survivors

An air and sea search was immediately started. Among the other ships involved were two British minesweepers, the *Ashton* and the *Leverton*, but it was too late. Within an hour the *Heraklion* had gone down, and only debris was found. It appeared at first that there might be no survivors from the 288 passengers or the crew, but when morning came some 47 people were found to have got ashore on Falconcra.

> **Liner destroyed by fire**
> The day before the *Heraklion* disaster, the Hamburg-Atlantic liner *Hanseatic* (formerly called both the *Empress of Japan* and *Empress of Scotland*) caught fire in New York harbour a few hours before she was due to depart for Germany. The fire was discovered at 7:30am on 7 September; fortunately, only three of the 425 passengers booked for the voyage had gone aboard. Flames quickly engulfed the 30 000 ton ship and she was abandoned. If the fire had started a few hours later a major disaster could have followed. It was the end of a long career for the *Hanseatic*, built in 1930; she was towed to Hamburg and broken up.

Admiral Nakhimov

31 August 1986

A Soviet cruise liner sinks

Collision in the Black Sea ends the life of a ship which was raised from the dead.

It is perhaps not surprising that the *Admiral Nakhimov* came to a dramatic and disastrous end; the ship had an extraordinarily chequered career. She was built by Bremer Vulkan in Vegesack, Germany, in 1925 as the *Berlin*, a liner of some 17 000 tons gross, destined for the luxury Bremen–Southampton–New York run operated by North German Lloyd.

The first incident in her long career happened in November 1928, when she went to the aid of the stricken Lamport liner, the *Vestris*, in the Atlantic. She succeeded in rescuing 23 passengers, but 112 people perished in the accident. The *Berlin* continued to operate on the Atlantic run until the outbreak of hostilities in 1939, by which time she had herself suffered a serious accident. On 17 July 1939 one of her boilers exploded while she was off the German coast, and 17 crew were killed.

Soviet claim

During World War II the *Berlin* operated for some years as a hospital ship. Towards the end of the war, in 1944, she became an accommodation vessel, and on 1 February 1945 she struck a mine off Swinemunde and sank. It seemed her life was at an end, but the Soviet naval authorities had other ideas. She was now in Soviet waters, and they claimed her, stating their intention to refloat her.

This happened, but not until 1949. The old liner was towed to the large Warnow shipbuilding yard at Warnemunde for repair. It was, almost incredibly, to be eight years before she emerged, now renamed the *Admiral Nakhimov* in honour of a naval hero killed in the Crimean War. The ship sailed round to the Black Sea and was operated by the Black Sea Shipping Company between Odessa and Batumi, calling at ports such as Sebastopol which must have been known to the man she was now named after. Part of her duties was to provide cruises for Soviet citizens who had earned the approval of the state.

On one such cruise, she left Novorossiysk just before midnight on 31 August 1986 bound for Sochi, carrying 888 passengers and a crew of 346, with Captain Vadim Markov as master. The cruise was to last less than an hour: despite receiving warnings, the large bulk carrier *Pyotr Vasyov* failed to alter course and rammed the *Admiral Nakhimov*, tearing a large hole in her side. The cruise ship immediately took on a list and sank within 15 minutes.

Given the speed with which the ship sank, a surprising number of people were saved: 836 in all, including the captain. Only 79 bodies were recovered and another 319 were listed as missing, presumed drowned. This time there was no recovery for the old ship.

> ### A change of policy
> This was one of the first disasters to occur within the Soviet Union to be announced, with details, to the outside world without delay. Regular press conferences were held in Moscow, and the Soviet press included eye-witness accounts of the sinking. After an inquiry, the captains of both vessels were sentenced to 15-year prison terms and given large fines.

Herald of Free Enterprise

6 March 1987

Disaster in Zeebrugge harbour

A cross-Channel ferry overturns after its main door is left open.

The *Herald of Free Enterprise* was one of several large 'ro-ro' ferries operated by the Townsend Thoresen company, shuttling back and forth across the English Channel carrying passengers and vehicles. The term 'ro-ro' is short for 'roll on, roll off' and indicates how these vessels operate.

Cars, buses and lorries drive straight into the capacious holds through huge doors at the bow or stern of the ship, are parked carefully both to even the load and to get the maximum number aboard, and then drive straight off at the other end. It is a convenient, quick system which is in use all over the world. There had been doubts expressed about the stability of these large ferries before the disaster at Zeebrugge.

The *Herald of Free Enterprise* was often used on the Dover to Calais run, but in early March 1987 was working to Zeebrugge, in Belgium, as relief for another vessel which was undergoing maintenance. On Friday 6 March she was due to leave Dover at 11:30am and arrive in Zeebrugge at 4pm (5pm local time), leaving again two hours later for the return crossing. The outward run was without incident. There would normally be few tourists at that time of year, but the passenger list was boosted by about 200 people taking advantage of a promotion run by Townsend Thoresen and the *Sun* newspaper under which they got the return trip for only £1.

There were delays in loading for the return journey, and the ship moved away from the dock at Zeebrugge about 20 minutes late. The deep water at Zeebrugge is confined, and large ferries such as the *Herald of Free Enterprise* have to reverse into a side dock, then move forward to go out of the harbour. The Herald completely the reversing manoeuvre, and started to go forward. As she did so, she started to roll. What happened next is described by Stephen Homewood, one of the ship's pursers, who wrote a book about the disaster:

'I felt the ship heel to port . . . the *Herald* righted itself, tilted a fraction to starboard, came back, and started to roll to port again. This time it did not come back.' What had happened was that the main bow loading door had been left open as the ship sailed. As she reversed, then went forward, water poured in through the open door, rapidly filling the ship beyond the level at which she could stay afloat. The *Herald* went over on her side, on a sandbank.

In the moments before she capsized, the *Herald* was travelling at about 18 knots. The open door meant that that bow deck acted like a 'spade', shovelling vast amounts of water into the ship. As the ship rolled, the water rushed to one side of the vehicle area, then rushed back to the other side. More water was pouring in by the second, and once the rolling started, nothing could have stopped it.

Desperate situation

Inside the ship there was chaos. As she went over, passengers were flung across the lounge, bar and other large spaces. The lights went out. What had been a floor was now a wall, and vice versa. In pitch darkness, with water rushing in, it was a desperate situation for the confused, disoriented passengers. Because the ship was still in harbour, rescue services were quickly on hand, but many people drowned in the few seconds after the ship tilted. The total death toll was 188.

There were many acts of great bravery in the hours that followed. Stephen Homewood himself saved a number of passengers. He received the Queen's Medal for Gallantry, as did a Belgian diver, Lt Guido Couwenburgh. Two George Medals — the highest peacetime award for bravery — were awarded, one posthumously to crew member Michael Skippen, and one to Andrew Parker, a passenger who formed a 'human bridge' to get others off the ship.

The inquiry into the disaster uncovered the fact that a number of Townsend Thoresen masters had expressed concern over the procedures for closing main doors: there was no direct link to the bridge, such as closed-circuit TV, by which the skipper could satisfy himself that the doors were closed. Masters had also complained about overloading with passengers, and a failure to supply ships with instruments to read the draught, which can crucially affect any vessel's stability.

Severe criticism

The company's management came in for severe criticism at the inquiry. It was described as 'infected with the disease of sloppiness from top to bottom'. Mr Justice Sheen said that the board of directors 'did not have proper comprehension of what their duties were . . . there appears to have been a lack of thought about the way in which the *Herald* ought to have been reorganised for the Zeebrugge run.' Noting that the suggestions put forward by ship's masters had been ignored, he said that the Townsend Thoresen management had shown 'staggering complacency'. The company was ordered to pay inquiry costs amounting to over £400 000.

Remaining ferries were fitted with bridge indicator lights showing whether main doors were open or shut, and a 'failsafe' system was introduced. The *Herald of Free Enterprise* was righted by lifting crane a few weeks after she sank, and was eventually towed to the Far East and scrapped.

Change of name

In the face of this damning indictment, it is hardly surprising that a few months after the Zeebrugge tragedy, in July 1987, Townsend Thoresen's owners, P&O, announced that the TT ships would no longer sail under that name but would operate as P&O European Ferries. The ships were rapidly repainted.

*A floating crane is brought alongside the capsized **Herald of Free Enterprise** for salvage operations.*

Dona Paz

20 December 1987

The largest death toll at sea

A crowded ferry collides with a tanker in a Christmas disaster.

The difficult waters around the islands of the Philippines carry considerable marine traffic, with numerous ferries shuttling between the islands. In the pre-Christmas period demand for places is high and passenger lists are almost impossible to keep accurately. Thus we may never know the full death toll from the sinking of the *Dona Paz*, but it seems certain that it was the highest of any maritime disaster so far.

The *Dona Paz* left the port of Tacloban, on the island of Leyte, on 20 December 1987 bound for the Philippine capital Manila. About two thirds of the way there, off the small island of Marinduque, on a dark, moonless night, the ferry, packed with people returning home or visiting relatives for Christmas, collided with the tanker *Victor*.

Few survivors

The collision was followed by a fire, and the ferry sank before any real rescue attempt could be mounted. When the area was searched by sea and air the following day, only 30 survivors were found. Most were suffering from burns: there was burning oil on the sea around the two vessels. To make matters worse, the rescue operation was hampered by thunderstorms.

The official count of passengers and crews for the two vessels was 1 556 but the actual total is almost certainly over 2 000. Many of the dead were never recovered. One survivor, Paquito Osabel, said 'I was sleeping when I heard an explosion. In just two seconds, there was a big fire on the ship and I heard everybody screaming and wailing. I jumped into the water'. He was lucky enough to be picked up by another ship two hours later, after clinging to a plank. Many hundreds were less fortunate.

Salem Express
15 December 1991

A Red Sea ferry sinks

Ship strikes coral reef off Egyptian coast.

The *Salem Express* operated a regular service across the Red Sea, carrying passengers and freight between Egypt and Saudi Arabia. She was often used by pilgrims travelling to or from the holy sites of Mecca and Medina.

On one such journey, in December 1991, the vessel struck disaster. She was carrying around 650 passengers and crew (reports put the number anywhere between 640 and 680) on the run from Jeddah in Saudi Arabia to the Egyptian port of Safaga. In poor weather conditions, she got off course and struck a coral reef, sinking rapidly. She was not far from Safaga and rescue operations were quickly put in hand. A US frigate, the *Aubrey Fitch,* and an Australian Navy vessel, the *Sydney,* on patrol in the area enforcing UN sanctions against Iraq, sent helicopters to assist.

The rescuers were hampered by strong winds and darkness — the ship struck the reef at around midnight — and there was considerable confusion. The most reliable figures indicate that 178 people had been saved, and that the death toll was about 480 — the worst maritime accident since that in the Philippines in 1987.

Space

Space has been famously called 'the final frontier'. If it is, then it is a frontier in both directions. As well as man escaping from the earth's protective atmosphere into the harsh space environment, there are plenty of small and potentially hazardous visitors trying to get in.

The first entry in this short section deals with examples of these visitations. Many hundreds of space fragments enter our atmosphere every day. Most are harmless and fail to reach the earth's surface, but some do, with spectacular results. The Tunguska meteorite (a fragment of a comet) which struck a remote part of Russia in 1908 caused enormous damage, undiscovered by the outside world for 20 years. Other large-scale meteorites have hit Arizona in the USA and south-western Africa. So far none has struck a densely populated area, but it could certainly happen, and the effects hardly bear considering. There is nothing we can do to prevent such a disaster.

Man's exploration of space dates back only 30 years. In that short time manned flights have reached, and landed on, the moon, and unmanned craft have travelled to the edges of the solar system, giving us for the first time close views of the other planets. The numbers of people carried by spacecraft have been relatively small, so there have been no very large-scale catastrophes, but there is evidence that dozens died in the Soviet accident described here when a rocket blew up on its launchpad.

The explosion of the *Challenger* moments after take-off from Florida in January 1986 stunned the world and set space travel back badly. As with so many other events described in this book, human frailty seems to have been a factor, with decisions taken for the wrong reasons.

Space exploration continues, and there will no doubt be other accidents as man reaches out towards the stars. As he does so, let him always remember that the stars can reach out to us too: we are lucky to have, in our atmosphere, such a protective guard at our frontier.

The Tunguska meteorite

June 1908

A destructive visitor from space

A vast chunk of comet debris crashes into the Siberian forests.

Space is not empty. It never has been. All around us are fields of meteorites, pieces of long-dead stars and comets, in orbits which constantly pass through our own. It has been estimated that up to 1 000 tons of space debris hits the earth's atmosphere every day. Most of these pieces are small, and the friction caused by their entry burns them up: these are the familiar 'shooting stars' we see. Occasionally something much larger gets caught, and collides with the earth. One of the largest on record is the Urals meteorite of June 1908.

Even today, the full facts are not known. The area where the meteorite impacted is still very remote: in 1908 it was even more so. No observer from outside Russia reached the scene until 1927. It was known that something had happened because of the atmospheric disturbance which took place. The impact threw vast amounts of dust into the stratosphere, reflecting sunlight from the light side of the earth into the darker side. But with communications more primitive than today, and Russia in turmoil as the rule of the Tsars came towards its end, no hard facts were likely to emerge.

Short summer

The area that the meteorite — thought to be part of Encke's Comet — struck is called the Tunguska Valley. For nine months of the year its climate is arctic; only for a few short weeks is there any real summer, and during that period growth of trees and vegetation is phenomenal. The area is named for the Tungus people, hunters and forest-dwellers.

It would appear that the Tunguska was struck by the largest space fragment to reach the earth's surface for centuries. It may have weighed as much as 10 million tons and been 350 feet (100m) across. The explosion was equal to perhaps three hydrogen bombs going off. It annihilated all life in an area 30 miles (50km) across. At the centre of this area there was nothing, just a vast, churned-up, scarred plain. Outside that were millions of trees — the area is mostly conifer forest — scattered like so many carelessly dropped matchsticks. As there is no large crater, the meteorite may have exploded before striking the ground.

A deafening roar was heard, and a huge pillar of fire was seen, by people hundreds of miles away. The shockwave was felt as a tremor from Irkutsk to Moscow. At the town of Kansk, 375 miles (600km) from the point of impact, the meteorite felt like an earthquake.

Ecology affected

It is not known if there were any human casualties. The area was sparsely populated, so there may have been a few. Large numbers of animals, including reindeer, bear and wolves, would certainly have died, and the ecology of the area was affected for scores of years. The incident is included here as a reminder to us that we are vulnerable to attack from space, and there is nothing we can do about it.

It is very unlikely statistically that a meteorite would hit a densely populated area, but it could happen, and if it did, it would be a disaster to rank with any in this book. If something the size of the Tunguska meteorite landed in the ocean, the waves set up would be catastrophically large and could affect many countries. If it struck the edge of either Polar icecap, enough ice could be melted to affect sea levels.

Stone showers

There have been many other recorded instances of space fragments striking the earth. They sometimes happen in 'showers', as in Kansas in 1948 when a shower of 100 stone fragments included one weighing a ton. Fortunately no-one was killed. The biggest meteorite known to be visible is a 60-ton lump that landed on farmland in south-west Africa. The biggest crater we have is in Arizona, where the dry desert atmosphere has preserved it. The rim is three miles in circumference, and the crater can be seen from orbiting spacecraft. It is believed to have been

caused by a huge meteorite fragment falling some 30 000 years ago.

The earth is largely protected by its atmosphere: the face of the airless Moon, scarred and pock-marked, shows us how fortunate we are to have this shield.

Man-made debris

There are now several thousand man-made objects orbiting the earth — satellites, parts of spacecraft, burned-out rocket motors and an assortment of tools and other debris. From time to time they fall back into the atmosphere, and occasionally one may reach the earth, but none has so far proved to be a major hazard, despite scare stories about nuclear fuel and radiation. There is far more danger from the natural debris of space.

The Nedelin disaster
24 October 1960

A Soviet launch pad explosion

Dozens of workers and military personnel killed.

The tragedy recounted here is headed 'the Nedelin disaster' because one of the few things known about it for certain is that Field Marshal Mitrofan Nedelin, commander of the Soviet Union's Strategic Rocket Forces, died in it. Other Soviet 'cover-ups' have been recounted in this book. Perhaps because of the ultra- sensitive nature of the technology involved in this one, no official Soviet account ever appeared. Marshal Nedelin's official obituary says that he died in the line of duty in an air crash.

The best account of what happened comes from a Soviet engineer called Tiktin who emigrated to Israel. An American aerospace engineer turned writer, James Oberg, an authority on Soviet space activities, devoted a chapter in his book *Red Star in Orbit* to the disaster in which Nedelin died, and Tiktin responded with a commentary.

moving alignments of the planets meant this was the last chance for two years: it had to be taken. The launch was set for the evening of 24 October.

When the countdown reached its final stage, however, the rocket's engines failed to ignite. The safe thing to do was to abandon the launch, but instead, Nedelin, as the senior officer present, ordered the engineers to go out with him and inspect the rocket on its pad, but while the inspection was underway, the rocket exploded, igniting a million pounds of kerosene and liquid oxygen.

Tiktin says that the explosion was caused because the final booster stage of the rocket failed to register the 'stand by' command and continued making its own independent countdown to ignition. When the clock ran down, instead of being on the verge of space, the booster was sitting on top of the other stages of the rocket.

How many died that day? We simply don't know. One report spoke of 'over 300' but that seems unlikely. It could have been 30, or perhaps 50. It would still be the worst single disaster of the space programme in terms of lives lost.

Political pressure

In1960, Soviet space engineers were some way ahead of their American colleagues, and there was considerable political pressure on them to stay ahead. They had already sent probes round the moon and were testing unmanned orbiting craft. It was decided to go for a really big one — a probe to Mars, to photograph and send back data on the 'red' planet.

The first two launch attempts succeeded only in reaching the upper atmosphere; in each case the booster rocket's final stage malfunctioned. A third attempt was to be made in October 1960. The constantly

The Soyuz XI tragedy
In June 1971 three Soviet cosmonauts, Georgi Dobrovolski, Viktor Patsayev and Vladislav Volkov, took the spacecraft Soyuz XI up to link with the orbiting space station Salyut, where they remained for 24 days. On 29 June the cosmonauts left Salyut to return to earth. Soyuz XI appeared to re-enter the atmosphere without trouble and made a normal soft landing but when the hatches were opened, all three cosmonauts were dead. They were apparently victims of a sudden decompression — a tragic end to a splendid mission.

The Challenger explosion

28 January 1986

A tragedy watched by the world

US spacecraft explodes shortly after lift-off, killing all seven crew.

By the time of the *Challenger* launch scheduled for late January 1986, space travel was becoming almost a commonplace. The USA and USSR were both regularly launching space shuttles, satellites and other craft. However, this launch was unique in one respect in that among the crew was Christa McAuliffe, a teacher from New Hampshire who won a national competition which drew 11 000 entries to find a schoolteacher to go into space and then come back and spread the space message afterwards. Before the launch she said she hoped to 'humanize the technology of space.'

The *Challenger* crew was said to be 'all American' — male and female, black and white and of several different faiths. One of their primary aims was to launch a communications satellite called TDRS-B, part of a link system between ground stations and orbiting spacecraft.

given to her by her class. She was never to eat it. The spacecraft launched at 11:38am into a clear blue sky, and at first everything seemed to be going well. Just over a minute into the flight, in full view of those watching — including Christa's husband, parents and children — and captured worldwide on television, *Challenger* exploded in a massive ball of fire.

As much debris as possible was recovered from the sea and a painstaking investigation started. The explosion was eventually found to have been caused by failure of the rubber rings designed to seal the joints between the different sections of the booster rocket. The unusually low temperatures on the launch pad had made the rubber stiff and brittle and gaps formed, allowing hot gases to get past.

It is believed that the spacecraft's structure was further weakened by severe wind buffeting about 40 seconds into the flight. At 58 seconds a flame broke through the weakened joint. It acted just like a blowtorch, after a further 14 seconds forcing its way into the main fuel tank. The liquid hydrogen and oxygen in the tank ignited, and *Challenger* was blown into a thousand pieces.

Sharp frost

The flight had problems before its final tragic moments. The launch was postponed several times due to minor technical difficulties, including a broken handle on a hatch, and once because of high winds. On launch day the weather in Florida was unusually bad. There had been a sharp frost and ice had formed on and around the spacecraft.

On the morning of 28 January, the crew went aboard and the countdown started. Christa McAuliffe was carrying an apple

NASA criticized

It was the first time American astronauts had been lost after take-off, though three others — Roger Chaffee, Gus Grissom and Ed White — were burned to death when their *Apollo* capsule caught fire during practice drills in January 1967.

The Presidential Inquiry into the *Challenger* disaster was severely critical of the management of NASA, the US space agency, describing it as 'lackadaisical' and the decision to launch *Challenger* as 'flawed'. It was revealed that engineers at

Morton-Thiokol, the company which built *Challenger's* rockets, had been warning NASA for three years that the rubber rings could cause problems, and on launch day had indicated that the very cold weather could have damaged the rings. No shuttle had ever been launched in such low temperatures.

On the night of the disaster, President Reagan said on US television: 'There will be more shuttle flights, and more teachers in space. Nothing ends here. Our hopes and our journeys will continue', but the loss of *Challenger* set the US space programme back several years.

Last moments

Tapes recovered from the wreckage of *Challenger* indicate that the crew had very little warning, if any, of the disaster. A minute after lift-off, ground control gave the order 'Challenger, go at throttle up' and at 68 seconds the commander, Dick Scobee, responded 'Roger, go at throttle up'. Three seconds later the pilot, Michael Smith, is heard to say 'uh-oh' and a second after that the explosion occurred. No trace of any of the crew was ever found.

*The **Challenger** lifting off and exploding.*

Sporting disasters

It is a curious reflection on our society that a section on sport needs to be included in this book at all. But sport does arouse strong feelings, and those feelings can sometimes overspill into violence. This has been particularly true of football in recent years, and five of the six entries in this section concern that game. Of those five, two arose directly through crowd trouble (Lima and Heysel) and two through crushing in crowded areas of stadia (Ibrox and Hillsborough). The fifth, Bradford, was a disastrous fire. None of these events is further back than 1964.

A great deal of thought has been given to the design of stadia and management of crowds in recent years, and all-seater grounds will be the norm in future, greatly reducing the risks from both rioting and crushing, though those risks can never be totally eliminated. There have been many other incidents as well as those described here, and while major national and international competitions continue to attract large numbers of people, trouble will continue. It would be ridiculous to play matches behind closed doors with no crowd. The alternative is to stop particular games, as has happened with the Scotland v England soccer match, not played for a number of years after regular crowd trouble in the early 1980s.

The sixth incident, the tragic crash at Le Mans in 1955, is from a sport where high-speed machinery is always likely to cause mayhem if it gets out of control. Here too safety provision has received much attention in recent years, and crowds are generally now further back from the track, making a repetition of Le Mans less likely.

It should not be thought that football and motor racing are the only sports where trouble has occurred. There have been riots at cricket matches in India, Pakistan and the West Indies and quite serious crowd disturbances at basketball and ice hockey matches, to name only a few. So far they have not resulted in major loss of life.

It could be said that all the incidents described here (with the possible exception of Le Mans) were avoidable, but human passions and emotions can never be fully controlled, nor indeed should they be. It seems inevitable that on occasion there will be tragic results. Top-class sport is high drama, and sadly, the drama is not always confined to the field of action.

The Le Mans crash

12 June 1955

A car spins into the crowd

*Tragedy strikes at the famous
24-hour motor race.*

The Le Mans 24-Hour Race is one of the sternest tests in motor sport. From 4pm Saturday to 4pm Sunday, sports cars with two drivers operating in relays race continuously round the famous French circuit. The race attracts many thousands of spectators and there is a full infrastructure of food outlets, bars and stalls to keep everyone fed, watered and entertained.

In the 1950s there was great rivalry between British, German and Italian cars, the principal marques contesting Le Mans being the famous names of Jaguar, Mercedes-Benz and Ferrari, with top racing drivers taking part. In the 1955 race Mike Hawthorn was driving for Jaguar, Juan Fangio for Mercedes-Benz and Luigi Castellotti for Ferrari. Le Mans has long straights where the cars can be unleashed, and even in 1955 top speeds of over 150mph (240kph) were attained; the winners' average speed was expected to top 100mph (160kph).

Expected pattern

The race settled into its expected pattern with the three 'big names' battling for the lead. Two and a half hours into the race, tragedy struck as a group of cars entered the pit straight. Here, the teams' service areas are on one side and opposite them is a grandstand with standing enclosure in front.

Hawthorn overtook the Austin-Healey of Lance Macklin and then turned into the pits. Macklin pulled over to go round Hawthorn's slowing car and was struck by Pierre Levegh's Mercedes, which was travelling at top speed. The silver Mercedes flew through the air, turning over and over. It jumped the barrier and plunged into the crowd before bouncing back onto the protective banking and bursting into flames, throwing out more wreckage as it did so. Levegh was killed instantly, but Macklin was unharmed; though his car was badly damaged, it stayed on the track.

Rescue services rushed to the scene of the Mercedes crash, clearing wreckage and taking away the dead and injured in fleets of ambulances. Difficult decisions had to be made. Should the race be stopped? What sort of announcement should be made? It was decided to continue the race and to make no announcement mentioning fatalities, in order to let the rescue services continue their work without being hampered by thousands of people trying to leave the circuit. Both these decisions were later criticized, but they were genuinely taken for the best reasons at the time. People on the far side of the track did not learn of the tragedy until many hours later.

Including those that died later of their injuries, the death toll reached 82: motor sport's worst single incident. A further 80 people were injured, some of them seriously. The French government launched an inquiry, but after examining the circuit, the Minister of Public Works, M Coniglion Molinier, said that the safety arrangements were as efficient as could be expected. The circumstance of a car flying into the crowd was impossible to counter.

Hollow victory
Shortly after the crash, Mercedes withdrew their two remaining teams from the race, which was won by the Jaguar driven by Hawthorn and Bueb, at an average speed of 106mph (171kph).

The Lima riot

24 May 1964

Sport's worst-ever tragedy

Football fanaticism in South America leads to riots and hundreds of deaths.

Football arouses passionate feelings in many countries, and nowhere more so than in South America where not only clubs but countries attract thousands of followers. On a few occasions it has, sadly, become literally a matter of life and death.

Such was the case in May 1964, when Peru met Argentina in an Olympic Games qualifying tie in the Peruvian capital, Lima. The stadium was packed with 45 000 people inside, nearly all of them supporting Peru. With only a few minutes of the match remaining, Argentina led 1-0. Then Peru mounted an attack and the crowd went wild with joy as the Peruvian winger, Lobatón, apparently scored the equaliser.

Goal disallowed

Their celebrations were premature. The referee, Angel Pazos from Uruguay, had disallowed the goal and given a free-kick to Argentina for a foul. The crowd's anger erupted into violence. Fighting broke out on the terraces and missiles rained down onto the pitch. A well-known local character, Matias Rojas, nicknamed 'The Bomb', got onto the pitch and rushed towards the referee. He was set upon by police with dogs.

This enraged the crowd, and spectators behind one of the goals broke down the crush barriers and surged onto the pitch. By now the two teams and the officials (Pazos and his two linesmen) had left the field and sought shelter in a locker room guarded by police. They were smuggled out two hours later.

Inside the stadium, police over-reacted to the situation, throwing teargas into the crowd and firing over their heads. This simply made matters worse, and panic ensued as people tried to get out of the exit doors, most of which were locked. Others attacked the police with whatever missiles they could find. In the awful crush, people were suffocated as they tried to leave the stadium.

Those who did get out marched on the presidential palace, waving flags and shouting 'Justice! Justice!' They wanted Peru's president, Fernando Belaunde Terry, to intervene to have the match declared a draw. Next day, the mob returned to the stadium, breaking down barriers and stealing trophies from the building.

It was some time before an assessment of the tragedy could be made. The exact number of dead is not known, but at least 300 people lost their lives that awful day. The Peruvian government was accused of brutality and lack of control, but the official line was that the riot was caused by the actions of 'left-wing extremists'; an ironic term to use about a soccer match where hundreds of people died. Writing about the tragedy in the *New York Times*, Robert Lipsyte perceptively said that: 'In countries where soccer is one of the few diversions and emotional releases for a poor and restless mass, the game takes on the proportion of a kind of controlled warfare'. There was certainly something akin to a battle in Lima on 24 May 1964.

Another riot

In Buenos Aires in 1968, when the crowd rioted during a league game between River Plate and Boca Juniors, a total of 73 fans were killed.

Disaster at Ibrox

2 January 1971

Fans are crushed on a stairway

Over 60 die after the traditional Glasgow 'Old Firm' game.

The two main football teams in Glasgow, Rangers and Celtic, always meet at New Year. This traditional fixture between rivals long known as the 'Old Firm' is eagerly awaited by their large and devoted followings. The games are played alternately at Ibrox, Rangers' ground, and Parkhead, the home of Celtic.

In January 1971 it was the turn of Ibrox to stage the game. This was in the days before the terrible tragedies of Bradford and Hillsborough which led to recommendations for all-seater stadiums, and enormous crowds packed the terraces for important matches. The 'Ne'er Day' game at Ibrox meant a crowd of 80 000 people.

Late equalizer

With a few minutes left to play, Celtic were ahead and Rangers fans, disappointed by the outcome, began to leave, pouring down the steep stairways of the Cairnlea Drive exit. As they did so, a great roar went up from inside the stadium. Colin Stein had equalized for Rangers. As the news came down the stairway, people tried to turn back up, to catch the last few seconds of the match. But more fans were starting to leave and a crush developed.

Inevitably, someone slipped. Some reports say it was a small boy. Mrs Elizabeth McKim, watching from her house in Cairnlea Drive, described what happened. 'There was a roar and fans tried to get back up. Suddenly the whole mass of people began swaying. I could hardly bear to watch. Within seconds people were tum-

bling down the stairway; all you could see were arms and legs.'

Glasgow hospitals were immediately put on alert for a major disaster. Fleets of ambulances sped to the ground to take the injured away, and it soon became clear that there were a number of deaths. It took some time to sort out the final toll, but eventually the total reached 66 dead, with 200 injured.

Tragic stories emerged. Five boys from the small town of Markinch, Fife, all died. The youngest victim was eight-year-old Nigel McPherson from Alberta, Canada. He and his father had come over to spend Christmas and New Year with Mr McPherson's parents, and being a keer. Rangers fan, Donald McPherson decided to give the boy a treat and take him to the game. A public appeal for the victims and their families was immediately launched, and over £250 000 was raised.

The inquiry into the tragedy questioned the layout and the steepness of the Cairnlea Drive stairway, which had been redesigned and strengthened after an incident in 1961 when two people died. It had two platforms to break the descent, but no-one could predict part of the crowd trying to turn back and go up again.

Ibrox today is a very different place. The stadium, one of the most modern in Europe, is all-seater and capacity has been much reduced. A tragedy along the lines of January 1971 is almost impossible to conceive.

Previous incidents

There had been crowd deaths at Ibrox before 1971. In 1902, 25 people were killed during a Scotland–England international when part of a grandstand collapsed. In 1961 two people died on the same stairway, and 24 were injured after the Ne'er Day game in January 1969.

The Bradford fire

11 May 1985

A grandstand becomes an inferno

A club's day of celebration is turned into tragedy.

Supporters of Bradford City FC were happy on Saturday 11 May 1985 as they made their way to the club's Valley Parade ground. The small, unfashionable West Yorkshire club had already gained promotion to the Second Division, and the last home game of the season, against Lincoln City, was to be something of a celebration.

A larger than usual crowd turned up that day and once the match had started, the gates into the ground were locked to prevent anyone getting in free. There was a carefree atmosphere as the game neared half-time. Then fans sitting at the back of the main grandstand noticed smoke curling up from beneath their seats. At first it was thought that it was a minor thing — perhaps a carelessly dropped cigarette end, nothing to worry about. Then they realised that the fire was taking hold and panic spread as people desperately tried to escape.

Television cameras were at the ground to record Bradford's hour of triumph, and found themselves recording instead the last terrible moments of fans' lives, as the fire raced through the old grandstand with frightening speed. The stand roof caught fire and dropped blazing chunks of felt onto people below.

Extinguishers removed

By the time the fire brigade arrived it was too late to save the victims. The grandstand was a mass of flames. There were no fire extinguishers nearby — the club had them, but they had been removed to the main clubhouse after fans had used them as missiles and set them off deliberately in the past.

Once the fire was extinguished, the grim task of recovering the bodies started. They were so badly burned that they could only be identified by meticulous examination of dental records and other forensic techniques. The only victim identified on the day of the fire was Samuel Firth, aged 86, a lifelong supporter and former chairman of the club. The final death toll was 56, including some children: one 11-year-old died with his father, grandfather and uncle. Over 200 were injured, many with severe burns.

An investigation established that the fire started in accumulated rubbish piled under the grandstand and not cleared for many years. Possibly ignited by a dropped cigarette, it burned rapidly and fiercely, and with much of the stand being wooden, there was little to check the spread of the fire. It ran the whole length of the stand within ten minutes.

There was great shock expressed that a sports arena could be so ill-equipped to deal with a major fire, but it seems simply to have been an eventuality that no-one had considered. The Bradford fire led to demands for safer stadia, and safety regulations were changed, but too late for the 56 who died and for those badly injured on that awful Saturday afternoon.

Brave young lady

Many people risked their lives trying to save others in the burning stand. One of the bravest was 10-year-old Joanne Barron. She saw an elderly man struggling to escape the flames, and in spite of suffering burns herself, went back to help him out, probably saving his life. She received an award for her bravery.

Riot at Heysel

29 May 1985

Tragedy at a European Cup Final

Death on the terraces as rival supporters come into conflict.

For most of the past 20 years, Liverpool FC has been one of England's great football teams. The club has won many trophies both in domestic competitions and in Europe, and in 1985 seemed poised on the brink of further glittering success, by winning through to the final of the prestigious European Cup to face the Italian club Juventus, from Turin.

The match was to be played at the Heysel Stadium in Brussels. Liverpool's supporters are devoted to their team and will follow them anywhere, and many thousands made the trip across the Channel, looking forward to another night of triumph as their heroes won the cup. Italian fans are no less passionate, and from across the Alps the Juventus supporters also converged on Brussels confident of success.

Supporters separated

The fans made their way to the stadium early, to be sure of getting a good place. As is usual, rival supporters were separated, with empty areas of terracing between them. But Heysel was an old stadium, and the barriers were inadequate. Liverpool fans began taunting the Juventus supporters, and then throwing things into the Italian section of the terracing. Finally, they broke down the barriers and charged towards the Juventus fans.

Some of the Italians panicked, and started running for the main exit from their section. In the confusion that followed, many fans were crushed or trampled underfoot. Others escaped on to the pitch. The Belgian police charged into the crowd, and further fighting broke out. For a time all was mayhem as medical services tried to get to the injured. The start of the match was delayed while order was restored, and intense discussions took place among officials of both clubs and of UEFA, football's European governing body.

It was decided that the match should go ahead. Frustration was mounting in the crowd, most of whom were unaware of the scale of the disaster, at the long delay, and there was a strong feeling that to let over 50 000 people out into the streets of Brussels without a match, and with fans from Turin bent on revenge, could lead to 'an unimagined and unmanagable crisis', in the words of the official statement.

Irrelevant result

The match started nearly an hour and a half late. Juventus won 1–0, but the result seemed almost irrelevant beside the grim statistics that were emerging. Over 500 people had been affected by the crush, and of these 38 were dead or dying, most of them Italians but also including some Belgian fans and one Frenchman.

There were immediate calls for English clubs to be banned from European competition: this was the worst incident of its kind but there had been many other instances of poor behaviour by English supporters. The ban was supported by the British government, and no English team competed in Europe for four years. The ban was not extended to clubs from Scotland, Wales or Northern Ireland. A number of Liverpool supporters were charged with assault and faced trial in Belgium.

The Hillsborough disaster

15 April 1989

Britain's worst sporting disaster

Overcrowded terraces at a cup-tie lead to nearly a hundred deaths from crushing.

Supporters of Liverpool and Nottingham Forest were eagerly looking forward to Saturday 15 April 1989. On that day their teams were to meet in a semi-final tie of the FA Cup, the winners going through to a place in the final at Wembley Stadium in May. Cup semi-finals are always played at neutral grounds, and this tie was at Hillsborough, the ground of Sheffield Wednesday. The match had long been a sell-out, with a capacity crowd of 54 000 expected.

In the week before the game, police advised supporters travelling by road from Liverpool to leave early, as there were road-works on the M62 motorway which could delay them; the alternative route, through Stockport on the A6, was also slow. Despite this, many fans arrived with only a few minutes to spare. At all major football matches, rival fans are kept apart, and many of the Liverpool supporters were using the Leppings Lane entrance to the ground. One Liverpool supporter described the scene there at 2:45pm, 15 minutes before kick-off time, as 'absolute bedlam, there was no control at all. I saw only one policeman and he was helpless to do anything. Fans were getting very anxious that they would miss the kick-off.'

men doing anything about it. They seemed happy to stand and let things happen.' Then, at about 2:55, an extra gate was opened. There was a concerted rush for this gate, where just one policeman was stationed. Hundreds of fans poured through the gate, joining those inside struggling to find a place on the terracing. A supporter said 'I was carried along with about 40 others, and we could have been crushed to death there, let alone inside the ground. You could not dictate where you went, you were just carried along against your will.'

Inside, the situation in that section of the terracing was getting desperate as the game actually started and more supporters tried to push in to see the action. The crowd at the front of the terracing became crushed against the barriers. In the words of one survivor, Stephen Hendry, aged 19, 'People had been put on the floor under the barriers and were getting trampled by fans, helpless in the surge . . . people were unable to breathe . . . fans climbed over the fence because of what was happening. The game was now an irrelevance.'

The match was in fact about ten minutes old, and as Liverpool attacked the Nottingham Forest goal — at the Leppings Lane end — the crowd surged forward again in excitement, causing further crushing at the front. More and more fans were trying to climb over barriers onto the pitch. Finally realising the seriousness of the situation, ground stewards and police opened a relief gate to let supporters through onto the pitch, and the game was stopped — temporarily, it was assumed.

The fatal gate

Another described how he was 'crushed against the walls . . . there were no police-

Unable to cope

However, the situation on the terracing was far worse than anyone realized.

A major tragedy of this kind was wholly unexpected, and medical services were quite unable to cope. Dr John Ashton, a senior lecturer at Liverpool University, who was watching the match, went onto the pitch to help and was appalled at the lack of aid available. 'At 3:30pm there were no medical personnel apart from one or two St John Ambulance men. There was no equipment and only one ambulance' he said later.

The vital resuscitation equipment did not arrive until about 4:15pm, too late for many of the casualties. However, until the terracing gate was opened, there was little or nothing rescue services could do to help the people being crushed on the terraces, and many must have died in those awful few minutes before the game was stopped.

The toll of life rose steadily. At first it was thought only a small number had died, but as the area was slowly cleared, more and more bodies were brought out. The final toll was 95, nearly all of them Liverpool supporters. It was Britain's worst sporting tragedy. There was severe criticism of the way South Yorkshire Police had handled the situation, particularly before the match, and of the apparent lack of proper medical facilities to deal with a major incident at a sporting occasion attended by over 50 000 people. Much of this criticism was upheld by the inquiry into the disaster and the report on football grounds prepared by Lord Justice Taylor, which led to a number of recommendations, the most important of which was that all major football stadia should have seated accommodation only, so that crushing of the kind seen at Hillsborough could never happen again.

> ### The Anfield shrine
> In the days after the tragedy at Hillsborough, Liverpool's ground at Anfield became a shrine for those who had died. On the Sunday morning, so many people gathered at the ground that it was opened, and supporters — not just from Liverpool but from many other clubs — began to lay wreaths and scarves on the pitch and the terraces at the famous Kop end of the ground. Eventually, half the pitch was covered in tributes to the dead, a very moving sight. A disaster fund for the bereaved and injured raised millions of pounds.

Scene of mourning outside Hillsborough Stadium.

Tsunamis

Tsunamis have been better understood in recent years. They were formerly called 'tidal waves' but it is now realized that they have nothing to do with tides. The word is Japanese for 'great wave in harbour' and it is in enclosed coastal areas that tsunamis do most damage.

A tsunami is a series of waves most commonly caused by violent movement of the seafloor. The movement can be produced by three different types of violent geologic activity. Submarine faulting, when a block of ocean floor is thrust upward or suddenly drops is accompanied by earthquakes. Landslides occuring underwater, or starting above water and plunging into the sea, also generate tsunamis, as does volcanic activity in nearshore or underwater volcanoes.

Tsunamis can measure as much as 100 miles from crest to crest and travel at up to 500 miles per hour in the deep ocean waters. In deep water they may be only a foot or two high, but as they move into shallower water they change. As they approach shore their forward speed drops to around 40 miles per hour, but the speed of the water particles themselves increases, and the height of the wave begins to increase dramatically.

In areas where tsunamis are common it is often thought that the water recedes before the tsunami arrives. But a tsunami is not one wave but a series, a 'tsunami wave train', and whether the water first rises or falls depends on what part of the tsunami wave train first reaches shore.

Tsunamis may be generated by local events as at the Lisbon earthquake in 1755, in which case they are very sudden, or they may travel thousands of miles across the ocean, like the two tsunamis which struck Hilo, Hawaii in 1946 and 1960.

Major tsunamis

Location of source	Year	Height m	Height ft	Location of deaths/damage	Deaths
Sea of Japan	1983	15	49	Japan, Korea	107
Indonesia	1979	10	32	Indonesia	187
Celebes Sea	1976	30	98	Philippine Is	5 000
Alaska	1964	32	105	Alaska, Aleutian Is, California	122
Chile	1960	10	30	Chile, Hawaii, Japan	5 000
Aleutian Is	1957	16	52	Hawaii, Japan	0
Kamchatka	1952	18.4	60	Kamchatka, Kuril Is, Hawaii,	many
Aleutian Is	1946	17	55	Aleutian Is, Hawaii, California	159
Nankaido (Japan)	1946	6.1	20	Japan	1 997
Kii (Japan)	1944	7.5	25	Japan	998
Sanrika (Japan)	1933	28.2	93	Japan, Hawaii	3 000
E Kamchatka	1923	20	66	Kamchatka, Hawaii	3
S Kuril Is	1918	12	39	Kuril Is, Russia, Japan, Hawaii	23
Sanriku (Japan)	1896	22	75	Japan	27 122
Sunda Strait	1883	35	115	Java, Sumatra	36 000
Chile	1877	23	75	Chile, Hawaii	many
Chile	1868	21	69	Chile, Hawaii	25 000
Hawaii Is	1868	20	66	Hawaii Is	81
Japan	1854	6	20	Japan	3 000
Flores Sea	1800	24	79	Indonesia	4–500
Ariake Sea	1792	9	30	Japan	9 745
Italy	1783	?	?	Italy	30 000
Ryukyu Is	1771	12	39	Ryukyu Is	11 941
Portugal	1775	16	52	W Europe, Morocco, W Indies	60 000
Peru	1746	24	79	Peru	5 000
Japan	1741	9	30	Japan	1 000+
SE Kamchatka	1737	30	98	Kamchatka, Kuril Is	?
Peru	1724	24	79	Peru	?
Japan	1707	11.5	38	Japan	30 000
W Indies	1692	?	?	Jamaica	2 000
Banda Is	1629	15	49	Indonesia	?
Sanriku (Japan)	1611	25	82	Japan	5 000
Japan	1605	?	?	Japan	4 000
Kii (Japan)	1498	?	?	Japan	5 000

Tsunamis

1883, 1896, 1958

Giant waves from near and far

The greatest wave ever known was a type of tsunami, although it did not travel any great distance. It happened in Lituya Bay in Alaska, which is roughly frying-pan shaped with a narrow entrance. On 9 July 1958 an earthquake dislodged a vast amount of rock and earth from hills around Gilbert Inlet, at the head of the bay. It is estimated that 80 million tons of rock fell up to 3 000 feet (900m) into the waters of the inlet.

This has been graphically described by the author Frank Lane as 'equivalent to the simultaneous launching of 2 000 battleships from a slipway half a mile high.' The effect was incredible. A tsunami raced across the bay and smashed against the opposite shore with a force that is impossible to envisage. Damage marks on the hills show that the water reached a maximum height of 1 700 feet (500m) — a wave a third of a mile high!

The area is unpopulated but heavily forested. After the wave retreated four square miles of forest had gone, the trees ripped out and strewn about or vanished beneath the waters of the bay. The effect of such a wave on a populated area, should such a thing ever happen, does not bear thinking about.

A massive tsunami struck the Sanriku coastal area of Japan following a major earth tremor beneath the sea here on 15 June 1896. A series of waves, travelling at about 60mph (100kph), reached heights of up to 75 feet (22m) and caused immense damage. Hundreds of boats were smashed to pieces, and as the waves swept inland they crushed houses like paper. The death toll reached over 25 000. Fishermen from the area who had been outside the earthquake zone were shattered when they returned to their home ports, for they had felt nothing unusual.

Tsunamis do not always cross the oceans. Their direction of travel is to some extent dependent on the alignment of the fault which appears in the sea-bed. Following the Good Friday 1964 earthquake in Alaska (see p53), the tsunami raced southward, down the coasts of Canada and the western USA, causing considerable damage and killing a number of people.

Tsunamis can also be created by volcanic disturbance, and here too they damage caused can be immense. Very few of the 36 000 people who are known to have died when Krakatoa erupted in 1883 (see p206) lost their lives directly as a result of the eruption. Most of them died when colossal waves hammered the islands around the area, inundating large areas. The same phenomenon has arisen at other major eruptions.

Tsunamis strike with tremendous force and there is no possible defence against them. There is now a well-established Tsunami Warning System around the Pacific, and the only precaution that can be taken is to evacuate areas most likely to be hit. These extraordinary earthquake waves will undoubtedly, however, continue to cause great damage to life and property in the future.

Hilo and the Hamakua coast

Hawaii, 1946

With no warning

A tsunami that travelled from Alaska on April Fool's Day.

The Hawaiian Islands are located in the centre of the Pacific, in the path of any tsunami, wherever its origin; the giant waves have struck many times over the centuries. One of the most vulnerable sites is the city of Hilo, second largest in the state, situated on the east coast of the island from which the state takes its name, at the centre of a deep crescent bay . . . a perfect tsunami target.

On this occasion it came from the north, following movement at the bottom of the Aleutian Trench. The earthquake in Alaska was measured by seismographs on Hawaii and on Oahu, but there was no warning system in operation at that time, so when the tsunami reached the east coast of the island of Hawaii five hours later, no one was prepared.

It reached there just after 7am as people were beginning to go about their daily business. In Hilo the first warning for most people was the withdrawing of water from the bay (and the harbour). At the breakwater the outward flow met an incoming wave and combined into a massive surge that rushed to the shore.

The greatest damage and loss of life occured in the bay front area known as Shinmachi, populated mainly by Japanese immigrants. The Wailoa River ran to one side of it — the wave travelled up the river smashing the buildings, and then withdrew carrying walls, roofs, refrigeration, furniture and struggling people in its flood.

The death toll in the Hawaiian Islands was 159, of which 96 were Hilo residents. There was tremendous damage to property, the business district of Hilo being almost completely destroyed. The island community was particularly distressed by the fact that the wave struck the school at Laupahochoe, north of Hilo, drowning 16 children and five of their teachers.

Wonderful escapes

But there were wonderful escapes as well as tragic losses. Because people did not realize how big the wave would be, some stood to watch events. Many were on the banks of the Wailoa River or on the bridge that spanned it when the third and largest wave arrived. The owners of a newly-opened café, situated at the crossroads next to the bridge, were extremely fortunate as the wave swept over them. They clung to the concrete uprights and were still there when the wave receded. In Laupahochoa some students climbed on to part of a cottage floor and floated on this improvised raft until rescued.

After the waters had finally receded the enormous damage could be assessed — as well as the tremendous force of the waves. In the Polalu Valley in the northeast of the island the water attained heights of 55 feet (17m). Photographs taken in Hilo show that the waves were more than 25 feet (8m) above normal sea level.

It was decided that the bay front area of Hilo should not be rebuilt, but left as a park. Lessons were learnt too from the buildings that survived. The most resistant were concrete structures and those on stilts, where the water could flow underneath. This influenced future design.

Valdivia

Chile, 22 May 1960

A great tsunami

Chilean coastal towns are battered by giant waves.

The coastal strip of Chile lies sandwiched between the high Andes Mountains and the deep Peru–Chile Track. It is an area of frequent seismic activity; earthquakes, volcanic eruptions and tsunamis occur with terrifying regularity. The city of Concepción had been rocked by a series of sizeable earth tremors during 21 May, including one which measured 7.5 on the Richter scale. Another of the same size occurred just after 3pm (local time) the next day, Sunday 22 May, to be followed only seconds later by an even larger quake with the same epicentre. This lasted for seven minutes and at its maximum, 3:15pm, it measured 8.5 on the Richter scale — more than 30 times the energy of the 7.5 earthquake. Many people fortunately left their houses when the first quake happened and were outside when the prolonged vibration occurred and many houses were destroyed. Coastal towns braced themselves for the wave that they knew must follow.

Gigantic wave

In Valdivia, on the Bay of Corral, the water rose by 16 feet (5m) in a few minutes, submerging many houses and harbour areas. The bay then emptied, the retreating waters taking a number of ships with them. A pause of half an hour followed — precious time for the people to get to safer places. Then the tsunami arrived.

A mass of water smashed into the bay, forming a gigantic wave over 30 feet (10m) high that pounded the harbour areas and rushed far inland causing great damage. Then, as fast as it had come, the water retreated again, scouring the floor of the bay and taking with it tons of debris from houses and streets. Swollen rivers fell into the empty bay as waterfalls, an extraordinary sight.

In came yet another huge wave, bringing some of the debris — including whole houses — back again and piling them in stacks along the harbour front. A tug was thrown right over the warehouses to land some way inland. The waves continued, though gradually abating, for more than 24 hours.

Smashed to matchwood

A French scientist, Haround Tazieff, was at the port of Corral and described how the tsunami appeared to him. 'The wave, like an enormous hand crumpling a sheet of paper, crushed the houses one after another, with a prodigious cracking of shattered timbers. In only 20 seconds it had heaped up perhaps 800 houses, smashed to matchwood, at the foot of the hill.'

The quake and tsunami caused widespread damage. Over 400 000 houses were destroyed along a 600-mile (1 000km) stretch of the coast of Chile. The 'breathing space' at least meant that casualties were relatively low. Only 150 people died in Valdivia and 5 000 in Chile as a whole, but the economic loss was immense.

Hilo
Hawaii, 1960

Disaster by night

After many false alarms, the citizens of Hilo were lured into a false sense of security.

The devastating earthquake described on p195 caused a Tsunami Watch to be started. A Tsunami Warning was issued at 6:47pm (local time) and the tsunami sirens along the coast at Hilo began to sound at 8:30pm. It had been estimated that the waves would arrive at around midnight, Hawaiian time.

Most people in Hilo were aware of the warning, but not all evacuated the low ground. Some actually went to the bayfront and the harbour area, confident that the waves would be small, as they had been following the warnings in 1952 and 1957.

Among the observers were some geologists. They waited on a bridge over the Wailuku River, with an escape route planned to higher ground. Two waves came into the bay, the second flooding the business district. The water withdrew from the bay, then flooded back with the third and biggest wave, which carried away part of the bridge on which the geologists had been standing (they had run when they saw it advance up the estuary); the city was flooded and plunged into darkness.

On this occasion the waves approached from a different angle and destroyed different parts of Hilo. Homes which had been merely splashed in 1946 were washed away in the 1960 tsunami. The café owners who had survived on the bridge over the Wailoa survived again, by amazing chance. Their home was lifted from its foundations but became wedged on a piece of higher ground instead of being carried out to sea.

The most remarkable escape however was that of Fusayo Ito who lived on the south side of the Wailoa River. She had decided to stay in her home, despite pleas from her daughter that she should leave. When the third wave hit she was knocked unconscious and recovered to find herself floating in water, in darkness. She could not swim, but clung to a piece of debris and was swept by the ebb of the tsunami into the ocean. She floated all night offshore until she was seen by a Coast Guard's patrol boat. She had been floating on a window screen from her house. Only a tiny woman like herself — a mere 4ft 11in tall — could have been kept afloat by such a flimsy structure.

Mrs Ito was a survivor. But 61 people were killed in Hilo that night, despite the Warning System. Property damage was estimated at as high as $50 million.

Information gathered by scientists during and after the tsunami led to an increase in understanding about how the waves behave. The waves had also caused great destruction in Japan — Japan and many other countries joined the Tsunami Warning System.

Tsunami Warning System
Most Pacific-wide tsunamis are caused by severe faulting on the ocean floor, accompanied by an earthquake of magnitude 7 or greater. A system of 62 tide stations and 77 seismic stations has been set up by the 24 member countries in the Pacific Basin. The detection of an earthquake sets off special seismic alarms and a decision is made as whether to announce a Tsunami Watch (followed by a Tsunami Warning). It is possible to predict the actual arrival time of the first tsunami waves. Unfortunately it is not at present possible to predict what size they will be.

Volcanoes

An erupting volcano is one of the most impressive and spectacular sights that nature can present. Whereas the equally powerful forces that lead to earthquakes happen underground, volcanic emissions are very visible, and the image of a cone-shaped mountain spewing forth molten rock and ash engraves itself indelibly on the mind of anyone fortunate enough to see it.

Provided, that is, you are not in line with the emission, for volcanoes can be exceptionally destructive. Their powers take several forms. As well as the lava flow issuing down the side of a volcano and burning up, as well as burying, everything in its path, there is the 'lahar', the flow of debris which combines with ice or water to form a sticky and often deadly mud, most recently seen in Colombia in 1985 with the eruption of Nevado del Ruiz. There is also the feared 'nuée ardente', the cloud of red-hot gas which kills by suffocation as well as by fire. One of these clouds, issuing from Mont Pelée, destroyed the town of St Pierre in a few minutes in 1902.

The million of tons of ash and dust which shoot skyward have their own effect. Caught up in the stratospheric winds, they have been known to circle the earth for several years, causing weather disturbances and spectacular sunsets. The cloud from the exceptional eruption of Tambora in Indonesia in 1815 was so powerful that the following year was known as the 'year without a summer'.

In his fine book on volcanoes, Cliff Ollier makes the bold statement that 'on balance, volcanoes do more good than harm.' This may seem surprising when set against the high casualty figures following the eruptions of Vesuvius, Krakatoa, Mont Pelée and others. What he had in mind was the highly fertile land that volcanic flows leave behind and the great natural beauty of most volcanic regions.

Our knowledge of volcanoes is still developing. Like earthquakes, they are a reminder of our earth's continuing evolution, and of the sheer power of untamed nature. We must accept this power — and the destruction that can follow it — as being in the rightful order of things. Volcanoes are not to be tamed.

Major volcanoes

Name	Height m	Height ft	Major eruptions (years)	Last eruption (year)
Aconcagua (Argentina)	6 960	22 831	extinct	
Ararat (Turkey)	5 198	18 350	extinct	Holocene
Awu (Sangihe Is)	1 327	4 355	1711, 1856, 1892	1968
Bezymianny (USSR)	2 800	9 186	1955–6	1984
Coseguina (Nicaragua)	847	1 598	1835	1835
El Chichón (Mexico)	1 349	4 430	1982	1982
Erebus (Antarctica)	4 023	13 200	1947, 1972	1986
Etna (Italy)	3 236	10 625	122, 1169, 1329, 1536, 1669, 1928, 1964, 1971, 1985	1992
Fuji (Japan)	3 776	12 388	1707	1707
Galunggung (Java)	2 180	7 155	1822, 1918	1982
Hekla (Iceland)	1 491	4 920	1693, 1845, 1947–8, 1970	1981
Helgafell (Iceland)	215	706	1973	1973
Hudson (Chile)	1 740	5 742	1971, 1973	1991
Jurullo (Mexico)	1 330	4 255	1759–74	1774
Katmai (Alaska)	2 298	7 540	1912, 1920, 1921	1931
Kilauea (Hawaii)	1 247	4 100	1823–1924, 1952, 1955, 1960, 1967–8, 1968–74, 1983–7	1991
Kilimanjaro (Tanzania)	5 930	19 450	extinct	Pleistocene
Klyuchevskoy (Russia)	4 850	15 910	1700–1966, 1984	1985
Krakatoa (Sumatra)	818	2 685	1680, 1883, 1927, 1952–3, 1969	1980
La Soufrière (St Vincent)	1 232	4 048	1718, 1812, 1902, 1971–2	1979
Laki (Iceland)	500	1 642	1783	1784
Lamington (Papua New Guinea)	1 780	5 844	1951	1956
Lassen Peak (USA)	3 186	10 453	1914–5	1921
Mauna Loa (Hawaii)	4 172	13 685	1859, 1880, 1887, 1919, 1950	1984
Mayon (Philippines)	2 462	8 084	1616, 1766, 1814, 1897, 1968	1978
Nyamuragira (Zaire)	3 056	10 026	1921–38, 1971, 1980	1984
Paricutin (Mexico)	3 188	10 460	1943–52	1952
Pelée, Mont (Martinique)	1 397	4 584	1902, 1929–32	1932
Pinatubo, Mt (Philippines)	1 462	4 795	1391	1991
Popacatepetl (Mexico)	5 483	17 990	1920	1943
Rainier, Mt (USA)	4 392	14 416	1st-c BC, 1820	1882
Ruapehu (New Zealand)	2 796	9 175	1945, 1953, 1969, 1975	1986
St Helens, Mt (USA)	2 549	8 364	1800, 1831, 1835, 1842–3, 1857, 1980	1987
Santorini/Thera (Greece)	300	984	1470BC, 1450BC, 197BC, AD46, 1570–3, 1707–11, 1866–70	1950
Stromboli (Italy)	931	3 055	1768, 1882, 1889, 1907, 1930, 1936, 1941, 1950, 1952	1986
Surtsey (Iceland)	174	570	1963–7	1967
Taal (Philippines)	1 448	4 752	1911, 1965, 1969	1977
Tambora (Sumbawa)	2 868	9 410	1815	1880
Tarawera (New Zealand)	1 149	3 770	1886	1973
Unzen (Japan)	1 360	4 461	1360, 1791	1991
Vesuvius (Italy)	1 289	4 230	79, 472, 1036, 1631, 1779, 1906	1944
Vulcano (Italy)	502	1 650	antiquity, 1444, 1730–40, 1786, 1873, 1888–90	1890

Vesuvius
Italy, AD79

The burying of Pompeii

Roman towns are preserved under a sea of lava.

There are few places in the world where you can go and see for yourself exactly what it was like at the time of a great natural disaster hundreds of years ago. Pompeii is one of them. The Roman town, buried under volcanic debris for many centuries, has been excavated with great care and you can now walk its streets, see the damage to the buildings, and even some of the dead at the moment of their interment.

Mount Vesuvius, above the Bay of Naples in southern Italy, was known to have been an active volcano, but the Romans who built the towns that spread below its slopes in the first century AD had no reason to fear a large-scale eruption. Pompeii was the principal town of the area, a flourishing place with fine villas, shops, public areas and baths with under-floor central heating. Nearby was its port, Misenum, and not far away was another town, Herculaneum.

The first signs of trouble ahead were felt in AD62, when sharp earth tremors affected the area. These were not associated with Vesuvius, which still showed no real sign of direct activity, but they were the forerunners of the great disaster to come. Over the next 16 years there were more rumblings and tremors, then in August 79 the volcano burst into life.

Pliny's writings

We have the writings of Pliny the Younger, historian and naturalist, as a vivid eye-witness account of those awful days. His uncle, Pliny the Elder, who as well as being a lawyer was in command of a fleet of galleys, set off across the bay to see what was happening, but could not land near Pompeii and had to continue for several miles to the south.

He landed at Stabiae and took refuge in a villa belonging to a friend. Later that night they tried again to reach Pompeii, but on the way the elder Pliny died, overcome by fumes. His nephew meanwhile was heading towards the countryside, with his mother and hundreds of others escaping the volcano. He described the scene as follows:

'Behind us, a thick and ominous smoke spread over the earth. We were enveloped by darkness, not as in a moonless night but the darkness of a sealed room. The cries of women and children and the shaking of men could be heard all the time.' Over Vesuvius was a vast cloud 'like an immense tree-trunk projected into the air and opened out with branches, sometimes white, sometimes dark and mottled. The cloud was riven by bursts of fire and revealed flashes brighter than lightning.' This is a common phenomenon in major eruptions.

Suffocating fumes

Hot ash and pumice rained down on the towns below and suffocating sulphurous fumes filled the air. As the ground shook and the debris crashed down, buildings collapsed, burying those inside. Others were burnt to death or suffocated. Of the population of around 20 000, fewer than a quarter are thought to have survived as the volcanic debris continued to fall for two days, covering Pompeii and Herculaneum with a shroud of grey. Later, heavy rain helped a thick tongue of mud and lava to flow down the mountain, further burying the towns below. Little wonder that Pliny described the scene as being 'as if the last eternal night had settled on the world.' For many thousands, it had.

Pompeii remained buried until the mid 18th century, when the Bourbon rulers of the area carried out some excavation (and took away such treasures as they found) but the main work started in 1861 under the direction of Professor Giuseppe Forelli. He found that the ash contained remarkably lifelike impressions of bodies at the moment they were engulfed, and developed a new technique of taking casts from these impressions.

These casts can be seen today — a family with arms round each other, people with arms raised to ward off the deadly ash, others with cloths to their mouths. There is a dog twisted grotesquely in the agony of its death-throes. You can also see preserved documents written on wax tablets, coins and household utensils.

The town was carefully excavated over a period of decades and many of its streets, houses, shops, inns and gardens are now once again open to view. You can walk among them, even see graffiti on the walls, and imagine for yourself what it was like that hot August day as the people of Pompeii realised that the mountain above them, on which they had cultivated vines, was destroying them under a smothering cloud of ash and fumes from which there was no escape.

More eruptions

Vesuvius has continued to be intermittently active. There have been at least 40 eruptions since AD79 including 1631 — when 18 000 people died — 1779, 1872 and 1906, all causing some damage and casualties. The most recent disturbance was in March 1944, and it is quite possible that the volcano could spew forth more ash or lava in the future. The area beneath is densely populated, and a major evacuation might well be necessary if a big eruption threatened.

Stefanoni's Storia d'Italia *showing the destruction of Herculaneum and Pompeii by Mount Vesuvius.*

Santorini

Eastern Mediterranean, 1500BC (approximate date)

The origin of the Atlantis legend?

A vast eruption changes the Aegean sea-scape.

There was certainly a tremendous volcanic eruption in the eastern Mediterranean in about 1500BC. The island of Thera (modern Santorini) was reduced to the small crescent shape it has today, curving round the volcano's crater or 'caldera'. Some 32 square miles (80 sq km) of the island disappeared beneath the sea as the volcano ejected vast amounts of matter — probably five times as much as Krakatoa.

A huge tidal wave must have been set up, and it has been postulated that this wave was responsible for the end of the Minoan civilization on Crete. Certainly volcanic matter has been found on that island, and if there was a wave, it must have been affected. Core samples show a possible ash layer 30 inches (75cm) deep in the Crete area, which would have had a disastrous effect.

There are no actual accounts of the eruption. This is not surprising as Thera itself would have been buried under ash and debris perhaps as much as 200 feet (60m) deep. Associations have been made between the Santorini eruption and the legend of the lost civilization of Atlantis. Could this be Atlantis? Plato's account of the size and age of Atlantis do not fit what we know of the geography and history of the known world. However, the town of Akrotiri, buried by the volcanic pumice, and the collapse of the caldera, do indicate a possible connection with the legend. Plato's description of a civilization that met its end 'with violent earthquakes and floods, in a single day and night of misfortune' would certainly fit the events which followed the eruption of the volcano in Thera.

Evacuation

Excavations on the island of Santorini have revealed finds which rival Pompeii — but without any bodies. The house walls are richly decorated, there are beautifully made jugs and pots, some filled with seeds. However, all jewels and money seem to have been removed, suggesting an evacuation before the catastrophe which buried the town in a fall of pumice 10 feet (3m) thick within a few hours. Further excavations may answer some of the questions which remain. Where did the people of this advanced civilization go?

Taupo

New Zealand, c.150AD

A whole island buried

Probably the greatest eruption of the last two millennia.

Studies by vulcanologists have led to the conclusion that the eruption of the volcano of Taupo, on the North Island of New Zealand, was perhaps the greatest of the past 2 000 years — even greater than Krakatoa. The volcanic debris can still be clearly seen.

There seem to have been eight massive eruptions in all over a period of a few years, ejecting about 14 cubic miles (60 cu km) of debris into the stratosphere. In addition, an enormous mass of hot ash and gases poured out of the volcano. This wave is estimated to have reached 300 feet (90m) in height and to have had a maximum flow of one million cubic yards *per second* — an almost unbelievable amount of matter travelling with immense force.

It changed the landscape north of the volcano for 200 miles (320km), leaving a grey, dead desert. The ash is thought to have covered virtually the whole of North Island with at least four inches (10cm) of material. If you visit the area today you will see not a mountain but Lake Taupo, which is the volcano's caldera. It is not known if the island was inhabited at the time.

Caldera

A caldera results when the top of the volcano collapses because the lava has retreated down the vent, or when a very violent explosion has blown off the top of the volcano. The caldera may become filled with fresh water, as at Lake Taupo, or by the sea, to form a protected bay, as at Santorini.

North Island

New Zealand is part of the Pacific crustal belt, land recently formed by active volcanism and the movement of the Earth's plates. The area around Lake Taupo continues to be volcanically active.

Mount Etna

Sicily, 1669

Catania is buried

*Europe's most active volcano
has struck many times
over the centuries.*

Etna is Europe's largest volcano, at just under 11 000 feet (3 330m) and also the most active. It has erupted countless times since records began, from AD122 up to its latest outpouring which began in April 1992. Its eruptions are called 'parasitic' because they issue from small fissures on the flanks of the mountain and not from its cone.

Catania, the principal town and industrial centre of Sicily and a major port, has suffered several times from the volcanic activity on Etna. The town was badly damaged in the AD122 eruption, and again in 1169, but the most serious damage occurred in March 1669.

During that month, Etna was extremely active, with loud rumblings and clouds of ash and gas belching forth from the summit. Finally, on 11 March, a major eruption took place. Vast clouds of ash spread out for 60 miles (100km) and lava began to flow down the mountain towards Catania.

For a time, the town wall stopped the flow, but in the end its force was too great and it overwhelmed the town. Many people escaped, but equally, many had no chance to flee and nowhere to go, and around 20 000 people lost their lives. A careful watch is kept on Etna but volcanoes are not easy to control.

Taming the lava flow

During the 1992 eruption attempts were made by the Italian Air Force to divert the flow of lava, by bombing it, away from the town of Zafferana. When this failed, a plan was made to place a 5 000lb (2 268kg) steel platform on the mountain near a tunnel where the lava had been accumulating. The intention was to load two-ton concrete blocks on to the platform, then winch them to the tunnel, forcing the lava to rise to the surface and cool down.

However, high winds forced the helicopter to jettison the platform before it could be placed by the tunnel.

Mount Laki

Iceland, 1783

The island's crops are poisoned

Eruption causes economic disaster and famine.

Iceland is a centre of volcanic activity: since the ninth century AD when the country was settled, about 30 volcanoes have been active. A very large proportion of the lava produced on earth in historic times has been produced in Iceland. In recent years, vulcanologists went there to study the birth of a new island, Surtsey, from volcanic material, and in the first half of 1973 the fishing port of Heimaey was badly damaged by ash and lava, despite continual pumping of sea-water onto the flow to cool and check it.

Laki is one of nearly 200 volcanoes, live, rumbling or thought extinct, on this relatively small island, and although not the best-known — Hekla takes that prize — is among the most active. It erupted with disastrous effect in summer 1783.

A fissure nearly 19 miles (32km) long opened up in early June, and enormous quantities of basaltic lava poured out. The lava continued to flow over a period of several months, and as well as causing serious flooding in several areas, the sulphurous fumes poisoned crops and killed half of the cattle, 75 per cent of the horses, and 80 per cent of the sheep on the island. Although the eruption itself took few lives, the famine that resulted led to the deaths of about 10 000 people — a fifth of the entire population. This was the greatest lava flow of historic times.

Hekla

This volcano has been built up by many eruptions. These have formed a ridge which splits during an eruption. An explosive eruption in 1104AD destroyed vast areas; in 1947 the column of smoke and steam from the eruption rose to 100 000 feet (3 048m).

Katla and Grimsvötn

These volcanoes are covered by ice, which melts when they erupt, causing catastrophic floods, known as *jökulhlaup* ('glacier bursts').

Tambora

Indonesia, 1815

The eruption that led to *Frankenstein*

A bigger blast even than Krakatoa affects the weather worldwide.

Tambora is one of the chain of active Indonesian volcanoes. Sited on the island of Sumbawa, it is known to have erupted a number of times, but its most devastating blast came in April 1815. This is thought to have been the greatest eruption between 1500 and 1835, when it was matched by Coseguina, in Nicaragua.

When Tambora blew its top, it put at least 40 cubic miles (160 cu km) of matter into the atmosphere. Ash was deposited over an area of a million square miles (2.5 million sq km). The effect on the surrounding area was naturally severe. The blast, hot ash, lava, floods and fire killed about 12 000 people on Sumbawa and neighbouring islands. Virtually all the livestock was killed, and crops were ruined. The resultant famine is thought to have led to a further 70 000 deaths.

Tambora lost a third of its height as a result of this massive explosion. The volcanic material thrown into the atmosphere was caught up in the stratospheric winds and circled the globe for two years. Its effect in 1816 was remarkable. In many countries this was known as 'the year without a summer'.

Snow every month

In the northern states of the USA, it snowed every month, even in July and August. It has recently emerged that the Far Eastern countries suffered similarly, with frost — unheard-of in summer — destroying crops in tropical areas and a great deal of cold, stormy weather throughout the year.

In Europe too it was a cold, gloomy summer. The harvest was a disaster and prices on the London Grain Market reached record levels as supplies dwindled. One curious story from that summer concerns the poet Byron and his friends the Shelleys, who were staying together beside Lake Geneva in Switzerland.

The weather was so bad that the party spent most of their time indoors, talking and writing. Byron composed a masterly poem called *Darkness* which, reflecting the mood of the weather, begins: 'The bright sun was extinguish'd, and the stars/Did wander darkling in the eternal space.' Mary Shelley was also taken by the sombre mood, and was inspired to write the classic horror story *Frankenstein*.

Great natural events have often inspired literature and art but can rarely have provided the impetus for such a tale!

Galunggung

Seven years after Tambora went up, Galunggung on Java, which is in the same chain, known as the Indonesian Arc, exploded through its crater lake, creating an enormous *lahar* (mudslide) which covered an area of country 15 miles (24km) in length. Over a hundred villages were destroyed and about 4 000 people died. In April 1982 Galunggung erupted again. Although many villages were covered with ash or lahars, 75 000 people were successfully evacuated and there was little loss of life. An airliner had a remarkable escape when ash from Galunggung blocked all four of its engines. It fell thousands of feet but the crew managed to restart two engines just in time.

Krakatoa

27 August 1883

The biggest bang of all

An explosion that echoed round the world.

The eruption of Krakatoa is one of those global events that etches itself into the consciousness everywhere. It is in every history book and the name has become a legend. Films have been made about it, books written about it, many paintings (real or imaginary) made of it, and the name seems destined to live for ever.

So, in truth, it should — as a warning as well as a reminder of what actually happened. Its echoes literally did carry round the world, as did the colossal cloud of ash and dust, producing dramatic sunrises and sunsets for years afterwards.

There was some warning. The island of Krakatoa lies between Java and Sumatra in Indonesia. Six miles (10km) long, it held a number of volcanic cones, as did two adjacent smaller islands, Danan and Perboewetan, but they were considered mild compared with others in the archipelago. The highest hill on Krakatoa, called Rakatam, was under 3 000 feet (900m) high. But in May 1883 Krakatoa began to serve warning of what was to follow, with a series of eruptions, some of which could be heard in the city of Batavia (now called Jakarta), nearly 100 miles (160km) away. Minor eruptions continued through the summer, but they were nothing when set beside the events of 26 and 27 August.

Permanent darkness

The major eruption started just after midday on Sunday 26 August, followed by further eruptions every few minutes. Huge clouds of ash and dust were flung miles into the atmosphere, and everywhere within 50 miles (80km) of Krakatoa was in permanent darkness for the next two and a half days. A British ship, the *Charles Ball*, was in the area at the time, giving us one of a number of remarkable eye-witness accounts. The ship's log records the scene: 'The intense blackness above and around us was broken by the glare of varied kinds of lightning; that and the continuous explosive roars of Krakatoa make our situation a truly awful one'. In the circumstances, that seems almost an understatement.

Later that day, Captain Wooldridge of another British ship, the *Sir Robert Sale,* noted in his log that 'the sky presented a most terrible appearance, the dense mass of clouds covered with a murky tinge, with fierce flashes of lightning'. Ships were covered with phosphorescent mud, and another observer, Robert Dalby, felt 'such a hurricane as no man had experienced before. The wind seemed a solid mass, roaring like an enormous engine and shrieking like a demon in torment. In the heavens there was a terrible commotion, clouds whirled around at terrific speed, and most of us thought we were in the vortex of a cyclone.'

It seemed impossible to believe that worse was to follow, but on Monday 27 August the volcanic activity reached an unprecedented crescendo. On that morning the central part of the island collapsed inward, into the hole created by the volcano, and the sea rushed into the abyss. The explosion that followed, described graphically later as 'Krakatoa's death cry', was the largest sound ever recorded on the earth. It was heard clearly as far as 3 000 miles (4 800km) away on Rodriguez Island in the Indian Ocean; the coastguard there reported it as gunfire.

Huge waves

In the area around Krakatoa, the devastation was colossal. Apart from the damage caused by the ash, dust and pumice from the volcano itself, there were many tsunamis created, and nearly 300 towns and villages suffered grievous damage from these waves, which reached over 100 feet (30m) in height. In the port of Merak, on Java, only two of the 2 700 inhabitants survived the tsunami. A Dutch gunboat, the *Berouw*, was lifted bodily by the wave and deposited a mile inland from its port of Telok Betong on Sumatra. The port itself was completely devastated.

The tsunamis travelled for thousands of miles before dying out, and were seen on the west coast of America and in other places around the Pacific, as well as in Australia. The huge cloud from the eruptions reached a height of 17 miles and then dispersed, following stratospheric winds right round the world and giving rise to strange atmospheric effects for several years. Vivid sunsets were seen as far away as Europe, and the dust had the effect of dimming the sun's rays so that a noticeable cooling was experienced in many countries.

Underwater crater

When the volcanic activity had died down and the island could be examined, its shape had been drastically altered. Instead of being mountainous, the principal feature was now a huge crater, water-filled and 1 000 feet (300m) deep. Danan and Perboewetan had simply disappeared. It was later estimated that over 7 000 million cubic yards of rock (5 600 million cubic metres) had been blasted into the air by the eruptions.

It was a long time before anything like a proper count of the dead and injured could be made. At least 36 500 people died, possibly more because of unreported deaths. Few of these deaths were directly as a result of the eruptions (Krakatoa was uninhabited) but were due to the tsunamis that followed and to destruction of buildings from the shockwaves. As well as those who died, thousands more were left homeless and ruined.

Krakatoa is a vivid example of the awesome powers constantly in motion under the earth's fragile outer crustal layer. It is the greatest eruption so far, but it could yet be exceeded.

Krakatoa erupting in La Nature.

Krakatoa's baby

Despite the devastation, the heat and the thick layer of volcanic ash and pumice, what was left of the island of Krakatoa slowly reverted to its former densely vegetated state. In 1927 vulcanologists observed that growth had begun from the caldera floor left behind by the 1883 eruptions. A new volcano was starting to emerge. It was called Anak Krakatoa, which means 'child of Krakatoa'. It is now several hundred feet high, and minor eruptions from it have already occurred. Krakatoa's death cry was a birth pang as well. The area continues to be studied, and a centenary conference held in 1983 presented new reports.

Mont Pelée

Martinique, 8 May 1902

A devastating holocaust

Only two people survive from a city of thirty thousand.

Martinique is a French colony in the Lesser Antilles group of West Indian islands. A small island with an area of about 420 square miles (1 100 sq km), it has a population of about 350 000, and its main products are sugar, cocoa and rum. Napoleon's famous empress Josephine was born in Martinique. Its capital today is Fort-de-France.

At the beginning of the 20th century, however, St Pierre was Martinique's principal city and seaport, a busy place with a population of 30 000, with many fine houses and well laid-out streets and avenues. The city lay below Mont Pelée, known to be a dormant volcano, but there had been no record of significant eruptions in living memory, so the devastating holocaust of May 1902 could hardly have been forecast.

In April of that year the sleeping giant began to reawaken. Steam rose from the summit, the earth rumbled and groaned, and a small amount of ash fell on the city. As the month went on the activity steadily increased, the smell of sulphur becoming so strong that people were obliged to wear wet handkerchiefs or cloths over their faces as a crude filter. Still there were no real fears of a major eruption, the local newspaper *Les Colonies* assuring its readers that their lives were not in danger and that St Pierre was safe. Unfortunately, that complacent view could not have been more mistaken.

On 5 May there occurred the first powerful eruption. Boiling mud issued from Mont Pelée to follow a valley two miles from St Pierre. A sugar mill in its path was completely destroyed and its 30 workers killed. There was great alarm in St Pierre, and some people left.

Relative calm

The city had two more days of relative calm, and even on 7 May *Les Colonies* ran an interview with a distinguished scientist, M. Landes, in which he said confidently that Mont Pelée 'presented no danger to the people of St Pierre.' In its editorial, the paper expressed surprised that people were leaving, saying: 'Where could one be better off than in St Pierre?' There was a further warning from the island of St Vincent, where on 7 May the volcano La Soufrière — part of the same chain as Pelée — erupted. Scorching hot dust (known to vulcanologists as a *nuée ardente*) covered the island and 2 000 people died.

On 8 May, Mont Pelée provided the answer to the newspaper's question — almost anywhere in the world! At 7:30am the volcano burst its sides, to terrible effect. An enormous explosion was followed by an eruption of molten rock, accompanied by a cloud of scorching gas and dust. Rushing down the slopes of the mountain, it was on the inhabitants of St Pierre before any action could be taken. Fire rained down from the sky, killing virtually all life over an area of about 10 square miles (25 sq km).

Lightning arch

The eruption was watched with horror from Fort-de-France, 14 miles (24km) away. Just before 9am a huge wave crashed onto the shore, then the watching people saw a colossal arch of lightning flash across the sky. A huge black cloud hung over St

Pierre, with lightning and thunder continuing. Later in the day there was a violent storm. Stones the size of large nuts landed on Fort-de-France.

St Pierre, meanwhile, had all but disappeared, burnt to unrecognizable twisted debris. Rescuers who cautiously approached later in the day could not find their way around, so great was the damage: streets and roads had simply vanished. The vicar of Fort-de-France, M Parel, wrote: 'The vivid colouring of houses has been turned to ashen grey . . . no living soul appears in this appalling desert of desolation.'

named Auguste Ciparis, he lay for three days without food or water before being rescued, badly burned. He survived and was pardoned. Ciparis later joined Barnum and Bailey's circus as 'the amazing survivor of Mont Pelée', taking the stage name Ludger Sylbaris. He died in 1929.

Following the eruption, Mont Pelée erected its own grotesque monument to the dead in the form of a spine of cooling lava within its crater. It survived for a year, reaching a height of over 1 000 feet (310m) before collapsing back into the volcano. Since then, Mont Pelée has been quiet, and St Pierre has been rebuilt.

Two survivors

There were, in fact, two people left alive. One was a shoemaker, Leon Comprère-Leandre, who lived on the edge of the city. He described how his throat and lungs were 'bursting with pain' and how, after an hour, he had recovered sufficiently to stagger to the next village, Fonds St Denis. The other survivor was a prisoner in the innermost cell of the city gaol, whose incarceration proved to be his salvation. A negro

Poisonous snakes
In the days before the major eruption, 50 people in St Pierre were killed by highly poisonous fer-de-lance snakes that made their way into the city. More than 100 of the six-foot (2m) snakes, stirred into unusual activity by the movements of the earth, invaded streets, houses, drains and sewers. Some snakes were caught or shot: others fell victims to St Pierre's semi-wild cats, noted for their size and ferocity.

Mount Pelée *erupts, by H C Seppings Wright after Marc Legrand (eyewitness), 1902.*

Kelut

Java, 1919

A catastrophic mud flow

Farmland is ruined and many lives are lost.

Kelut is another of the Indonesian Arc of volcanoes, and is another example of a volcano erupting through its crater lake. Its 1919 eruption displaced almost the entire lake — an estimated 38 million cubic metres of water which combined with earth and other material to form a catastrophic mudflow or 'lahar'.

The lahar flowed outward, collecting more material and expanding until it covered 50 square miles (80 sq km) of productive land. Over a hundred villages and small settlements were partially or completely buried and 5 500 people lost their lives.

Before the eruption, walls 10 feet (3m) high had been erected, but proved useless. Afterwards a different system was tried. A tunnel was driven into the crater in order to lower the level of water in the lake. When Kelut next erupted, in 1966, the tunnel worked and the lahar was much less powerful, but it was found that the eruption had severely damaged the tunnel. A new tunnel has since been constructed.

Parícutin

Mexico, 1943

A new volcano is formed

Amazing growth as a unique natural phenomenon is observed.

Parícutin is not, strictly speaking, a catastrophe, but it is such an extraordinary story that it deserves to be included. On 5 February 1943 tremors commenced. They increased in intensity until on 19 February there were several hundred. The following day, at about 4pm, a volcano was born in a cornfield!

At first a small fissure was noticed, then a column of smoke, and then a small hole, from which smoke and ash was emitted. By next morning a perfect miniature volcano cone 30 feet (10m) high had formed in the field. By midday it was up to 150 feet (45m) and after a week it had reached 400 feet (130m).

Over the course of the next six months, Parícutin (named after the nearest village) continued growing, and throwing out more and more matter. It was estimated to be ejecting at about 2 400 tons a minute. The countryside around was covered in ash over an area 35 miles (60km) in diameter. Everyone was moved out so there were no human casualties.

Parícutin reached a height of 1 500 feet (450m) and continued to be regularly active until March 1952, when it seemed to have blown itself out. By then it was estimated to have ejected 3 000 million tons of rock and ash.

Mount St Helens

USA, 18 May 1980

The biggest logging operation ever

Millions of trees are felled as the volcano blows its top and carpets a large area with ash.

Mount St Helens, in the Cascade Range, Washington State, in the north-west USA, was much photographed as a beautiful symmetrical snow-cone just under 10 000 feet (3 000m) high. That was before May 1980. Now it is truncated, with a vast scoop out of its northern side.

The mountain was known to be volcanic — the Klickitat Red Indians called it Tah-one-lat-clah, or 'Fire Mountain' — but the last recorded activity was in 1857. In March 1980 it began to show signs of activity. From then on there were small eruptions of steam and dust, accompanied by rumblings. Aware that a major eruption could take place, vulcanologists put the mountain under constant watch.

Evacuation order

As activity steadily increased, 1 000 people living around the foot of Mount St Helens were evacuated and warning signs were erected to keep sightseers at a safe distance. By mid-May a fracture nearly three miles (5km) long had appeared, and then the northern face of the mountain began to bulge outward. Clearly something pretty big was about to happen.

St Helens blew at 8:30 on the morning of Sunday 18 May. The eruption, one of the most closely observed of modern times, was dramatically captured on film, deliberately by photographers stationed round the mountain and accidentally by the pilot of a light aircraft flying over it, who was lucky to escape.

Forced outward by the tremendous pressures inside, the bulge broke through the side of the mountain and an enormous rockfall starting sliding down it. With the hole thus opened, the molten material inside blasted out with terrific force. David Johnston, a 30-year-old vulcanologist stationed on a nearby ridge, just had time to shout into his radio 'Vancouver, this is it!' before the fiery plume hit him. He was never found.

Devastated landscape

The volcanic material started landslides and mudflows as well as ejecting large amounts of ash and dust. About a cubic mile of matter was forced out of the mountain, and the landscape was devastated over an area of 232 square miles (1 000 sq km). Everything was dead and grey: 150 miles (250km) of prime fishing rivers had been buried, together with 26 lakes, and it is estimated that over a million animals and birds died. A huge mudflow travelled for 28 miles (45km) down the Toutle River and eventually blocked the shipping channel of the Columbia River.

The area was heavily forested, and the felled trees — snapped off by the blast and debris — presented an extraordinary sight. The eruption felled 130 000 acres (52 000 ha) of forest, containing perhaps six million mature trees — enough timber to build 250 000 houses. Many of these trees have been salvaged, so Mount St Helens carried out the biggest and most rapid logging operation ever seen!

Ash spread for many miles, covering everything. The town of Yakima (population 50 000), 100 miles (160km) east of St Helens, removed 600 000 tons of ash from its streets, houses and gardens. The clean-up operation took 10 weeks and cost $2.2 million. Life was most unpleasant during this period. The *Columbian* newspaper reported from western Canada that 'the ash was everywhere, kicked up by traffic and continually blown about by the wind. When it rained, the powder and moisture combined to make a muddy substance that defied windscreen wipers and window cleaners. People were urged to stay indoors. If they had to venture out, they were advised to wear surgical masks, or at least hold a wet cloth over mouth and nose.'

Harry's mountain

The loss of life was relatively light, due to the warnings given and the evacuations. In all, 60 people died, though the figure could have been higher if it had been a weekday, when 300 forestry workers might have been in the area. One who died was 84-year-old Harry Truman, who lived in a cabin at the foot of the mountain. He said he loved the place and refused point-blank to move. His body was never found.

Harry's mountain is now 1 300 feet (400m) lower than before, and has a crater over a mile wide with walls 2 000 feet (600m) high. Inside the crater, a lava dome 600 feet (180m) high has formed. There have been several further small eruptions and activity will probably continue for some time. St Helens has naturally been the focus of intense activity as vulcanologists take the rare opportunity of studying the activity and effects in the period immediately following a large eruption.

Although this was a large eruption, it was not amongst the biggest ever. Krakatoa pushed out 18 times as much matter, and Tambora 80 times as much. The effects of the St Helens blast were magnified because most of the matter came out horizontally, spewing directly over the surrounding area rather than shooting into the atmosphere. Even so, its ash has circled the globe seven times.

Genesis situation

The eruption naturally attracted great coverage and some public alarm was expressed. Wildlife biologist Bill Ruediger put things into perspective very well: 'Although it's unique as far as our lifetimes are concerned, it's the way nature is. Every couple of thousand years she cleans the slate again. What we have here is almost a Genesis situation.'

Quite a thought. As if to back him up, within a month of the blast small plants appropriately called fireweed started pushing through the ash. Nature was getting to work on the clean slate.

Longest word
The eruption gave medical experts the chance to parade what is thought to be the longest correct word in the English language. They said people were suffering from pneumonoultramicroscopic-silicovolcanoconiosis. Put more simply, it means inhaling contaminated air from a volcano. An uncommon name for an unusual ailment.

Nevado del Ruiz

Colombia, 13 November 1985

A giant lahar

A town is devoured by vast mudslides.

Nevado del Ruiz is the northernmost of the many volcanoes in the Andean chain running up the western side of South America. Reaching to a height of 17 700 feet (5 400m) it is, most of the time, a beautiful snow peak. Occasionally, as on 13 November 1985, it turns into a killer. There had been signs of activity on the mountain for some time, and discussions had taken place as to the advisability of evacuating the people in the towns and villages round its flanks. Evacuation is a complicated and expensive business, however, and the authorities hesitated.

In the afternoon of 13 November the activity increased, and a further meeting was held to discuss evacuation. One of the towns on the agenda was Armero, whose prosperity, ironically, was based on the rich soil left by a previous eruption, in 1845. By the time the decision was taken, it was too late. Armero could not be contacted.

In the evening a large column of ash, steam and rocks was ejected from the volcano. The hot ash, falling on the mountain side, melted part of the mountain's icecap, and the combined water and ash flowed ever more rapidly downward, into the valley of the Lagunillas River, towards Armero.

No escape

The waves of mud, or lahar, hit the town at about midnight. Many people were in bed, and for them there was no escape. Those that did try to flee found themselves overtaken by the lahar and buried. Houses collapsed, burying those inside, as the lahar swept on, engulfing the whole town in mud which set like cement and was up to 11 feet (3.5m) deep.

By the time rescuers reached the town next day, it was too late. A dreadful toll had been exacted and 23 000 of Armero's people lay buried under the mud. One small girl came to symbolize the battle for survival. Rescuers found 12-year-old Omayra Sanchez buried up to her neck in rapidly solidifying mud. She had her feet on her aunt's dead body. For three days the rescue teams tried to get her out without injuring her further, while she remained cheerful and brave. Finally, she turned her face to them and said quietly 'God is calling me now', and she died of heart failure. The whole country mourned her, for her struggles had been seen on television.

Likely lahar paths were known before that terrible night. As with other disasters, it is easy to be wise after the event, but if only someone had been brave enough to give the order for evacuation, many thousands of lives might have been saved.

Lake Nios

In August 1986, there was a very large eruption of poisonous gas from this crater lake in Cameroon, West Africa. There was no lava, no ash, no rocks hurled into the air, just the deadly gas cloud. It covered an area of six square miles (15 sq km) and killed at least 1 500 people and many thousands of animals.

Windstorms

It could be argued that of all the great natural forces, wind is the most fearsome. The destructive power of a hurricane or cyclone is immense and there is something particularly relentless about fierce winds which batters the spirit as well as the body into submission.

Wind, at its strongest and most powerful, can spread fire with astonishing speed. It can send waves and rainstorms across the land with unstoppable force. Of itself it can destroy the strongest building that man has put up. Photographs of towns in hurricane and cyclone areas after the wind has passed show houses reduced to shattered piles of timber and brick as if trodden underfoot by a giant.

This section covers great winds and their effects in many parts of the world. It looks back at winds which may well have changed the course of history, by stopping the mighty fleets of Kubla Khan from conquering Japan and by reducing the ambitions of Philip of Spain's Armada to broken ships and frightened men desperately seeking whatever shelter they could find.

Several Caribbean hurricanes are covered. Each year the islands between South and North America, and parts of the USA, wait anxiously for the hurricane warnings. Winds of up to 200mph (320kph) can wreck the fragile economy of islands with only one or two crops, and can wipe out whole communities. The same applies to the typhoons and cyclones of the east. It is impossible for a young nation such as Bangladesh to cope with the devastation caused by winds such as that which struck in April 1991. Here, as elsewhere in the book, we find international aid being freely given, though it can only minimise the effects, and the next typhoon may be only a few short months away.

The capricious tornadoes or 'twisters' are also included. Often highly localised, they too can be extraordinarily destructive. They are most often associated with the southern states of the USA, but Britain also suffers a surprising number with tornadoes, and some examples are included here. Still in Britain, the great storm of October 1987 which laid waste to historic landscapes in south-east England is included.

Finally there is the Christmas Day hurricane of 1974 that reduced much of the town of Darwin in Northern Australia to rubble. Disasters appear particularly poignant at this time of year, but the wind can bring tragedy at any time. Its behaviour is never predictable and there are some very curious tales of its antics included in these pages.

The Beaufort scale

Beaufort number	Wind speed m/sec	kph	mph	Wind name	Observable wind characteristics
0	1	< 1	< 1	Calm	Smoke rises vertically
1	1	1–5	1–3	Light air	Wind direction shown by smoke drift, but not by wind vanes
2	2	6–11	4–7	Light breeze	Wind felt on face; leaves rustle; vanes moved by wind
3	4	12–19	8–12	Gentle breeze	Leaves and small twigs in constant motion; wind extends light flag
4	7	20–28	13–18	Moderate	Raises dust, loose paper; small branches moved
5	10	29–38	19–24	Fresh	Small trees in leaf begin to sway; crested wavelets on inland water
6	12	39–49	25–31	Strong	Large branches in motion; difficult to use umbrellas; whistling heard in telegraph wires
7	15	50–61	32–38	Near gale	Whole trees in motion; inconvenience walking against wind
8	18	62–74	39–46	Gale	Breaks twigs off trees; impedes progress
9	20	75–88	47–54	Strong gale	Slight structural damage occurs
10	26	89–102	55–63	Storm	Trees uprooted; considerable damage occurs
11	30	103–17	64–72	Violent storm	Widespread damage
12–17	≥ 33	≥ 118	≥ 73	Hurricane/ typhoon	

Sir Francis Beaufort

Admiral Sir Francis Beaufort was born in 1774 in Ireland. He joined the Royal Navy as a boy of 13 and saw active service in several areas. He was wounded twice, at Cornwallis in 1795 and later off the coast of Asia Minor when attacked by pirates while engaged on surveying work.

He developed the Beaufort scale while working on shore telegraphs in Ireland in 1806, and refined it during his period as Hydrographer to the Navy (1829–55). The scale was internationally recognized in 1874 and further refined in the 1920s. Francis Beaufort died in 1857: the Beaufort Sea in the Arctic is also named after him.

Hurricanes through history

From 1274 to 1889

Mighty winds stop naval fleets

From Kubla Khan up to modern times, the wind has wrecked plans for invasion and conquest.

Wherever in the world very strong winds blow, the underlying meteorological cause is similar. The names vary — hurricane, typhoon, cyclone etc — but the pattern is the same. These windstorms occur when millions of tons of very warm air rise from a warm sea and the deflecting effect of the Earth's rotation (known as the Coreolis force) starts the whole mass whirling. Hurricanes are formed in an area from five to 20 degrees either north or south of the Equator. They do not form nearer to the Equator, as the Coreolis force there is almost negligible.

Meteorologists are still uncertain as to how exactly hurricanes start. Their progress is better understood. They usually start moving over the sea at about 12mph (20kph), this rate increasing with hurricanes travelling north. The 'Long Island Express' of 1938 (see p222) reached a speed of 60mph (95kph). At the centre of a hurricane, its 'eye', the air is calm while all around is violence. Hurricane warning services have been developed in several parts of the world, but despite this, such winds still cause vast amounts of damage. In past times they have also been responsible for altering the course of major conflicts.

The kamikaze

Violent winds are a common occurrence in the western Pacific, where they are often called typhoons. The Japanese word *kamikaze,* more recently used for suicide pilots, actually means 'divine wind' and has its origin, it is thought, in two events in the late 13th century.

In 1274, Kubla Khan, head of the great Mongol Empire, sought to invade Japan. He assembled a mighty fleet of nearly 1 000 ships carrying 40 000 men, and set sail from Korea. The Japanese waited, and prayed. Their prayers were answered by the *kamikaze,* which wrecked the great fleet, sinking hundreds of ships and drowning at least 13 000 men.

Seven years later, in 1281, Kubla Khan tried again. This time his fleet was of incredible size: over 4 000 ships carrying an invasion force of nearly 150 000 soldiers which would have been unstoppable. Twice the invaders reached Kyushu, the most southerly of Japan's islands, and were resisted, with great losses on the Japanese side. In August they tried again, but the *kamikaze* was waiting. According to contemporary records almost the entire fleet was sunk with the loss of over 100 000 men. Most were drowned but those who struggled to the shore were killed by Japanese soldiers. Not surprisingly, the Mongols never tried to invade Japan again.

The Spanish Armada

The great fleet assembled by King Philip of Spain to invade Britain in 1588 was decimated by gales, though technically not by a hurricane. Harried by the British fleet through the Channel and into the North Sea, the Spaniards decided to run for home the long way, round the north of Scotland. They hit a run of very bad weather. Modern meteorological study has shown that in August and September 1588 no fewer than 22 depressions tracked in from the Atlantic across Britain and out over the North Sea.

The Spanish ships were caught out time and again. Early on, one report from a ship's log says 'From 13–18 August we experienced squalls, rain and fog with heavy sea, and it was impossible to distinguish one ship from another.' The British admiral Sir Francis Drake noted on 15 August 'A great storm for the time of year.' Winds probably gusted up to 80mph (130kph).

When the battered fleet reached Ireland things were no better. In Blasket Sound on 21 September (the autumn equinox, noted for gales) the mournful tale continues. 'It began to blow with most terrible fury. There sprang up so great a storm with a sea up to the heavens that our cables could not hold and we were driven ashore.' The Armada lost more ships in that storm than in the battle with the English fleet. It is possible that this storm was the remnant of a tropical hurricane.

During the American War of Independence in 1780, hurricanes hit the British, French, Spanish and Dutch fleets: the Spanish attack on the British base at Pensacola, Florida, was abandoned after many of the ships were badly damaged by the storm.

Samoan incident

There was a curious incident in 1889, when a German force of three ships attacked Samoa, in the Pacific. Villages were shelled, and three American and one British warships were ordered to Samoa. As the seven ships manoeuvred in preparation for battle, a hurricane struck the area. The American and German ships sank, and hostilities were forgotten as sailors helped each other. The British vessel, the *Calliope*, with stronger engines, put to sea and rode out the storm. Shortly afterwards the Treaty of Berlin was signed, bringing peace to Samoa. Once more the wind had had the last word.

Task Force typhoon

In December 1944, US Task Force 38 was very badly damaged by a typhoon off the Philippines. Of the 90 ships in the Task Force, 18 were sunk or seriously damaged, 146 aircraft were lost and 800 men killed. War plans had to be altered.

A British hurricane

26–7 November 1703

Damage on land and a maritime disaster

*Great destruction as a fierce
wind batters southern Britain
and the surrounding seas.*

The great storm of November 1703 was
recorded in considerable detail by the
writer Daniel Defoe, author of *Robinson
Crusoe*. He travelled round the country
after the storm, talking to people and
noting the damage he saw. We can thus get
an accurate picture of what happened.

It is clear that a wind of exceptional force
blew across southern Britain. The storm
centre seems to have passed across
Lancashire and Yorkshire, with the fiercest
winds to the south. There had been strong
winds for several days before the hurricane
struck, on the night of 26–7 November. It
reached the west of England around
midnight, London at about 3am, and
cleared the Kent coast an hour or so later.

In the capital, many houses lost their
roofs, part of St James' Palace collapsed,
and between 20 and 30 people were killed
by flying debris. Thousands of trees were
felled. Defoe rode round Kent, where the
scene must have been much like that of
October 1987: he counted 17 000 trees
down before giving up, and also noted over
1 100 houses, out-houses and barns 'blown
quite down' in a scene of 'general desolation'.

Lead carpet

Large buildings of the time commonly had
roofs containing substantial sheets of lead,
and there are several stories of these sheets
being moved bodily for some distance. At
Berkeley in Gloucestershire, 26 sheets of
lead, joined together, were blown off the
church roof and landed 30ft (10m) away
in the churchyard. At Leamington Hastings in Warwickshire, six sheets, weighing
about 2.5 tons, were rolled up like a carpet
and blown 150 yards (45m) by the wind.

About 150 people were killed on land,
but the wind caused a major maritime disaster. Hundreds of ships tried to ride out
the storm in anchorages such as Spithead,
and failed, and it is estimated that 8 000
lives were lost, including at least 1 500 men
of the Royal Navy. The Eddystone lighthouse off Cornwall, built in 1699 by the
eccentric designer Henry Winstanley, was
totally destroyed, taking Winstanley —
who was there at the time, having boasted
that his tower would withstand the fiercest
storm — with it.

Many ships were wrecked on the no-
torious Goodwin Sands, off the Kent coast.
The storm also destroyed some 400 windmills, some of them catching fire as the
friction generated in the machinery by the
excessive speed of rotation created heat.
The Bishop of Bath and Wells, Dr Kidder,
and his wife were victims of the storm,
killed when chimneys crashed through
their roof. This was one of the commonest
causes of death and injury on that terrible
night.

The Mayor's rescue

One of the heroes of the storm was Thomas
Powell, Mayor of Deal in Kent. Seeing the
plight of shipwrecked sailors on the sands,
he offered local men five shillings (25p), a
considerable sum at the time, for each man
rescued, and more than 200 were saved in
this way. Powell acted because Customs
officers refused to do anything to help the
stranded sailors, who would have been
drowned when the tide rose again to cover
the sands.

British tornadoes

From 1091 to 1981

A surprising frequency of storms

---

*Violent winds cause damage,
death and destruction.*

It is not generally appreciated that Britain has one of the highest annual densities of tornadoes of any country in the world, due to its position at the eastern edge of a major oceanic tornado track. In more recent years, with more attention paid to the phenomenon and more careful recordings, over 100 tornadoes a year have been recorded. In 1981 there were more than 150, with 100 of them hitting an area from North Wales to Eastern England on one day, Monday 23 November.

There are records of tornadoes going back to 17 October 1091, when a 'whirlwind' struck London, demolishing or severely damaging over 600 houses. Two people were killed at the church of St Mary le Bow. Another famous tornado occurred on Sunday 21 October 1638 at the small, picturesque village of Widecombe-in-the-Moor, in Devon. The church was full, and service had just begun when a violent wind arose, very suddenly. There was a tremendous explosion, which wrecked the church. It is recorded that the congregation 'fell down into their seats, and some upon their knees, some on their faces, and some on each other, with a great cry, they all giving themselves up for dead'. Little wonder that the people were 'sore affrighted' and thought that the wrath of God had descended upon them.

Work of the Devil

The tornado was accompanied by ball lightning. People were hurled into the air, some having their brains battered out on stone pillars, others surviving unhurt. One lady, a Mistress Ditford, 'Had her gowne, two waistcoates, and linen next her body burned clean off.' About 60 people were killed, and the poem composed about the tragedy by the village schoolmaster can still be seen at the (new) church today. For a long time afterwards, it was believed that the Devil haunted Widecombe.

October seems to be a prime tornado month in Britain. On 27 October 1913, a tornado rushed up the English–Welsh border for over 100 miles from Barry to Chester, killing five people and causing great damage. Another series of severe tornadoes swept from Buckinghamshire to Cambridgeshire, a distance of 65 miles (105km), on 21 May 1950. They were accompanied by black clouds, torrential downpours of rain, lightning and huge hailstones of up to two inches (5cm) diameter. Whole orchards were wrecked in this storm and many houses lost their roofs.

London was hit by at least 30 tornadoes between 1900 and 1981. One of the most violent was on 8 December 1954 when many trees were blown down, houses were damaged, and 12 people were injured. The Royal Meteorological Society now has records of about 2 000 tornadoes of various strengths.

Death by hailstone

In May 1140, the scribe John of Worcester tells us, there was 'a very violent whirlwind' at Welsburn in Warwickshire (a village now called Wellesbourne). He speaks of 'a hideous darkness extending from the earth to the sky' — an excellent description of a twister — and says that 40 houses were severely damaged and that an unfortunate woman was killed when struck by a large hailstone.

Galveston's great storm

8 September 1900

The Texas town is inundated

A hurricane from the Gulf of Mexico brings appalling floods, killing thousands.

The Gulf of Mexico is prime hurricane country. Violent storms form over its waters every year. Their track then varies; some move east, or north-east towards Florida, while others head more directly north towards the coastal towns of Texas. The storm of 8 September 1900 left in its wake one of the greatest natural disasters the USA has suffered.

Hurricane warning was rudimentary at that time; furthermore, the town of Galveston was largely built on a low-lying barrier island, with underlying sands. Much of the problem arose not from the hurricane's wind, which certainly caused a great deal of damage, but from the enormous flood waves brought with it. The town was simply inundated.

As if that were not bad enough, the hurricane was accompanied by tremendous rainstorms. One estimate indicates that as much as 2 000 million tons of water fell on the area, adding to the rapidly rising floods. With the wind having already weakened many houses, the floods found easy prey as they rushed inland.

Darkest horror

When the storm had passed, Galveston had lost over 3 000 houses and 6 000 of its population were dead. The town had a population of about 40 000 at the time, and most of the survivors were either homeless or living in damaged houses. Businesses of all kinds were wrecked, roads and railways cut. Writing in *National Geographic* magazine after visiting Galveston, W J McGee was moved to record that: 'The darkest horror of American history has fallen on our southern coast; a city comparable in population and wealth with Ephesus and Sodom of old, with Herculaneum and Pompeii of appalling memory, and with earthquake-wrecked Lisbon of later centuries, is blotted out in a night . . . the morning's sun rises on a scene of suffering and devastation hardly paralleled in the history of the world.'

Sea wall

A little over the top, perhaps, and the people of Galveston might not have welcomed the comparison with Sodomites, but the town certainly suffered grievous damage that September day. If anything good comes out of disaster, in this case it was a determination to make Galveston as weatherproof as human engineering could devise. Between town and sea, Galveston built a vast sea wall 11 miles (18km) long. At its foot is a 'riprap' of loosely piled granite up to 40 feet (12m) wide and three feet (one metre) high. The wall itself is of concrete, 16 feet (five metres) wide at the base and rising 20 feet (six metres) in a backward-sloping concave curve.

It was tested to the full when Hurricane Carla, the fiercest since 1900, struck in September 1961. The hurricane centre was some miles away, but Galveston was still battered. By various means, quite a lot of water did get in, but the wall kept most of it out, and only two people are known to have died in Galveston as the result of Carla's efforts.

The Long Island Express

21 September 1938

The eastern USA is ravaged

A severe hurricane continues much further north than usual.

Most Caribbean hurricanes hit the southern states of the USA, or are deflected eastwards out into the Atlantic, where they lose their force. Those that strike land can cause immense damage.

On 2 September 1935 a violent hurricane hit Florida. Its winds were estimated to have reached over 200mph (320kph) and at Long Key a barometric reading of 26.35 inches of pressure recorded at the time is still the lowest ever recorded in the Western Hemisphere. During that storm over 300 people were killed, including more than 200 veterans of World War I who were on vacation.

Unusual combination

On 20 September 1938 an unusual combination of pressure zones, with high pressure to both west and east, left a developing hurricane with only a relatively narrow channel to follow — up the eastern seaboard of the USA towards Long Island, thus earning its nickname of the Long Island Express. The hurricane was travelling at 60mph (100kph) with winds of much greater force circulating within and around it. The observatory at Blue Hills, Massachusetts, recorded a sustained wind of 121mph (190kph) for five minutes, and a peak gust of 183mph (290kph).

The worst of the storm struck Long Island and New England, causing immense damage. Houses were blown down and flattened, and an estimated 275 million trees were lost to the storm. In many places, their ripped-up roots damaged power cables and gas or water pipes. The storm affected seven million people, and the damage to property, land and business was later estimated to be $350 million, greater than any other American natural disaster.

White windows

The force of the wind carried sea salt some 120 miles (200km) inland where it whitened windows in Vermont. Felled trees cut the lines to over half a million telephones and for a time after the storm messages from Boston to New York had to be sent across the Atlantic and back again! The insurance companies faced claims from the owners of 25 000 cars which were severely damaged. One of the strangest tales was that of a two-storey house in Madison, Connecticut which was blown half a mile and turned upside down, but without a single window-pane being broken.

The Long Island Express took 600 lives. Other storms have killed more people, but this one is remembered, perhaps because of its unusual track and because it struck at an area normally safe from such destruction.

Naming the wind

Hurricane forecasting has taken place since 1898, and since 1960, weather satellites have given us the ability to see large weather systems developing. Until 1978, hurricanes were given only girls' names, but since then boys' names have been used as well. If a hurricane proves particularly devastating, its name is not used again for ten years.

Typhoon Vera

Japan, September 1959

One of the worst storms of the century

Three prefectures including the city of Nagoya suffer great damage and loss of life.

Typhoons in September are a regular occurrence in Japan. They usually cause damage and casualties, but occasionally the islands are struck by a storm of exceptional ferocity, against which no defence is proof. Such a storm hit the island of Honshu in late September 1959.

There had already been one typhoon earlier in the month. On 17 September a storm swept across the sea between Korea and Japan. Many small boats were sunk and 15 people were reported killed. But this was nothing compared with what was to come when Typhoon Vera arrived.

The typhoon struck Honshu, Japan's largest island holding its main cities and ports, late on 26 September with tremendous winds registering up to 135mph (210kph) on a 450-mile (700km) front. The western prefectures of Aichi, Gifu and Mie suffered most damage. This area contains the major industrial city and port of Nagoya, with a population of two million, and also other substantial towns including Kuwana and Nagishima.

Torrential rain

The typhoon arrived at the worst possible time, when the tide was already high. The winds swept huge waves up to 15 feet (4.5m) high inland, drowning low-lying areas, while continuing to batter houses where the sea could not reach. The typhoon was accompanied by torrential rain

causing very serious flooding. Early reports said that 90 per cent of Kuwana was under water and that parts of Nagoya were buried under mud, silt and debris. An initial death toll of about 800 was given, but this was to prove an underestimate. It took some time for rescue teams to reach the area, and they found many houses under water up to roof level. The damage was said to be the worst experienced since the end of hostilities in 1945.

As more reports came in, it became clear that a major disaster had struck western Honshu. Nearly 300 ships and boats were sunk and hundreds more damaged, destroying fishermens' livelihoods. In and around Nagoya, the amount of damage was almost impossible to take in. Thirty thousand homes were destroyed, another 80 000 badly damaged and over a million people were either homeless or facing the long job of restoring their damaged homes.

Town submerged

Three days after the typhoon struck, the death toll passed 3 000 and was still rising. A reporter who commandeered a small boat to reach the town of Nangyo, not far from Nagoya, spoke to the mayor there, who was in despair, saying 'I feel as if my arms and legs have been cut off — the entire town is submerged.' In Nagoya itself, floods caused by the typhoon and the swollen rivers Kiso and Nagara extended from the sea front for ten miles inland. In the harbour area alone 12 000 houses were completely under water. A relief base at Tshushima had to be abandoned when it was flooded.

Rescue workers flying over the area could see many people stranded on rooftops who had been without food or water for three days. Disease, particularly dysentery, began to add to the casualty figures as desperate people drank polluted water. The relief operation was one of the largest ever mounted for a natural disaster in Asia. The army was mobilised and 9 000 men were sent to the affected areas with trucks, barges, helicopters, landing craft and other aids. An emergency session of the Diet, Japan's parliament, voted £4 million for immediate work. The US Navy sent an aircraft carrier to help.

National emergency

On 1 October, five days after the typhoon, the floods had still not subsided in many places, and thousands of people were taking what shelter they could in higher buildings, schools and factories. It was estimated that 250 000 people still had no proper shelter. By now nearly 1 000 cases of dysentery had been reported. The death toll had risen to 4 000 with a further 1 100 missing; it was expected that most of those would also be dead. The number injured was reported as 15 000.

The disaster was treated as a national emergency. Many areas only reclaimed from the sea in the past century were once again under water, and the task of rebuilding the shattered city of Nagoya and the other towns in the three prefectures would take years. (Nearly seven centuries earlier, the invading fleets of Kubla Khan had felt the tremendous force of a typhoon in the waters off Japan. When a storm as violent as Vera arrives, it is as if all the cursed forces of war strike in a single night.)

Worst storm
The final casualty figures exceeded the previous worst Japanese storm this century, the Muroto typhoon of 1934. That storm left 3 000 people dead, thousands more injured, and destroyed many houses, but Typhoon Vera caused death, injury and destruction on an even greater scale.

Hurricane Camille

USA, 16 August 1969

The greatest storm of its kind

Southern and eastern States are battered by winds reaching 200mph.

Hurricane Camille gathered its strength over Cuba on 15 August 1969. By the time it left that island to track north across the Gulf of Mexico, its winds had reached 115mph (185kph) and had caused serious damage to Cuba's tobacco and coffee bean crops. That was, however, just a mild foretaste of what was to come.

Camille smashed into Mississippi and Louisiana on 16 August, and left a vast trail of destruction as the winds reached 200mph (320kph). Huge oil tankers snapped their anchor chains and were driven ashore; smaller boats were flung through the air. Coastal towns suffered severely.

In Pass Christian, Mississippi, every house was damaged; the same was true of Biloxi, and Gulfport was also largely wrecked. In the latter town, 23 people who had ignored warnings and had instead started a 'hurricane party' were found dead; the town suffered serious problems from looters in the days that followed and martial law had to be imposed.

Violent rainstorm

Camille continued its assault, tracking north then east over Virginia, where a rainstorm of extraordinary force deposited 10 inches (25cm) in an hour in some areas. The town of Richmond was seriously affected, with the historic 'Tobacco Row' warehouses badly damaged. The James River flooded, affecting a number of towns and villages.

The hurricane left over 300 people dead and nearly 100 000 homeless. Property damage was estimated at over $6 million in south-east Louisiana alone, and at $18 million in Virginia. The US government declared Mississippi and Louisiana as disaster areas and a large-scale Federal Aid programme got under way immediately with each state receiving an advance payment of $1 million for essential work in restoring services and repairing roads, bridges and railway lines.

Dr Robert Simpson of America's National Hurricane Centre described Camille as 'probably the greatest storm of any kind that has ever affected this nation'. There was considerable criticism afterwards about the lack of proper warning. Some of the casualties could perhaps have been avoided if people had taken notice of warnings, but you cannot force people to move if they are unwilling. Since 1969, hurricane warning systems have been greatly improved, but should a wind of that ferocity come again, and it is almost certain that at some time it will, there is still very little that those in its path can do except flee.

Low pressure

As hurricanes draw up water from the sea, the atmospheric pressure within them falls. When Camille was at its height, a pressure of 26.61 inches (901 millibars) was recorded at the storm centre. Among USA storms, only the 1935 Labour Day hurricane was lower — it dropped to 26.35 inches (892mb). Normal atmospheric pressure at sea level is 29.92 inches (1013mb). The British record low is 27.33 inches (925.5mb) in Scotland on 26 January 1884.

Midwest tornadoes

2–3 April 1974

More than 100 'twisters' strike

Five American states are declared disaster areas as violent winds cause major damage.

In early April 1974 a series of tornadoes of ferocious strength hit the American Midwest. Eleven states were affected, and in five of them — Alabama, Indiana, Kentucky, Ohio and Tennessee — damage was so bad that President Nixon granted disaster status, making large-scale federal aid available for rescue and rebuilding. Ohio was the worst affected state. Xenia, a town of 25 000 people, was devastated, with houses, offices and other buildings completely smashed. Bundles of banknotes from one of the town's banks were found several days later 200 miles (320km) away. The tornado hit the town at 4:40pm A survivor described the experience: 'I saw the dark cloud, then it must have touched down and I knew it was time to go. Seven of us got down on the floor of the kitchen. The windows went all at once, you could hear them breaking all over the house. Then all I could hear was the wind. Mud and glass were flying around, hitting everybody. The rushing wind went on and on'. Only 30 people were killed in Xenia, but thousands were left homeless.

Clear warning signs

Tornadoes in this part of the world are usually formed through a collision between weather systems carrying warm air up from the Gulf of Mexico and much colder air down from the Rocky Mountains. The warm air, seeking to rise, is trapped until it finds an escape. If this escape is a small 'hole' in the cold clouds the hot air rushes upwards in a swirl, forming the tornado. There is often thunder and lightning, rain and hail. The warning signs are clear from the ground — a dark black cloud and a feeling of humid heat. The late afternoon, between 4pm and 6pm, is prime 'tornado time', and March to July are the months when they occur most, the temperature gradient over the area being greatest in those months.

Tornadoes are capricious. Houses are at risk because there is a pressure differential between the near-vacuum inside the twister and the rooms of the house. Air is sucked out of the building, which can literally blow apart in seconds. Other houses may be untouched, or partially damaged. There are numerous stories of tornadoes lifting people, cars, even trains in the air and depositing them some way away unharmed except for the shock.

Communities badly affected by the April 1974 tornadoes included Brandenburg, Kentucky, which virtually disappeared; Depaun, Indiana; and Jasper, Alabama, where a radio announcer told his audience: 'We can't talk to the police department about the tornado — the building just blew away.' Tornadoes were seen to go down one side of a 1 000-foot (300m) deep canyon in Tennessee and up the other wide, and clean over Betty Mountain in Georgia, which is 3 300 feet (1 000m) high.

Storm cellars

When the clearing-up operation got under way, it was found that 324 people had been killed, many thousands were homeless and property worth an estimated $400 million had been destroyed. Yet these states are used to tornadoes and know how to cope with them. Many houses have 'storm cellars' specially constructed for tornado shelter. Your best chance of survival in a tornado is to get into a hole, ditch, or below ground in some way. Large, open-plan buildings like schools, swimming pools and sports halls are severely at risk.

On this occasion the force of the wind was just too great for even strongly-constructed buildings. Since 1974 the early warning systems have been improved, but damage and loss of life could never be totally eliminated.

There was a very severe tornado on 18 March 1925. It formed in the middle of the day over Missouri and in the next three hours travelled over 200 miles, crossing southern Illinois and finally blowing itself out just inside Indiana. It was exceptional in every respect, being up to a mile wide at times and travelling at up to 70mph (110kph). According to contemporary reports, the storm cloud was so close to the ground there was no room for the normal 'twister' vortex.

Blown up a tree

The tornado struck towns and villages with no forewarning given and caused tremendous damage. About 3 000 houses were wrecked and 689 people were killed. Property loses totalled $17 million.

On 25 April 1955 the village of Udal, Kansas, was shattered by a violent twister. Of its 200 houses, 170 were completely destroyed, but one was left undamaged — another example of the capricious nature of tornadoes. Eighty people died and others had amazing escapes. One man, Fred Dye, was blown up into a tree, suffering only minor injuries. The village barber, Henry Norris, was asleep when the tornado hit and woke up, unhurt, in the street, with no idea how he got there.

There was another severe tornado strike on 11 April 1965 — Palm Sunday. A total of 37 twisters ravaged the Midwest, killing 270 people. There was an even worse disaster on 18 March 1925 when one very large tornado whirled across much of Illinois, Indiana and Mississippi. Over 600 people were killed. The April 1974 tornadoes were however notable for the very large area they covered and the amount of damage inflicted.

Franklin's whirlwind

Benjamin Franklin experienced a small tornado in 1755, and as was his nature, immediately carried out an experiment. He wrote: 'As it is a common opinion that a shot fired through a water-spout will break it, I tried to break this little whirlwind by striking my riding-whip frequently through it, but without any effect.' The well-known story *The Wizard of Oz* is based on a tornado. The heroine Dorothy and her dog Toto are drawn up into a twister which takes them 'over the rainbow' to the magical land of Oz.

Modern scientists also chase tornadoes. Teams from the national Tornado Intercept Project go out with a mechanism called TOTO (Totable Tornado Observatory), a cylinder packed with recording instruments, which they try to place in the path of a twister. Much valuable information has been gathered in this way.

Better buildings

Modern buildings in tornado-prone areas are designed to cope with the effects of the twisters' attack. Buildings properly designed and built of reinforced steel and concrete now often survive almost undamaged. This technology dates back to the 1930s, and one of its first tests was in Albany, Georgia on 10 February 1940. The new Hotel Gordon survived a tornado intact while buildings all around it were flattened. Similar scenes were recorded in Topeka, Kansas, during a severe tornado on 8 June 1966. New buildings at Washburn University had only glass damage, while older buildings were severely affected.

Hurricane Fifi

18 November 1974

Honduras is devastated

A small nation is physically and economically shattered by the effects of a tropical storm.

Honduras is one of the poorer nations of Central America. Politically unstable, and heavily reliant on foreign aid, its home economy largely rests on the production and export of bananas; some 15% of the world crop originates here. The hurricane which swept across Honduras in November 1974 wiped out virtually a whole year's crop, a catastrophic disaster for such a small state.

Radio services in the area broadcast warnings the night before Fifi arrived, but few real precautions were taken. The hurricane arrived in the early hours of 18 November. Winds reaching 140mph (225kph) were accompanied by torrential rains — it is estimated that as much as 24 inches (60cm) of rain fell in 36 hours.

Bodies burnt

The town of Choloma was particularly badly affected, losing half its population of 6 000 and virtually all of its houses. Many died not directly because of the wind but when a vast flood of water from the Choloma River surged through the town, battering houses and covering everything in mud.

The hurricane swept right through the country. There was great destruction in and around the second city, San Pedro Sula. In this area alone it was estimated that 400 000 people were left homeless and at risk from disease and starvation.

Rescue services did not arrive in some areas for several days, and those who had survived the wind and flood were left clinging to roofs or trees. Nearly all main roads were cut and many bridges fell.

Food was sent by other Central American nations, by Mexico, Cuba, the USA and Britain. Asked about the threat of starvation, the then US Ambassador, Philip Sanchez, said: 'You ask how people can starve in three or four days. These people were hungry before the hurricane'. A terse comment on a desperate situation. The full toll from the capriciously-named Fifi is hard to establish, but it is thought that perhaps 10 000 died.

Banana crop destroyed

The economic effects were particularly severe. Much of the banana crop was controlled by Honduran subsidiaries of two large American companies, Standard Fruit and United Fruit. Standard's extensive plantations in the Aguan Valley were almost totally destroyed, and of the 28 000 acres cultivated by United Fruit, 20 000 were flooded and a further 5 000 flattened by the wind. The roads and railways used for taking the bananas to the ports were also destroyed. It would take years to rebuild the industry.

Hurricane Janet

Severe storms affect the Central American countries in most years, though the warning system is now much improved. On 27 September 1955, Hurricane Janet took a swipe at Mexico. The town of Chetumal was directly in the hurricane's path and took the full force of the storm. Next day, only four of its 2 500 houses were left standing.

A Christmas Day hurricane
25 December 1974

Devastation in Darwin

The Northern Australian town is battered by ferocious winds.

Christmas is a memorable time of year for people in many countries throughout the world: a time for rejoicing, for celebrations and for family reunions. The people of Darwin, the largest town in Australia's Northern Territory, will however remember Christmas 1974 for the wrong reasons. On that day the town and the surrounding area were battered by Hurricane Tracy, a wind of ferocious force. Ships in the harbour were sunk or tossed onto rocks, and the town was devastated. The tragedy provided a severe initial test for Australia's new Natural Disaster Organization, set up only two months beforehand.

Before the wind struck, Darwin was a thriving town of about 40 000 people, a centre for the agricultural and mining country round about and a major port. After Tracy had done her worst, more than half the population were homeless and 90 per cent of the buildings had been destroyed or damaged. The town's meteorological station recorded a windspeed of 137 knots before it stopped working.

Risk of disease

With high temperatures and humidity, there was a serious risk of disease spreading rapidly. Potable water was in very short supply and in the days immediately following the hurricane, more children were hospitalized through drinking polluted water than through the direct effects of the wind.

There was also a serious shortage of acceptable food, and a major airlift was started to evacuate thousands of people until the town could begin to be restored. The hurricane had severed all main power lines. Seven ships of the Royal Australian Navy anchored in Darwin harbour bringing emergency generators and other vitally needed equipment. Within a week, nearly 20 000 people had been airlifted out of Darwin to temporary homes elsewhere.

Photographs of the wrecked town shocked the world. It looked as if it had been hit by a massive explosion. Whole streets were flattened, with houses reduced to piles of rubble and timber. There was inevitably some loss of life, though not, perhaps, as much as might have been feared. About 50 people died in the town itself and 25 or so more in the harbour area and on vessels moored there.

The rebuilding of Darwin began under the guidance of a specially constituted commission set up by the Australian government. The town was redesigned as a smaller community, with houses built, as far as possible, to reduce the risk of such severe damage occurring again in future. The population level was set at 10 000 but its position as the principal town of a large state means that Darwin will almost certainly grow beyond this.

Santa has arrived
Mrs Vivien Buffery told after the hurricane of how she had taken refuge in a shed with her two small children, Louise and Jean. When they asked her what had happened, she told them that Santa Claus had arrived and landed on the roof. 'They seemed to accept it' she said. It was not Santa, however, but Tracy, bringing gifts that nobody wanted.

Hurricane David

29–30 August 1979

Disaster strikes Caribbean islands

Loss of life and severe economic damage as two hurricanes batter the West Indies.

Hurricane David — and to a lesser extent Hurricane Frederick, which rapidly followed it — seriously affected two countries with very similar names, so a word of explanation about them may help. Dominica is a small island in the chain that runs south through the Caribbean. A former British colony, it gained independence in 1978. The island, which is mountainous, has a population of about 80 000. Its economy is based on the production of bananas and coconuts.

The Dominican Republic is the eastern half of the large island also containing Haiti. A former colony of Spain, it has suffered considerable internal unrest for most of this century. The island has a population of about 7 000 000. Like Dominica, it is mountainous. Sugar is the main export crop, and tourism is also very important to the country's economy.

The Caribbean sees the formation of hurricanes every year. They mostly track north towards the Gulf of Florida, and the most violent storms can cause terrible damage to the islands as they pass over. Hurricane warning systems have improved greatly, but there is still little that can be done in the face of the most severe winds. Hurricane David certainly fitted into that category.

No reports

The hurricane battered Dominica on 29 August 1979. There were virtually no re-ports from the island for two days, as all communication lines had been cut. A radio link was restored with the arrival of the Royal Navy destroyer *Fife*. She reported that damage was so widespread her crew were having to concentrate on one area of the island's capital, Roseau. Their most urgent job was to try to repair the roof of the Princess Margaret hospital, blown off by the hurricane.

The people of Dominica — and its neighbouring islands, Guadeloupe and Martinique — received 48 hours warning of the hurricane. But the storm was moving along a front 300 miles (480km) wide, with winds of up to 150mph (240kph). The government of Dominica reported that up to 60 000 people were believed to be homeless — three-quarters of the entire population. The vital banana crop was wrecked, as it was on Guadeloupe and Martinique also, and these small, poor islands faced economic disaster.

Typhoid epidemic

When reporters reached Dominica some days later they were appalled at the scale of the damage. One described the island as looking as if a nuclear bomb had hit it. The death toll was estimated at over 1 000 and there were growing fears of a typhoid epidemic as people drank polluted water. Most of the houses in Roseau were either destroyed or seriously damaged, as were all the schools and hospitals on the island. An international relief effort was mounted, with naval craft providing manpower. Teams of sailors searched wreckage for survivors and helped to restore basic services to the shattered island.

Hurricane David moved north-westward after leaving Dominica and took an equally severe toll of the Dominican Republic. The capital, Santo Domingo, was declared a disaster area as the hurricane struck, causing great destruction through wind and floods. On 12 September the country's government reported 1 300 dead, over 50 000 injured, 100 000 homeless and 500 people still missing. Most of the sugar cane crop had been destroyed.

Within days, Hurricane Frederick also passed through the Caribbean. It was much less violent than David and on Dominica, there was little left for it to destroy, but it set the relief operation back. In the Dominican Republic, towns and villages were left without power for several weeks. This added to the problem as there was virtually no way to boil water, and without that precaution disease spread quickly. Cases of dysentery and gastro-enteritis were soon reported among children and the elderly. Hospitals were also without power and were unable to treat the injured properly. There were even reports of emergency operations carried out without anaesthetic.

Cut by glass

Statistics alone cannot give any impression of what it is like to suffer the battering of one of these exceptionally violent storms. The wind makes conversation impossible — apart from the terrible roaring noise, it distorts the facial muscles. No structure is totally safe and the light houses common in this part of the world soon succumb. Hurricanes are frequently accompanied by torrential rainfall and tidal waves batter coastal areas, adding to the damage and misery. Flying debris is a serious danger, and after David had passed there were reports of numerous casualties on Dominica cut by glass slivers.

For countries whose economy is at best precariously based on one main crop, with smaller subsidiary crops, a disaster of this kind takes many years to recover from, even with generous international aid. Crops still have to be replanted, houses and public buildings rebuilt, and services restored. News of such disasters also affects tourist confidence, further depressing the economy of the area.

Continuing north

Hurricane David continued up the eastern seaboard of the USA, causing considerable damage in Florida. The wind had diminished to a mere 90mph (140kph) but still caused widespread flooding and damage to property. People living on the coast were told to evacuate their houses. States as far north as New York were affected by torrential rainfall as the hurricane gradually died. Fifteen people were killed in the USA.

The one the weathermen missed

England, 15 October 1987

Famous landscapes damaged

Violent wind strikes an unprepared people.

Although the loss of life in the 1987 English hurricane was relatively light — 19 people lost their lives — it created an enormous impact, partly because of the severe effect it had on a number of very famous landscapes, and partly because of claims that it had not been properly forecast.

To take the second point first, it is true that a TV weatherman denied that there was a hurricane on the way on the day before it struck. He did forecast strong winds, and was defended after the storm by the director-general of the Meteorological Office, who said 'The Met Office said there would not be a hurricane, and there was no hurricane'. This is skating on somewhat thin ice, to mix metaphors. The criteria for hurricane-force winds is a sustained 73mph (117kph) and that ferocity was certainly reached, and recorded, at a number of places including Gorleston in Norfolk and Dover in Kent, where the peak gust was 85mph (135kph). The forecast was hampered by the withdrawal of a French weathership from the Atlantic and a strike in France which delayed advance forecasting information.

No trains

The storm intensified as it crossed England from the south-west, and the worst of the damage was in the most densely populated part of the country, the south-east area, particularly Sussex and Kent. The day after the storm, nearly all main roads in Kent were blocked by debris, especially fallen trees, and no trains could be run anywhere on British Rail's Southern region, or out of Liverpool Street Station in London to the Eastern Region, again because of trees on the lines.

Three million households and businesses were without electricity and 150 000 telephone lines had been cut. Villages, especially in Kent, were cut off from the outside world, with no power and roads impassable through debris. What seemed most shocking of all was that prized landscapes and gardens were utterly devastated by the force of the wind.

Toys Hill in Kent, owned by the National Trust, was almost stripped of its superb trees. The park surrounding Petworth House, landscaped by Capability Brown in the mid 18th century, was similarly affected. The trees lost included the largest sweet chestnut in Britain. At Scotney Castle, another National Trust property, the long driveway was invisible under a mass of fallen trees and branches. A 300–year–old lime tree, 110 feet (35m) high, was blown down. The famous trees after which the town of Sevenoaks in Kent was named were badly affected. There were two lines of seven oaks, and of the 14, nine were lost. They have since been replanted but it will be many years before they form a cohesive group again.

Damage at Kew

The Royal Botanical Gardens at Kew, west of London, suffered grievous damage. The gardens are world-renowned for their rare trees, shrubs and plants; the deputy curator, Alan Beyer, described it as 'the worst day in the entire history of Kew'. Over 500 trees, many of them very rare specimens, were destroyed and hundreds more damaged, including some dating from before the establishment of the gardens in 1759. The artist Robert Games constructed a large carved mural from wood taken from some of these trees, as a memorial to them.

There was undoubtedly very severe damage to many woodlands, but naturalists urged that some of the fallen timber should be left, as it provides a valuable habitat for many forms of life. It was also pointed out that storms such as this occur with reasonable regularity, and that woods would recover, given a little help: replanting should not be rushed. Instant replacement of landscapes that have taken centuries to evolve is simply impossible, and it is thought that as many as 15 million trees may have been lost in this storm.

Saving windmills

One of many stories of bravery came from Sussex, where a group of determined people worked in awful conditions for several hours during the night to save the historic pair of windmills on the South Downs called Jack and Jill. The wind was causing the mill sails to turn despite the brakes being on, and the friction thus created inside was threatening to cause a fire. A small blaze did indeed start, but thanks to the efforts of a human chain of people using water from a house 40 yards (35m) away, it was brought under control. Meanwhile gravel was piled around the braking mechanism to reinforce it and stop the sails. Considerable damage was caused, and the sails were jammed, but at least the mills were saved. Hundreds of mills had been lost in the great storm of 1703.

The 1987 hurricane brought communities together through hardship in the same way as a war does; a similar thing happened in the 1953 floods. The wind was of a force that might be thought quite common in other parts of the world, but for southern England it was exceptional, and it will long be remembered.

Storms in 1990

Another severe wind struck southern England on Thursday 25 January 1990. This one was forecast correctly but it still caused a great deal of damage, and actually led to more deaths than the 1987 storm. Roads were blocked by overturned vehicles, those affected including a number of motorways. The Selborne Yew, a tree in Hampshire believed to be 1 500 years old, was overturned, after surviving the storms of 1287, 1703, 1666 and 1987. In a unique rescue operation, the tree was lifted, carefully pruned, and set back into its hole, and is apparently still alive. During the storm the well-known actor Gordon Kaye was seriously injured when part of an advertising hoarding came through the windscreen of his car.

The storm was followed by further bad weather, with gales, torrential rain and snow. On 26 February 1990 a number of coastal areas suffered inundation, the worst affected being Towyn in North Wales, where hundreds of people had to be evacuated. A relief fund was set up and the government gave £150 000 to help with rebuilding work.

Illustrations on following page show storm damage in London.

Bangladesh inundated

30 April 1991

A cyclone causes massive loss of life

Vast areas are drowned by one of the century's most powerful windstorms.

The Bay of Bengal area has long been liable to assault by cyclones, but that of 30 April 1991 was one of the most powerful, possibly the strongest of all, this century. The full death toll may not be known for several years, as the after-effects of the disaster including disease and malnutrition continue to take their toll.

Winds measured at up to 145mph (230kph) hammered into the densely-populated coastal areas of Bangladesh at the end of April, accompanied by waves up to 20ft (6m) high, and with heavy rain both during and after the storm. A vast area of low-lying land, including a number of islands, was totally inundated, and ten million people were made homeless — nearly 10 per cent of Bangladesh's entire population. For a young country without major resources of its own it was far more than they could cope with, and an international programme of aid was immediately started.

Short history

Bangladesh (the name means 'Free Bengal') only came into being in 1972. Before that the area was known as East Pakistan. In its short, turbulent history, two leaders have been assassinated, another deposed and charged with corruption, and martial law has been imposed for lengthy periods. The first free elections were held only a month before the typhoon: Khalida Zia,

widow of one of the former leaders, was elected as prime minister. It is little wonder that the country, one of the world's poorest and most densely-populated, with an average life expectancy of only 50 years, found it impossible to cope with a natural disaster of this scale.

To make matters even worse, the floods came just before the harvest was due, so that reserves of food were already at a low level. Thousands of head of livestock were also killed by the typhoon or flood, and their bloated corpses added to the threat of disease. A journalist visiting the area the day after the typhoon struck described it as 'looking like the whole area had been carpet-bombed, with damaged houses and craters made by the tidal surge. People were wearing torn, dirty clothes and appeared to be in shock'. Hardly surprising, when you try to imagine what had befallen them.

Used to tragedy

The Bay of Bengal area is subject not only to attack from the sea in the form of typhoons but also to regular flooding as the deltas of the two great rivers in the area, the Ganges and the Brahmaputra, overflow as a result either of massive snowmelt from the Himalayas or from the monsoon rains. There were terrible floods in 1974, only two years after the state of Bangladesh had been established. The monsoon went on for seven weeks, a longer period than usual, with up to five inches of rain a day falling. By mid-July half the country — an area of 15 000 square miles (37 500 sq km) — was under water and 800 000 houses had been destroyed. Not unnaturally, the people have developed a somewhat fatalistic attitude. The next disaster is never, it seems, very far away.

Estimates of the numbers of lives lost rose steadily in the days after the typhoon. A week later, the official death toll was put at 125 000, but it was expected to go far higher than that as more accurate reports came in from the areas affected; the final toll will almost certainly be over 200 000.

Relief could come only slowly, too slowly for many of those affected. The scale of the disaster, the size of the affected area and the difficulties in communication caused by the flood meant that aid workers could only scratch at the surface of the problem. One said 'You need at least 200 helicopters for this operation and at present we have two', graphically illustrating the impossibility of dealing with a tragedy of this scale.

Two villagers carry their possessions on their heads to cross the flooded garden of a mosque.

Index

Note: Entries in **bold type** refer to article headings on the pages given. Entries in *italic type* refer to named aircraft, ships and spacecraft, and also to publications. Where it is thought helpful, countries or states are added to place names eg Abercarn, Wales; Anchorage, Alaska.

A
Abbott, Eban 166, 167
Abd al-Latif 41
Abercarn, Wales 127
Aberdeen 112, 134, 135, 146
Aberfan 121, **132**
Abraham 104
Abrolhos Island, Brazil 165
Acapulco 58
acquired immunity deficiency
    syndrome — see AIDS
Acre 41
Adelaide 101, 102
Admiral Nakhimov 157, **172**
Aegean Captain **74**
Aegean Sea 171
Aeroflot 13, 22
Afghanistan 154
Afrique **165**
Agadir **52**
Aichi, Japan 223
AIDS 139, 141, **144**
air crashes 7–28
Air India 23, 26
    Flight 182 crash **23**
Air New Zealand 18, 19
Airleys Inlet, Australia 101
Airolo, Italy 33
airships 8
Airspeed Ambassador 10, 11
Aki, Keiti 53
Alaska earthquakes
    April, 1946 194
    April, 1964 **53**, 193
Albany, Georgia 227
Aleutian Trench 194
Alexander Keilland oil rig 135
Alexandria 41
Alfonso, King of Castile 141
All Saints Flood, 1570 107
Allah Bund 44
Allonne 9
Alma Ata 13
Alpert, Micky 98
Alyeska Consortium 81
Amasya, Turkey 42
American Airlines 17
American football 98
American Hospital,
    Yokohama 50
American mining disasters
    126

American War of Independ-
    ence 218
ammonium nitrate 131
Amoco Cadiz **72**
Amsterdam 15, 107
Anatolia earthquake, 1668 **42**
Anchorage, Alaska 21, 53, 54
Ancona 163
Andersen, Thomas 162
Anderson, Warren 76
Andes Mountains 195
Andrea Doria **169**
Andrews, Thomas 160
Anfield Stadium, Liverpool
    190
Anglesea, Australia 101
animal behaviour patterns 57
Ankara 42
Antarctica 18, 19
anthrax 75
Apollo spacecraft 181
Archbishop of Canterbury
    141
Ark, The 104
Arkansas River 110
Armada, Spanish 217, 218
Armenian earthquake, 1988
    60
Armero, Colombia 213
Arno, River **116**, 117
Arqa, castle of 41
Artsruni 40
Arzamas, USSR 155
Asbury Park, New Jersey 167
Ashton (minesweeper) 171
Ashton, John 190
Astor, J J 160
Aswan Dam 120
Athens 71, 171
Atlantic Empress **74**
Atlantic Ocean 23, 25
Atlantis 201
Aubrey Fitch (US frigate) 175
Auckland 151
Austin-Healey cars 184
Australian bush fires 93, **101**
Australian Natural Disaster
    Organization 229
avalanches 29–36
Avers, Switzerland 30

B
Baalbek 41

Bagmati River, India 153
Bahrain 170
Band Aid 91
Bangkok 28
Bangladesh **235**
Banmukhi, India 153
Barcelona 143, 163
Barclay Currie shipyard 170
Bardari, Captain 72
Barnsley 122
    mining disaster **122**
Barnum and Bailey's circus
    209
Barracuda Tanker Company
    68
Barron, Joanne 187
Basilicata hills 149
Basra 170
Batavia 206
Batumi, Russia 172
Bay of Bengal 43, 235
Bay of Biscay 165
Bay of Corral 195
Bay of Naples 44, 199
Bayazid, Sultan 42
Beaufort, Sir Francis 216
Beaufort Sea 216
Beaufort scale **216**
Beaumont, Texas 74
Beauvais 9
Bedegene 41
Bedreno, Italy 33
Beijing 56
Belgrade 10, 23
Bengal 86
Bengoechea, Fernando and
    Juan Manuel 77
benzene 129
Berkeley, Gloucestershire 219
Berlin — see *Admiral
    Nakhimov*
Berlin, Treaty of 218
Bermuda 68
Berouw (Dutch gunboat) 207
Bethel, Alaska 21
Bethlehem Steel Company 74
Betty Mountain, Georgia 226
Beyer, Alan 232
Bhopal 65, **75**
Biafra **89**, 90
Bibby Line 171
Bible, The 83, 104
Big Thompson River **119**

Bihar 86, 145, 153, 155
  rail disaster, 1981 **153**, 155
Biloxi, USA 225
Bingham, Utah 33
Black Death 139, **140**
Black Sea 136, 155, 157, 172
  Shipping Co 172
Blantyre mine disaster **123**
Blasket Sound, Ireland 218
Bligh Reef, Alaska 81
Blue Hills, Massachusetts 222
Blue Riband 163
Boca Juniors FC 185
Boccaccio 140
Boeing aircraft company 24
Boeing aircraft
  707 airliner 22
  727 airliner 16
  737 airliner 20
  747 airliner 15, 21, 23, 24
  767 airliner 28
Bolu, Turkey 42
Bombay 143, 170
Bonales, Martin 137
Bonelli, Maria 117
Bordeaux 165
Boston 93, 98, 119, 222
  Cocoanut Grove fire **98**
  molasses flood 119
  Piedmont Street 98
Bouch, Sir Thomas 146, 147
Bradford FC fire 93, 183, 186,
  187
Bragg, Robert 16
Brahmaputra River 235
Brandenburg, Kentucky 226
Bremen 172
Bremer Vulkan shipyard 172
Britannic 159
British Airtours 20
British Airways 24
British European Airlines 10,
  12, 14
  Flight 548 crash **12**
British hurricanes
  November, 1703 **219**
  October, 1987 **232**
British India Line 158, 170,
  171
British Petroleum (BP) 68
British tornadoes **220**
Brooks, Flight Engineer 19
Broughty Ferry, Scotland 147
Brown, Capability 232
Brown, John & Co 163
Brown, Samuel 122
Brussels 12, 188
  Heysel Stadium 183, **188**
Bryukhanov, Viktor 79
bubonic plague 139, 140

Bucigross, Captain 99
Buenos Aires 164, 185
Buffalo 14
Buffery, Vivien 229
Burntisland, Scotland 146
Burton, S H 111
Busby, Sir Matt 10, 11
Busby Babes 10
Busby Island, Alaska 81
Bush, George 63
butane gas 134
Byrd, Richard 19
Byron, Lord 205

C
Cabaud, Henry 167
Cadiz 164
Caerphilly, Wales 127
Caffa 140
Cairo 41
Calabria 43
Calais 173
Calalzo, Italy 115
Calamai, Captain 169
Calcutta 86
California Institute of
  Technology 39
Californian 160
Calliope 218
Camorta **158**
Canadian Pacific Airlines 16
Canadian Pacific Line ships
  162
Canvey Island 112, 114
Cape Hallett 19
Cape of Good Hope 72
Cape Verde Island 165
carbon monoxide poisoning
  149
Cardington 8
Carey, Roy 134
Carpathia 160
Carroll, Lewis 66
Caruso, Enrico 49
Cascade Mountains, USA 33
Casma, Peru 35
Caspian Sea 62
Castellotti, Luigi 184
Catania, Sicily 43, 203
Celtic FC, Glasgow 186
Ceylan 165
Chad 89
Chaffee, Roger 181
Challenger spacecraft 177, **181**
Chang Heng 44
Chapel of St Laurentius 30
Charles II, King 94
Charles Ball 206
Chelyabinsk, USSR 155
chemical waste dumping 67

Cheng-chou, China 105
Cherbourg 159
Chernobyl 65, **78**
Cherrapunji, India 111
Cherry, Illinois 126
  mining disaster 126
Chetumal, Mexico 228
Chiang Kai-shek 106
Chicago 17, 72, 93, 96, 97,
  100
  City Hall 96
  DC 10 air crash **17**
  DeKoven Street 96
  fire, 1871 **96**
  First National Bank 96
  Iroquois Theatre fire **97**
  O'Hare International
    airport 17
  Opera House
Chicago Daily Tribune 96
Chimbote, Peru 35
Chinese famine 91
Chinese Seismological
  Service 57
Chiso Chemical Company 66
cholera 86, 88
Choloma, Honduras 228
Christian Aid 89
Christmas Day hurricane,
  Darwin **229**
Cimabue 116
Ciparis, Auguste 209
City of Savannah 167
Clacton 112
Clare Valley, Australia 102
Cleland Conservation Park,
  Australia 102
Club Cinq-Sept fire 99
Clyde River 158, 162, 163,
  170, 171
coal mining 34, 56, 121–8,
  131–3, 136
Cockatoo, Australia 101
Cocoanut Grove fire 93, **98**
Coleman, Vincent 130
colliery waste tips 132, 133
Collins, Jim 18, 19
Columbia River 211
Columbian (newspaper) 212
Compagnie des Chargeurs
  Réunis 165
Comprère-Leandre, Leon
  209
Concepción, Chile 195
Cook, Marshall 98
Copenhagen 23
Coreolis force 217
Cork, Ireland 159
Coseguina, Nicaragua 205
Cousins, Greg 81

Couwenburgh, Guido 174
Crefisul Bank, São Paulo 100
Crescent City, California 54
Cuba 164, 225
Cummins, Nicholas 88
Cunard Line 157, 159, 160, 163
Curaçao 74
Curtis, Bradley 20
cyclohexane 71
Cyprus 41

D
Daijingu shrine, Yokohama 51
Daisetsu Maru 168
Dakar 165
Dalby, Robert 206
Dale Dyke, Yorkshire 111
Damascus 41
Danan, Indonesia 206, 207
Dara **170**
Dartmouth, Canada 129
Darwin, Australia 215, 229
Darwin, Charles 44
Dau, Enrique 137
Davies, Lord Justice Edmund 132
DC8 aircraft 16
DC10 aircraft 14, 17, 18, 19
de Chauliac, Guy 140
de Pombal, Marques 46
Defoe, Daniel 141, 219
Demavend, Iran 62
Demirel, Suleyman 136
Department of Transport, British 25
Depaun, Indiana 226
Detroit 14
Dillard, James 17
dioxin 70, 71
Ditford, Mistress 220
Dixon, William 123
Dobrovolski, Georgi 180
Doll, Sir Richard 77
Dominica 230
Dominican Republic 230, 231
Dona Paz ferry 157, **175**
Dordrecht 107
Dover 173, 232
Drake, Sir Francis 218
Drayton Park station, London 152
Dubai 170
Dukla Prague FC 10
Dundee 146, 147
Düniberg (mountain) 31
Dutch State Mining Company 71
Dvin earthquake, 893 **40**

Dye, Fred 227
Dymond, Thomas 122
dysentery 224

E
earthquake severity measurement **38**
earthquakes 37–64
    historic **43**
    major (table) **39**
East Lyn River, Devon 111
East River, New York 158
Eastern Mediterranean earthquake, 1202 **41**
Eddystone Lighthouse 219
Edinburgh 146, 148
    Rosebank Cemetery 149
Edinburgh, Duke of 151
Edwards, Duncan 11
Ekofisk oil field 135
Elizabeth II, Queen 133, 151
Ellis, Cyril 151
Ellis, Donald 73
Elm, Switzerland 31
Elson, Captain 170
Empire Guillemot 170
Empire Star 165
Empress of Australia 50
Empress of Britain 162
Empress of Ireland 158, **162**
Empress of Japan 171
Empress of Scotland 171
Encke's Comet 178
ENEL electricity company 115
Engin, Cevat 136
environmental disasters 65–83
Ephesus 221
Eritrea 91
Ermenonville, Forest of 14
Erto, Italy 115
Erzincan earthquake, 1992 **64**
Erzurum earthquake, 1983 64
Ethiopia famine **91**
Euphrates, River 104
European Cup (football) 10, 188
Evans, Edward 14
Exxon company 81
Exxon Valdez **81**

F
FAA — see Federal Aviation Administration
Fairfield shipyard 162, 171
Falconcra, Cyclades 171
famine 85–91
Fangio, Juan 184

Father Point, Canada 162
Feast of the Immaculate Conception 95
Federal Aviation Administration, USA (FAA) 17, 22, 24, 25
Felixstowe 112
Feodosiya 141
fer-de-lance snakes 209
Ferndale, Wales 127
Ferrari cars 184
Ferrero, Elias and Ramon 77
Fez, Morocco 45
Fife, HMS 230
fire disasters 93–102
First National Bank of Chicago 96
Firth, Barber and Company 122
Firth, Samuel 187
flagellants 141
Flanders gripe 142
Fleet, Frederick 160
Flixborough 71
floods 103–20
Florence 103, 116, 117, 118, 140
    Bardini Museum 116
    floods, 1966 **116**
    National Library 117
    Palazzo del Duomo 116
    Ponte Vecchio 116, 117, 118
    Santa Croce 117
    Santa Teresa prison 117
    Science Museum 116
    Uffizi Gallery 116
Fonds St Denis, Martinique 209
Ford, Henry 88
Forelli, Guiseppe 200
Fort-de-France, Martinique 208, 209
Forth River 146, 147
Framlingham, Australia 101
Frank, Canada 34
Frankenstein 205
Frankfurt 25, 26
Franklin, Benjamin 227
Friuli earthquake, 1976 **55**

G
Galileo 117
Galunggung 205
Galveston, Texas **221**
Games, Robert 233
Gandhi, Indira 153
Ganges, River 235
Garmab, River 47
Gemona 55

Geneina, Sudan 120
General Slocum **158**
Genoa 163, 169
George V, King 128
George Medal 113, 151, 174
Ghiberti 116
Gifu, Japan 223
Gilan, Iran 62, 63
Gilbert Inlet, Alaska 193
Gilmour Joseph 123
Giotto 116
Givaudan 70
Glasgow 123, 158, 186
    Cairnlea Drive 186
    Celtic FC 186
    Rangers FC 186
glasnost 13, 172
Golden Gate Park, San
    Francisco 49
Goodwin Sands 219
Gorbachev, Mikhail 13, 60,
    61
Gorleston, Norfolk 232
Gormec, Turkey 33
Gothenburg 108
Graf Zeppelin airship 8, 9
Grand Banks, off Canada 162
Grand Camp (freight ship)
    131
Grand Canary 15
Graubunden 33
Great Fire of London **94**
Green Monkey Disease 143
Grenoble 99
Gretna 148
Griffiths, Peter 57
Grimsvötn, Iceland 204
Grissom, Gus 181
Grosse Island, Canada 88
Grote Mandrenke (Great
    Drowning), 1362 107
Grubbs, Victor 15, 16
Gruinard Island 73
Guadalajara, Mexico 137, 138
    gas explosions, 1992 **137**
Guadeloupe 230
Gulf of Florida 230
Gulf of Martaban 158
Gulf of Mexico 221, 225, 226
Gulf of Po Hai 105
Gulf War 83
Gulfport, Louisiana 225
Guli, Captain 165
gun cotton 129

H

Hacihamza, Turkey 42
Haile Selassie, Emperor 91
Haiti 230
Hakodate, Japan 168

Halifax, Nova Scotia 121, 129,
    130
    harbour explosion, 1917
    129
    St Vincent's Academy 130
Halifax, Viscount 87
Hamakua, Hawaii **194**
Hamburg 171
Hamburg–Atlantic Line 171
Hamilton, Scotland 123
Haneda Airport, Tokyo 24
Hannibal 32
Hanseatic 171
Harrison, J W 130
Harwich 112
Hastings, Warren 86
Havana 164
Hawthorn, Mike 184
Hazelwood, Joseph 81, 82
Heathrow Airport, London
    12, 14, 23, 25
Heimaey, Iceland 204
Helsinki 25
Hendon 8
Hendry, Stephen 189
Heraklion (ferry) **171**
Heraklion, Crete 171
Herald of Free Enterprise 157,
    173
Herculaneum 199, 200, 221
hexane 137
Heysel Stadium, Brussels 183,
    188
Hidaka Maru 168
High Blantyre, Scotland 123,
    124, 125
    mining disaster, 1877 **123**
High Flyer (freight ship) 131
High Flyer, HMS 129
Hillsborough Stadium,
    Sheffield 183, 186, **189**
    Leppings Lane entrance
    189
Hilo, Hawaii 191, **194**, **196**
Hindenburg airship 9
Hindu Kush 154
Hokkaido, Japan 168
Holma, John 151
Homewood, Stephen 173,
    174
Honduras 228
Hong Kong 28
Honkeiko mine disaster 128
Howden, Yorkshire 8
Huang He — see Yellow
    River
Huaraz, Peru 35
Huarmey, Peru 35
Hundred Years War 141
Hunstanton 112, 113

hurricanes
    Camille **225**
    Carla 221
    David **230**, 231
    Fifi **228**
    Frederick 230, 231
    Janet 228
    Labour Day, 1935 225
    naming 222
    through history **217**
    Tracy **229**

I

Ibo people 89
Ibrox Stadium, Glasgow 183,
    186
ICMESA 70
Ile de France 169
Il'khan Kuchan 47
Ilyushin aircraft
    Il-18 13
    Il-62 13
    Il-76 61
Imo (freight ship) 129
Imperial Hotel, Tokyo 50
Incirharmani mine disaster,
    Turkey **136**
Indian famines **86**
Indian High Commission 23
Indonesian Arc 205, 210
industrial disasters 121–38
Industrial Revolution 121
Inglis, A & J, shipyard 158
Inonu, Erdal 136
Institutional Revolutionary
    Party, Mexico 138
International Atomic Energy
    Authority (IAEA) 79
International Civil Aviation
    Organization (ICAO) 13,
    22
International Federation of
    Airline Pilots Organiza-
    tions (IFALPA) 22
International Monetary Fund
    59
Iran earthquake, 1990 **62**
Irish potato famine 85, **87**
Irkutsk 178
Iroquois Theatre, Chicago
    93, **97**
Ismay, J Bruce 159, 160
ISNV Line 163
Istanbul 14, 42
Italian Line 169
Ito, Fusayo 196
Izmir 42

J

Jack, Jim 25

Jack and Jill windmills 233
Jaguar cars 184
Jakarta 206
James River 225
Japan Air Lines 24
  Flight 123 crash, 1985 **24**
Jasper, Alabama 226
JAT airline 23
Jeddah 20, 175
Jimenez, Fernando Perez 137
Joelma Building, São Paulo
  93, **100**
John of Worcester 220
Johnson, Lyndon 54
Johnston, David 211
Johnstown, Pennsylvania 103,
  109
José I, King 46
Josephine, Empress 208
Juventus FC 188

K
Kabul 154
Kamchatka 21
Kamensk-Shakhtinsky, USSR
  155
kamikaze wind 217
Kamon-no-Kami, Li 51
Kanamori, Hiroo 39
Kansk 178
Kansu, China 47
  earthquake, 1920 47
Karachi 170
Kashmir 86
Katha, Iceland 204
Kaye, Gordon 233
Kellogg mine disaster, USA
  126
Kelut **210**
Kendall, Captain 162
Kennedy, Edward 89
Kew Gardens 232
Key, Stanley 12
Key West, Florida 164
Khartoum 120
Khowyter, Mohammed Ali 20
Kidder, Dr 219
Kidwai, S R 153
Kiev 79
Kim Chang Kyu 22
Kimpo Airport, Seoul 21
King's Lynn 112
Kirghis 140
Klickitat Indians 211
KLM airline 15, 16
Klochko, Mikhail 67
Kmitrin, General 155
Kodiak Island, Alaska 53
Korean Air Lines 7, 21, 22
  airliner shot down **21**

Korem 91
Korramshahr 170
Kouchner, Bernard 63
Krakatoa 193, 197, 201, 202,
  205, **206**, 212
Kubla Khan 215, 217, 224
Kuchan earthquake, 1893 **47**
Kuwait **83**, 170
Kuwana, Japan 223
Kyshtym radiation escape 65,
  67

L
La Befana 117
La Compania, Santiago 93,
  95
La Rochelle, France 165
La Soufrière volcano 208
Lagunillas River 213
lahar 205, 210, 213
Lake Geneva 205
Lake Michigan 96
Lake Nasser 120
Lake Nios 213
Lake Taupo 202
Lakehurst, New Jersey 9
Lamport Line 172
Lanarkshire Miners Union
  124
Landes, M 208
Lane, Frank 193
Lapp people 78
Larne 112
Las Palmas 15
Las Vegas 100
Lassa Fever 143
Lauda, Niki 28
Lauda Air crash, 1991 **28**
Laupahochoe, Hawaii 194
Lawson, James 146
Le Mans motor race 183, **184**
Leamington Hastings,
  England 219
Lechuga, Ignacio Morales
  137
Legionnaire's Disease 143
Leicestershire 171
Leming, Reis 113
Leninakan 60, 61
Leningrad 13, 79
Leppings Lane, Sheffield 189
Lesser Antilles 45
Letham, Iain 134
Leukerbad avalanches **30**
levées 110
Levegh, Pierre 184
Leverton (minesweeper) 171
Lewis Bay, Antarctica 19
Lewis Merthyr Consolidated
  Collieries 127

Lima 36, 46, 183, 185
  football riot **185**
Lincoln City FC 187
Lipsyte, Robert 185
Lisbon, 43, 45, 46, 191, 221
  earthquake, 1755 **45**, 52,
  55, 191
Little Tobago 74
Lituya Bay, Alaska 193
Live Aid 91
Liverpool 162, 188–90
  Anfield Stadium 190
  Football Club 188–90
Lobatón (footballer) 185
Lockerbie 7
  air crash, 1988 23, **25**
Lockheed TriStar aircraft 20
loess 42, 105
London 8, 23, 25, 26, 93, 94,
  97, 107, 108, 112, 141,
  171, 219, 220, 232
  Grain Market 205
  Great Fire, 1666 93, **94**
  Heathrow Airport 14, 23,
  25
  Liverpool Street Station
  232
  London Bridge 94
  Pudding Lane 94
  St James's Palace 219
  St Mary le Bow church 220
  St Paul's Cathedral 94
  Thames Street 94
  underground railways 145,
  152
  Wembley Stadium 189
Long Island 222
Long Island Express
  hurricane 217, **222**
Long Key, Florida 222
Longarone, Italy 115
Longtown, England 25
Lord, Stanley 160
Los Angeles 15, 17, 48, 68
Los Rodeos Airport, Tenerife
  15
Loushan, Iran 62
Love Canal 67
Lovelace, Colorado 119
Lowland Cavalier (oil support
  vessel) 134
Lusitania 158, 159, **163**
Lynmouth, Devon 103, **111**

M
Mablethorpe 112
Macklin, Lance 184
Mad Hatters 66
Madison, Connecticut 222

Madras 158
Madrid 46, 77
   Trade Fair 77
Maiano, Italy 55
Makalle, Ethiopia 91
malaria 86
Mali 90
Mallet, Robert 44
Malta 26
Manchester 10, 11, 20
   air crash, 1985 20
Manchester United FC 10,
   100
   air crash at Munich 10
Manila 175
Manjil, Iran 62
Mannington mine disaster,
   USA 126
Mao Tse-tung 106
Marinduque, Philippines 175
Markinch, Scotland 186
Markov, Vadim 172
Marmolada 32
Marseilles 140, 165
Martin, Ramos 164
Martinique 208, 209, 230
Mauritania 90
Mauritania (liner) 159
McAuliffe, Christa 181
McDonald, Alexander 124
McDonnell Douglas 14
McGee, W J 221
McIntosh, Don 28
McInulty, Andrew and Joseph
   124
McKenna, Reginald 128
McKim, Elizabeth 186
McMahon's Creek, Australia
   102
McMurdo Sound, Antarctica
   18, 19
McPherson, Donald and
   Nigel 186
McWade, Frank 8
Meakin, George 148, 149
Mecca 170, 175
Medina 175
Melbourne 102
Melo, Vota 100
Mendez, Angela 58
Merak, Java 207
Mercalli, Giuseppe 39
Mercalli scale 38, 39
Mercedes-Benz cars 184
Mercury, Freddie 144
mercury poisoning 66
Mesopotamia 104
Messina, Sicily 47
   earthquake, 1908 47
meteorites 178, 179

methane gas 134, 136
methyl isocyanate (MIC) 75,
   76
Mexican rail disaster 153
Mexico City 58, 59, 137, 138
   earthquake, 1985 58
   Juarez Hospital 58
MGM Grand Hotel, Las
   Vegas 100
Michaelangelo 116
Microbiology and Virology
   Institute, Sverdlovsk,
   USSR 73
Mie, Japan 223
Milan 70, 71
Milford Haven 68
Minamata 65, 66
Miners Federation of Great
   Britain 128
Mino, Japan 44
Misenum 199
Mississippi River 43, 110
Mogul empire 86
Moiseyev, General 155
molasses flood, Boston 119
Molinier, Coniglion 184
Monarch of Bermuda 167
Moncton, Canada 130
Monongah, West Virginia 126
Mont Blanc (freight ship) 129,
   130
Mont Pelée 197, 208
Mooney, Mr 99
Moorgate station, London
   145, 152
Morales, Dr 35, 36
Morro Castle 157, 166
Morton-Thiokol company
   182
Moscow 13, 22, 60, 155, 172,
   178
   Narodny Bank 60
Mount Ararat 104
Mount Buffalo 102
Mount Erebus 18, 19
   air crash, 1979 18
Mount Etna 43, 203
Mount Fuji 24
Mount Gabar 33
Mount Hekla 204
Mount Katmai 53
Mount Laki 204
Mount Macedon 102
Mount McKinley 53
Mount Osutaka 24
Mount Ruapehu 151
Mount St Helens 211
Mount Toc 115
Mountain Ash, Wales 132
Mr Bluebeard (pantomime) 97

Mulgrew, Peter 18, 19
Munich 10, 11
   air crash, 1958 10
Murmansk 22
Muroto, Japan 224
Murphy, Ed 81

N
Nablus 41
Nagishima, Japan 223
Nagoya, Japan 223
naming of hurricanes 222
Nangyo, Japan 223
Nantucket Lightship 169
Naples 199
Napoleon 208
Narendra, Hanse 23
Naringal, Australia 101
NASA 181
National Coal Board, UK 71,
   133
National Geographic magazine
   221
Natural Disaster Organiza-
   tion, Australia 229
Nebukawa, Japan 50
Nedelin, Mitrofan 180
Neumann, Frank 39
Nevada de Huascarán 29, 34,
   35
   avalanche, 1962 34
   avalanche, 1970 35
Nevado del Ruiz 197, 213
New Madrid, Missouri 43
New Orleans 110, 164
New York 21, 25, 88, 129,
   158, 159, 163, 166, 169,
   171, 172, 222, 231
   East River 158
   Harbour 158, 171
   St Mark's School 158
   Throg's Neck 158
New York and Cuba Mail
   Steamship Co 166
New York (liner) 159
New York Times 185
Newcastle upon Tyne 141,
   165
Newport, Scotland 146
Newport News, USA 166
Newson, Leslie 152
NGI Line 165
Niagara Falls 67
Niger 90
Nile, River 120
Nixon, Richard 226
Noah's Ark (steamboat) 110
Noah's Flood 103, 104
Norabhur 40
Norris, Henry 227

North German Lloyd Line 172
North Sea 103, 107, 108, 112, 113, 121, 134, 135
  floods **107**, **112**
  Piper Alpha rig disaster **134**
North Slope oil field, Alaska 81
Nottingham Forest FC 189
Novorossiysk, Russia 172
nuclear incidents 67, 78
nuée ardente 208
Nypro company 71

O
O'Hare International Airport, Chicago 17
O'Leary, Mrs 96
Oahu 194
Oak Ridge, Tennessee 67
Oaks colliery disaster **122**
Oberg, James 180
Occidental Petroleum 134
Odessa 172
Ogden, Mahlon 96
oil blowout off California 72
oiled birds 69
Ojukwu, Emeka 89
Olcer, Ozer 136
Old Trafford, Manchester 11
Oldham River, Canada 34
Ollier, Cliff 197
Olympic 159
Olympic Games 185
Omsk 13
Operation Faith, Bhopal 76
Orissa, India 86
Orkney 112
Orly Airport, Paris 14, 20
Orr, John 25
Osabel, Paquito 175
Osaka 24
Otsuki City 24
Ottawa 23
Ovanes 40
Owari, Japan 44
Owen, Wilfred 142
Owens Valley, USA 44

P
P & O European Ferries 174
P & O Line 157, 174
Pacific (tug) 72
Pacific Ocean 21
Pacific Rim fault 53
PanAm airline 15, 16, 23, 25, 26
  Flight 103 23, **25**, 26
Panama Canal 49

pandemics 139–44
Pangloss 46
Paramount 167
Parel, M 209
Parícutin **210**
Paris 14, 20, 52
  Orly Airport 14, 20
Parker, Andrew 174
Parkhead Stadium, Glasgow 186
Pass Christian, Mississippi 225
Patna 86
Patsayev, Viktor 180
Pazos, Angel 185
Pemex oil company 137
Pensacola, Florida 218
Pepys, Samuel 94
Perboewetan, Indonesia 206, 207
Perth, Scotland 146
Petworth House 232
Philip, King of Spain 215, 217
Piave River 115
picric acid 129
Pictou (munitions ship) 129, 130
Pinillos, Izquierdo & Co 164
Piper Alpha oil rig 121, **134**
Piraeus 74, 171
Pittsburgh 43, 109
Plato 201
Plattenbergkopf rockfall **31**
Pliny the Elder 199
Pliny the Younger 199, 200
Plurs rockfall 31
Pluton 163
pneumonic plague 140
pneumonoultramicrosco-picsilicovolcanoconiosis 212
Polalu Valley, Hawaii 194
Pompeii 199, 200, 201, 221
Ponte Vecchio, Florence 116–18
Port Glasgow, Scotland 164
Port Richardson, Alaska 53
Port Royal, Jamaica 43
Porth, Wales 127
Powell, Thomas 219
Prague 10, 13
Pravda 13
Prince William Sound, Alaska 53, 81, 82
Princess Victoria (ferry) 112
Principe de Asturias **164**
Principessa Mafalda **165**
propane gas 134
Pudding Lane, London 94
pulmonary oedema 75

Pyotr Vasyov 172

Q
Qazvin 62
Qinghai Province, China 105
Quebec 162
Queen (rock group) 144
Queen Elizabeth 169
Queen's Medal for Gallantry 174
Quintinshill, Scotland 145, **148**
Qus 41

R
R100 airship 8
R101 airship 7, **8**
radiation escapes 67, 78
Radio Moscow 61
Raelca company 77
Rafsanjani, Hojatolislam 63
rail disasters 145–55
Ramadan 64
Rangers FC, Glasgow 186
Rangoon 158
Rann of Kutch 44
Ranrahirca, Peru 34, 35, 36
Rapsa company 77
Rasht, Iran 62
Rayment, Kenneth 10
RBMK-1000 reactor 78
Reagan, Ronald 182
Real Madrid FC 10
Rebecca Shoals light, Florida 164
Red Crescent 62, 63, 64 120
Red Cross 89, 131, 137
Red Star Belgrade FC 10
Redfoot Lake, Mississippi 43
Réunion Island 111
Reggio, Sicily 47
Rhône River 140
Richmond, Nova Scotia 129, 130
Richmond, Virginia 225
Richter, Charles 39
Richter Scale 39
Rio de Janeiro 165
Risca, Wales 127
River Plate FC 185
Riyadh aircraft fire **20**
road disasters 145, 154
Roberts, James 146
Roch, André 32
Roche-Bonne Reef, Bay of Biscay 165
Rocky Mountains 226
Rogers, George 166
Rojas, Matias 185
Rome 118

Roseau, Dominica 230
Ross, James Clark 19
Ross Dependency, Antarctica 19
Roten, Stephen 30
Rotterdam 72, 107
Roudbar-e-Alamut, Iran 62
Royal Australian Navy 229
Royal Botanical Gardens, Kew 232
Royal Meteorological Society 220
Royal Moroccan Army 52
Royal Scots Regiment 148
Rshtunishki, Bishop Grigor 40
Ruediger, Bill 212
Rufino, José 100
Rugiati, Pastrengo 68
'Run for the World' appeal 91
Russell & Co shipyard 164

S
Safad 41
Safaga, Egypt 175
safety curtain in theatres 97
Sagami Bay, Japan 50
Sahara Desert 85
Sahel famines **90**
St Fort Station, Scotland 146
St James's Palace, London 219
St Lawrence River 88
St Mark's School, New York 158
St Mary le Bow Church, London 220
St Paul's Cathedral, London 94
St Petersburg 79
St Pierre, Martinique 197, 208, 209
St Valery-sur-Somme 9
St Vincent 208
St Vincent's Academy, Halifax, Nova Scotia 130
Sakhalin Island 21, 22
Saladin 41
Salang Tunnel 145, **154**
Salem Express (ferry) **175**
Salyut space station 180
Samashpur, India 153
Samoa 218
San Andreas Fault 44, 48
San Francisco 44, 48, 49
  City Hall 48
  earthquake, 1906 **48**
  earthquake, 1989 49
  Golden Gate Park 49

Nob Hill 48
World Fair 49
San Pedro Sula, Honduras 228
Sanandaj, Iran 62
Sanchez, Omayra 213
Sanchez, Philip 228
Sandhaven (oil support vessel) 134
Sanriku, Japan 193
Santa River, Peru 34, 35
Santiago 93, 95
Santo Domingo, Dominican Republic 230
Santorini **201**, 202
São Paulo 93, 100
São Tomé 89
Sap Gulch, USA 33
Scobee, Dick 182
Scotney Castle 232
sea disasters 157–75
Sebastiao Point, Brazil 164
Sebastopol 172
seismology 37, 39
Selborne Yew 233
semtex 25
Senegal 90
Senghenydd mine disaster, Wales **127**
Seoul 21
septicemic plague 140
Seslice, Turkey 33
Seven Stones rocks 68
Sevenoaks 232
severity of earthquakes, measuring 38
Seveso 65, **70**
Shannon, Ireland 23
Shaw, Edward 127
Shcherbak, Yuri 79
Sheen, Mr Justice 174
Shelley, Percy and Mary 205
Shenshi earthquake, 1556 **42**
Shinsei Maru 168
Shipbuilder magazine 160
Shoak, Sudan 120
Siena 140
Silius Italicus 32
Simpson, Leslie 18
Simpson, Robert 225
Singapore 74
Sir Robert Sale 206
Sirnak, Turkey 33
Sittingbourne, Kent 114
Skegness 112
Skippen, Michael 174
Skopje 55
slate mining 31
Smart, David 146
Smbat I 40

Smillie, Robert 128
Smith, Edward J 159, 160
Smith, James 146
Smith, Michael 182
Snowdrop, The (inn) 30
Sochi 13, 172
Sodom 221
South Downs avalanche 30
South Fork Dam, Pennsylvania 109
South Magnetic Pole 18
South Pole 19
South Wales coalmining 127, 128
South Wales Coalowners Association 128
South Yorkshire Police 190
Southampton 159, 172
Soviet air disasters **13**
Soyuz XI spacecraft 180
space disasters 177–82
Spanish cooking oil tragedy **77**
Spanish 'flu epidemic 139, **142**
Spitak 60
Spizhenko, Yuri 79
sporting disasters 183–90
Stabiae 199
Staines Trident aircraft crash **12**
Standard Fruit Company 228
Star-Spangled Banner, The 98
Staten Island, New York 88
Stein, Colin 186
Stockholm (liner) 169
Storstad (Norwegian collier) 162
Straits of Dover 43
Stranraer, Scotland 112
SU-15 fighter 21, 22
Sudan floods **120**
Suez Canal 72
Sumbawa 205
Sun (newspaper) 173
Surtsey 204
Sverdlovsk 65, **73**
Swinemunde 172
Sylbaris, Ludger 209
Sydney, Australia 16
Sydney (Australian Navy ship) 175

T
Tabas, Iran 63
Tacloban, Philippines 175
Tagus River 45
Tah-one-lat-clah — see Mount St Helens
Takahama, Captain 24

Tambora 197, **205**, 212
Tang-shan 56, 57
  earthquake, 1976 **56**, 128
Tangiwai Bridge, New
  Zealand **151**, 153
Taupo **202**
Tay Rail Bridge 145, **146**
Taylor, John 141
Taylor, Lord Justice 190
Tazieff, Haround 195
Tees River 112
Tehran 62, 63
Telok Betong 207
Tenerife 15, 16
  air crash, 1977 **15**
  Los Rodeos airport 15
terrorist attacks 7, 23, 25, 26,
  154, 170
Terry, Fernando Belaunde
  185
Texas City 121, **131**
Thain, James 10, 11
Thames Barrier 112
Thames River 108, 112
Tharos (oil support vessel)
  134, 135
Thomson, Lord 8, 9
Three Mile Island 79
Throg's Neck, New York 158
Ticino Alps 33
Tigré 91
Tigris, River 104
Tiktin 180
Times, The 57, 88, 128
Tinsley, James 148, 149
Titanic 157, 158, **159**, 161,
  162
TNT 129
Tockachi Maru 168
Tokat, Turkey 42
Tokyo 21, 24, 50, 51, 153
  earthquake, 1923 **50**
  Grand Hotel 51
  Haneda Airport 24
  Imperial Hotel 50
  rail crash 153
  Twelve Storey Tower 50
Tomaszewski, Stephen 98
Topeka, Kansas 227
  Washburn University 227
Tornade Intercept Project
  226
tornadoes
  British **220**
  Midwest USA **226**
Toronto 23
Torrey Canyon **68**
TOTO (Totable Tornado
  Observatory) 227
Toutle River 211

Tower of London 94
Towering Inferno (film) 93,
  100
Townsend Thoresen line 173,
  174
Towyn, Wales 233
toxic fumes in aircraft 20
Toya Maru **168**
Toys Hill, Kent 232
Trans-Australia Airlines 16
Trans-Siberia railway disaster
  155
Treviso, Italy 115
Trident aircraft 12
  crash, Staines, 1972 **12**
Trident nuclear submarine
  22
Tripoli 41
TriStar aircraft 20
Truman, Harry 212
Tshushima, Japan 223
tsunamis 44, 45,52, 53, 54,
  191–6
  major **192**
  warning system 193, 196
Tuareg people 90
tuberculosis 90
Tungus people 178
Tunguska meteorite 177, **178**
Tupolev aircraft
  Tu-104 13
  Tu-124 13
  Tu-134 13
  Tu-154 13
Turin 188
Turkish Airlines 14
  DC10 crash, France, 1974
    14
Turkish earthquake, 1992 **64**
Turkish mine disaster, 1992
  136
Turkish–Aegean tectonic
  plate 62
Turner, William 163
Turtle Mountain, USA 34
Typaldos Line 171
typhoid 88, 90
typhoons
  Muroto 224
  Vera **223**
Tyre 41
Tyrolean avalanches,
  1916–18 **32**

U
Udal, Kansas 227
UEFA 188
Ufa, Russia 155
Uffizi Gallery, Florence 116

Ugarto, Father 95
Union Carbide Corporation
  75, 76
Union Oil Company 68
United Fruit Company 228
United Nations Disaster
  Relief Organization 62
United States
  Defense Intelligence
    Agency 73
  Geological Survey 34, 35,
    36
  National Academy of
    Sciences 54
  National Hurricane
    Centre 225
  Senate Committee on
    Refugee Peoples 89
  space administration
    (NASA) 181
  Task Force 38, 218
  Weather Bureau 33
Universal Colliery,
  Senghenydd, Wales **127**
University of Bradford 73
Upper Beaconsfield,
  Australia 101
Upper Volta 90
Ur 104
Ushant 72

V
Vaiont Dam, Italy 103, **115**
Valdez, Alaska 53, 81, 82
Valdivia **195**
Valley of Assassins, Iran 62
van Schaick, Captain 158
van Zanten, Jaap 15, 16
Vancouver 23
Varig Airlines 20
Vegesack, Germany 172
Venice 55, 120
Venoil/Venpet tanker collision
  74
Vestris 172
Vesuvius 197, **199**
Victoria, Queen 145, 147
Vidaurri, Guillermo 137
Vienna 28, 79
volcanoes 197–214
  major **198**
Volkov, Vladislav 180
Voltaire 45, 46
Volturno 162
Vulovic, Vesna 23

W
Wailoa River, Hawaii 194, 196
Wailuku River, Hawaii 196
Ward Line 166

Warms, William 166, 167
Warnemunde 172
Warnow shipbuilding yard 172
Washburn University, Kansas 227
Washington DC 43
Wattstown, Wales 127
Welansky, Barnett 99
Wellington, New Zealand 151
Wellington, Washington State 33
Wellington Snowslide 33
Welsburn (or Wellesbourne), Warwickshire 220
Wembley Stadium, London 189
West Lyn River, Devon 111
Whangaehu River 151
White, Ed 181
'white death' avalanches 32, **33**
White Star Line 159
Widecombe-in-the-Moor, Devon 220

Williams, Gwyneth 132
Williams Field, Antarctica 18
Wilmott, Robert 166, 167
Winchester Cathedral 140
Windscale 79
Winstanley, Henry 219
Wizard of Oz (book and film) 227
Wood, Charles 87
Wood, Harry 39
Wooldridge, Captain 206
Woolley, Sir Leonard 104
World Cup (football) 62
World Health Organization 144
Wren, Sir Christopher 94
Wright, Frank Lloyd 50
Wyatt, Vivian 73
Wyler Valley, Switzerland 30

X
Xenia, Ohio 226

Y
Yakima 211

Yamakazi, Kaichiki 168
Yanik, Salih 136
Yarmouth, Norfolk 112
Yarra Dam, Australia 102
Yellow River 103, **105**
Yellow Sea 105
Yerevan 60
Yokohama 50, 51
   American Hospital 50
   Daijingu shrine 51
   earthquake, 1923 **50**
Yokota 24
Yu, Son of Heaven 105
Yungay, Peru 35, 36

Z
Zafferana, Sicily 203
Zanjan, Iran 62, 63
Zdarsky, Matthias 32
Zeebrugge 157, 173, 174
Zia, Khalida 235
Zonguldak, Turkey 136
Zuiderzee 107